The Faber Pocket Guide to Handel

Edward Blakeman is a commissioning and programme Editor at BBC Radio 3, where his responsibilities include the broadcasts of the annual season of BBC Proms. Before joining the BBC, he freelanced as a flute player, writer and presenter, held a research fellowship at the Royal Northern College of Music, and was Head of the Wind Department at the London College of Music. He is a member of the Council of the Royal Philharmonic Society, editor of various music editions, and author of a recent book: *Taffanel – Genius of the Flute* (OUP).

THE FABER POCKET GUIDE TO
Handel

Edward Blakeman

faber and faber

First published in 2009
by Faber and Faber Ltd
Bloomsbury House
74–77 Great Russell Street
London WC1B 3DA

Typeset in Janson by RefineCatch Limited, Bungay, Suffolk
Printed in England by CPI Bookmarque, Croydon

A CIP record for this book
is available from the British Library

ISBN 978–0–571–23831–6

2 4 6 8 10 9 7 5 3 1

For Helen and Laura

Contents

Foreword

This gem of a book sets out all that the general reader, or the singer like myself, needs to know about Handel's life and works. It is clear, concise, packed with easily digestible information and full of pointers to further reading, either in books, the Internet or on the various web-sites of museums and galleries, and it gives lists of recommended recordings. The industry of the man is extraordinary – I mean of Handel, but in fact Edward Blakeman has read and listened to more Handel than most of us knew existed and deserves tremendous applause for rendering down all the information he has absorbed into such accessible morsels.

I was particularly fascinated by the list of Handel's operas, with the dates of their first performances and their revivals. They were really the popular music of their time, and from his golden age during the 1720's and until the 1740's, the extent of the list takes one's breath away. Then it all ceased and no Handel operas were staged anywhere in the world for nearly two-hundred years.

I realise that I was almost a pioneer of Handel opera performance in modern times. When I studied at the Royal Academy of Music, Sir Anthony Lewis, a great Handel scholar, was Principal and almost my first operatic role was in Handel's *Imeneo* – practically a first performance – and Sir Anthony also conducted Handel's oratorio *Athalia* in which I sang an aria beginning 'Blooming virgins', repeated three times, and causing me great problems of giggle control! As a young professional, I also sang Handel operas at the Barber Institute in Birmingham and at the Unicorn Theatre in Abingdon; both institutions had begun pioneering productions of Handel in 1959, the bicentenary of his death. And *Messiah*, of course, has been with me throughout my career – an enduring joy. So with Edward's book as a guide, I shall look forward to discovering more of this great man's music.

FELICITY LOTT DBE

Introduction

This book has grown from many years of enjoying Handel's music and from one particular year of concentrated listening. I hope it may appeal to music lovers who want to embark on their own listening journey and would appreciate a few pointers on the way. Not so long ago such a journey would have been impossible: at the last major Handel anniversary in 1985, the tercentenary of his birth, most of his operas had never been recorded. Now, 250 years after his death, all are available on CD, and many may even be sampled in bite-sized chunks on the Internet (see the section on 'Handel online' at the end of this book for some guidance on this).

I mention Handel's operas in particular, because that was where I started my own listening – and I'm glad I did. They are absolutely central to what made Handel tick as a composer, and when you move on to any of his other works, you can hear the supreme man of the theatre still at work. But if I had been writing this book in 1908 instead of 2008, it would have been inconceivable to devote a sizeable chapter to the operas: they had been completely forgotten. A hundred years ago Handel was known largely for his oratorios – and only that small selection of them that had been sanctified by the Victorians. Christopher Hogwood's biography of Handel quotes a revealing notice from *The Times*, reporting on a concert of Handel's chamber music organised by the young Arnold Dolmetsch in 1893: 'Handel is known to so many people only as a composer of oratorio that there is an element of novelty in a programme which includes none but his instrumental works.'

As for Handel the man, he had been effectively emasculated. Gone was any whiff of the theatre: he was seen as a religious composer who had ministered to the spiritual needs of his audiences, with a character that was correspondingly without blemish. Handel's contemporaries had a much more rounded view of him, however. And so, alongside my year's listening, I went back to the accounts of those who wrote about him from first-hand knowledge: men like the music historians John Hawkins and Charles Burney; the biographers John Mainwaring and William Coxe; and Handel's long-time assistant, John Christopher Smith, who worked with him from 1716 onwards, joined from 1720 by his son, also (confusingly) named John Christopher Smith.

Handel had the distinction of being the first composer ever to have a biography written about him. Entitled *Memoirs of the Life of the Late George Frederic Handel*, it appeared in 1760, the year after his death: though published anonymously, its author was the Reverend John Mainwaring, later Professor of Divinity at Cambridge, who had worked closely with John Christopher Smith, the younger. Despite Mainwaring's clerical background he knew how to tell a good story with lots of colourful detail – some of it wrong, but enough right for him to remain a key primary source on Handel.

William Coxe was also a clergyman, and more significantly the stepson of John Christopher Smith, the younger. After Smith died in 1795, Coxe resolved to produce a book that would do justice both to his stepfather and to Handel. His *Anecdotes of George Frederick Handel and John Christopher Smith* was published in 1799: once again, although not correct in every detail, it is a valuable document and complements Mainwaring's account.

In the mean time three other books had appeared that added significantly to knowledge both of Handel's life and of his works. One was by the music historian John Hawkins, who took advantage of the many conversations he had had with Handel when writing his five-volume *magnum opus* published in 1775: *A General History of the Science and Practice of Music* devoted a large section to Handel, placing him vividly in the context of the other composers and performers of his time.

Not to be outdone, the other great music historian of the age, Charles Burney, who also knew Handel well, produced his own definitive account in 1789: *A General History of Music from the Earliest Ages to the Present Period.* Burney was particularly interested in Handel as an opera composer, studying the scores and providing a commentary on almost all of them. He had previously written 'A Sketch of the Life of Handel' and 'The Character of Handel as a Composer' as introductory chapters to *An Account of the Musical Performances in Westminster Abbey . . . in Commemoration of Handel,* which described the series of Handel celebration concerts in 1784 and provided a commentary on the works performed.

I have quoted freely from Mainwaring, Coxe, Smith, Hawkins and Burney throughout this book – and also from one of Handel's female friends, Mary Delany, who merits a chapter all to herself. I have also dipped into the rich compendium of contemporary sources in Otto Deutsch's *Handel : a Documentary Biography,* published in 1955. I hope that these eyewitness accounts will enable you to immerse yourself in the sights and sounds of Handel's world while you listen to his music. The only missing element is what might have been gleaned from Handel's own diary or journal (none exists), or from his letters (they are few and unrevealing). So there is always an aura of enigma surrounding him. Read on . . .

Pocketing Handel

This book may fit into your pocket, but Handel himself won't be so easily contained. That's one of his attractions: he's one of the most elusive, as well as one of the most intriguing, of the great composers.

It doesn't take long before you encounter various contradictions. Take his birth date, 23 February 1685. Not only does John Mainwaring, his first biographer, get the day wrong, giving it as the 24th; there was also a mix-up over old and new calendars which meant that for a long time the year was thought to be 1684. This is the year that you will see on Handel's tombstone and monument in Westminster Abbey, and thus the series of grand Commemoration Concerts to celebrate the centenary of his birth took place in 1784, a whole year too early.

Then there was his death date, 14 April 1759. Nearing the end, Handel had expressed the pious wish, according to Charles Burney, 'that he might breathe his last on Good Friday, "in hopes", he said, "of meeting his Good God, his sweet Lord and Saviour, on the day of his resurrection".' In fact Handel died on Saturday, the following morning, at about 8 a.m., but once again there was some confusion. Mainwaring's biography gave 14 April, the date duly carved on the Abbey tombstone and monument, but the Good Friday myth was made, and Burney believed it to be true. Consequently when he had an engraving of the Westminster Abbey monument made for his book on the 1784 Commemoration Concerts, Burney had the artist change the date to Good Friday, 13 April. This engraving was then reproduced in a succession of books (including one as recently as 1984, issued by the Royal Society of Musicians), thus perpetuating the confusion.

Meanwhile, what's in a name? The various forms of Handel, Haendel, Händel and Hendel are not in themselves surprising, but if you look inside the name you find that when he himself anglicised it (he was naturalised in 1727), he signed himself George Frideric Handel. But Frideric was a German name, an alternative to Friedrich (as he used to sign himself) or Friederich (as he was baptised). Why didn't he sign himself Frederick; why only anglicise two thirds of his name? Incidentally, the name Frideric means 'peaceful ruler' – a sobriquet that would have brought a smile to the faces of contemporaries contemplating the volatile Mr Handel!

So when the *New Grove Dictionary of Music* confidently begins its article by describing him as an 'English composer of German birth', perhaps it should also give an alternative: 'German composer of English naturalisation'. He shared this ambiguity with the British monarchy of the time. When Queen Anne died in 1714, the crown passed from the House of Stuart to the House of Hanover, and the German Elector became the English King George I – somewhat reluctantly, as he chose to make frequent trips back to Hanover, and never won the hearts of the British.

Handel himself was only too happy to remain in England, but instead of pursuing the customary musician's position at court – all expenses paid – he adopted what now seems a very modern lifestyle and freelance career promoting his own operas commercially. Practical and pragmatic, he was mainly self-financing, made all his own administrative arrangements, was involved in his own publicity and promotion, organised the publication of his works, and even sold them himself at his house in Brook Street. Everyone who met him was impressed by his imposing physical presence, forceful person-ality, eccentric speech and trenchant opinions. You couldn't miss him – he was larger than life.

Handel's music too is larger than life – nobody has written more thrillingly for a great occasion – but it is also heart-rending, and must surely betray a depth and complexity that lay behind the composer's bluff exterior. The absence of revealing diaries or letters, however, means that our knowledge of Handel's private life remains shadowy. And even if you discount the notion that a composer's personality has any relevance his music, a further ambiguity still awaits in the music itself. The variety of Handel's invention and imagination may seem inexhaustible, but then you suddenly realise that something sounds familiar: it's one of Handel's borrowings, material recycled either from himself, or from another composer. Not all is original. But why did Handel borrow? (More about that in the chapter on 'Handel's borrowings'.)

How then (excuse the pun) do you get a handle on Handel? If this was a pocket travel guide, there would no doubt be an opening section on how to journey to the chosen destination and where to start sightseeing. For Handel, the music is both the journey and the ultimate destination, and the next chapter will begin to explore that. But there are also some places well worth visiting, in person if possible, or via the Internet if not, to connect with Handel the man, as well as the music. Westminster Abbey is a good place to begin (find www.westminster-abbey.org and enter 'Handel' in the search box). This is where the wonderful *Coronation Anthems* were first performed in 1727 for the crowning of King George II and Queen Caroline, and where the first of them, *Zadok the Priest*, has been sung at every coronation since. As noted above, it is also where Handel is buried, at the foot of the monument in the South Transept. Just over a century later when Charles Dickens died, the novelist Samuel Butler commented sniffily: 'They buried Dickens in the very next grave, cheek by jowl with Handel. It does not matter, but it pained me to think that people who could do this could become Deans of Westminster.'

The church of St George's, Hanover Square, near Bond Street in Central London was only just being built when Handel came to live in the area (visit www.stgeorgeshanoversquare.org and follow the links for 'History' and 'Handel at St George's'). Handel immediately became involved in advising on the installation of the church's organ and in appointing successive organists, and he attended services there regularly.

Nearby, at 25 Brook Street, is the house where Handel lived and worked from 1723 to the end of his life. The house was new when Handel bought it and the whole Mayfair area was only just being developed residentially. It is now a museum (opened in 2001) occupying the upper floors of No. 25 and No. 23, with the early Georgian interiors restored as closely as possible to those that Handel would have known. A collection of portraits of Handel and his contemporaries evokes the world in which he lived and there are also regular concerts and special exhibitions (see www.handelhouse.org). Incidentally, another flamboyant musician, the rock star Jimi Hendrix, lived briefly at No. 23 at the end of the 1960s.

The Foundling Museum, in Brunswick Square, Bloomsbury, is another London location with particular Handel associations (visit www.foundlingmuseum.org.uk and follow the link for 'Handel'). He was a governor and benefactor of the Foundling Hospital, established by Thomas Coram, which devoted itself to 'the maintenance and education of exposed and deserted young children'. Handel donated an organ to the chapel, gave an annual benefit performance of *Messiah* (which provided an important source of income), and eventually bequeathed the score and parts of *Messiah* to the Foundling Hospital in his will. The museum, opened in 2004 on the original site, now also houses the extensive Gerald Coke Handel Collection of manuscripts, printed music, libretti, books, paintings, engravings and other memorabilia. There is a permanent exhibition gallery and occasional special exhibitions.

The Foundling Hospital Chapel and its organ no longer exist, but in North London, at Stanmore, is a church and an organ that Handel knew well during his time working for James Brydges, Duke of Chandos: St Lawrence Whitchurch (visit www.little-stanmore.org and follow the link for 'History'). Bridges almost entirely rebuilt the church in 1715, after he bought the Cannons estate, and he had a new organ installed two years later. It has now been carefully restored and was used for Paul Nicholson's CD set of the complete Organ Concertos, among other recordings (see the section on 'Orchestral music').

Venturing further afield, the way to get right back to Handel's roots is to visit his birthplace in Halle in Germany. The house itself has had a chequered history since Handel's times, but now, restored and extensively developed since the Second World War, it is an important museum (see www.haendel-in-halle.de). Halle itself is home to an annual Handel Festival each June and to the scholarly and publishing activities of the Georg-Friedrich-Händel-Gesellschaft, an international society founded in 1955.

Halle is close to Leipzig where J. S. Bach spent much of his career, but the two composers never met. Bach travelled to Halle in 1719 to meet Handel, only to find he had already left for England. The story goes that ten years later, when Handel was back in Halle to see his mother, one of Bach's sons, Wilhelm Friedemann, brought an invitation to Handel to visit his father in Leipzig. Handel declined. Once again, how intriguing.

Picturing Handel

Many images of Handel exist – he certainly had more portraits painted than any other musician of his time – but what did he actually look like?

According to the music historian, John Hawkins, writing not long after Handel's death:

> Few of the pictures extant of him are to any tolerable degree likenesses . . . the most perfect resemblance of him is the statue on his monument, and in that the true lineaments of his face are apparent.

Handel himself was responsible for this monument. On 11 April 1759, only three days before he died, he modified his will for the fourth and final time, including the clause:

> I hope to have the permission of the Dean and Chapter of Westminster to be buried in Westminster Abbey in a private manner at the discretion of my Executor, Mr. Amyand, and I desire that my Executor, may have leave to erect a monument for me there.

Handel duly provided six hundred pounds for the monument, which was designed by Louis-François Roubiliac and installed in the Abbey on 15 July 1762.

So if you want to see Handel, you should really go to Westminster Abbey. The only problem is that when you get there, the monument is in a recess halfway up the wall in the South Transept (above his grave, which is immediately beneath your feet), so all you can do is gaze upwards: you can't really look Handel straight in the eye. However, if you study the photograph of the monument on the Abbey website (www.westminster-abbey.org/visitor/plan-of-the-abbey/12169) you do begin to feel that this was a real person. Granted, he is pointing at what appears to be an angel sitting in a cloud playing a harp hovering just above his head, but he is standing in front of an organ, surrounded by other musical instruments and with a score of *Messiah* open at the aria 'I know that my Redeemer liveth'. The composer's head is bare – no sign of the customary formal wig – as if this was a private moment of work and inspiration at home. As for Handel's face, it was supposedly modelled from a death mask which has since been lost (although photographs exist from earlier in the twentieth century) and it bears out Hawkins' description:

> His features were finely marked, and the general cast of his countenance placid, bespeaking dignity attempered with benevolence, and every quality of heart that has a tendency to beget confidence and insure esteem.

This was actually Roubiliac's second monument of Handel. The first was a statue for Vauxhall Gardens, which is now located in the Victoria and Albert Museum in London (visit www.vam.ac.uk and follow the links for Handel and Roubiliac). On 18 April 1738 the *London Daily Post* reported:

> We are informed from very good Authority; that there is now finished a Statue of the justly celebrated Mr. Handel, exquisitely done by the ingenious Mr. Raubillac [sic], of St. Martin's Lane, Statuary, out of one entire block of white Marble, which is to be placed in a grand Nich, erected on Purpose in the great Grove at Vaux-hall-Gardens, at the sole Expence of Mr. Tyers, Undertaker of the Entertainment there; who in Consideration of the real Merit of the inimitable Master, thought it proper, that his Effigies should preside there, where his Harmony has so often charm'd even the greatest Crouds into the profoundest Calm and most decent behaviour; it is believed that the Expence of the Statue and Nich cannot cost less than Three Hundred Pounds.

The statue was unveiled on 1 May that year, and showed Handel seated, in informal clothes and again without a wig – this time he wears a soft cap. He is playing a lyre and leaning on a pile of books. At his feet sits a cherub, with a viol, oboe and flute, writing down the music that Handel draws from his lyre. One of the books is identified as the score of *Alexander's Feast*, Handel's setting of the ode by Dryden, which was completed the previous year, 1737. The lyre identifies Handel with the heroic figures of Apollo and Orpheus, and Roubiliac may also have been making a connection with Dryden's text: 'Timotheus plac'd on high . . . with flying fingers touch'd the lyre'. Music historian, Charles Burney, however, cast a more literal eye over the statue and was unimpressed:

> The musician is represented playing upon a Lyre. Now if this statue should be preserved from the ravages of time and accident 12 or 4000 years, the Antiquaries will naturally conclude that the instrument upon which Handel acquired his reputation was the Lyre; though we are at present certain that he never played on, or even saw a Lyre, except in wood or stone.

Burney does rather seem to have missed the point there! Nevertheless, the question remains: what do these and other representations of Handel really tell us about him? Among the many portraits are some significant ones commissioned by his friends and some he owned himself. They were mainly by German artists, or artists associated with Germany, until later in his life when Handel sat for the Englishman Thomas Hudson. Here are four of them:

*c.*1726. Portrait by Balthasar Denner of Handel aged about forty. Owned by Handel and now in the National Portrait Gallery (NPG 1976). It shows him in three-quarter profile, dressed in formal attire and full wig, staring confidently out of the canvas at the artist. (View it at www.npg.org.uk/live/search and follow the link for Handel.)
*c.*1730. Portrait by Philip Mercier of Handel in his mid-forties. Owned by Handel and now in a private collection. It shows him in the act of composing, gazing thoughtfully at the artist, in informal attire and wearing a cap instead of

a wig. He is seated beside a harpsichord, resting his head in his left hand, and holding a quill pen, with an unfinished piece of music in front of him. (View it at www.haendel.haendelhaus.de/de/biographie/portraets and follow the link to 1726–31, No. 6.)

1749. Portrait by Thomas Hudson of Handel aged sixty-four. Owned by Handel and probably given to his relatives in Halle in 1750 – his last visit to Germany – and now in the Staats- und Universitätsbibliothek, Hamburg. It shows him seated in formal attire and full wig, corpulent, his right hand braced on his thigh with thumb extended, his left hand holding a sheaf of music. He is looking forcefully out of the picture to the right of the artist – a man of strong character and natural authority. (View it at www. haendel.haendelhaus.de/de/biographie/portraets and follow the link to 1748–9, No. 15.)

1756. Portrait by Thomas Hudson of Handel aged seventy-one. Commissioned by Charles Jennens (librettist of *Messiah*). Now in the National Portrait Gallery (NPG 3970). A full-length portrait, it shows him formally attired, with full wig, seated next to a table on which is a copy of *Messiah*. His right hand rests on the handle of a walking-cane and his left hand is tucked into the front of his jacket. He appears to stare placidly at the artist, but he is blind. (View it at www.npg.org.uk/live/search and follow the link for Handel.)

An engraving by Jacobus Houbraken, *c.*1738, should also be mentioned. It was issued to subscribers to the printed score of *Alexander's Feast*, which was published by Handel himself and available from his house in Brook Street. It therefore presumably had his approval as a fair likeness, although according to Hawkins, 'the features are too prominent', and indeed it is anything but flattering. It is now in the Gerald Coke Collection at the Foundling Museum in London. (View it at www.npg.org.uk/live/search and follow the link for Handel and D3214.)

Even less flattering are various caricatures of Handel, notably one entitled *The Harmonious Boar* by Joseph Goupy, satirising Handel's prodigious appetite – both for food and for big musical effects. It pictures him with a pig's head, sitting on a wine barrel, squeezed in behind the keyboard of an organ and surrounded by more food, drink, drums, horn, trumpet and bassoon, among other things. Goupy, a friend of Handel's, is reported to have penned it in outrage after being invited to dine with Handel one evening and discovering that he had been served a very plain and frugal meal, while Handel had excused himself and retired to an adjoining room where he enjoyed a sumptuous spread! It is now in the Fitzwilliam Museum in Cambridge. (View it at www.fitzmuseum.cam.ac.uk/opac/search/cataloguedetail.html and follow the links for Handel and Goupy.) A later version of this caricature was entitled *The Charming Brute*. It is now in the Gerald Coke collection at the Foundling Museum. (View it at www.wikipedia.org and search for Joseph Goupy.)

So how do these portraits accord with the descriptions Handel's contemporaries gave of him? Well, the wig was certainly important, according to Charles Burney:

> Handel wore an enormous white wig, and, when things went well at the Oratorio, it had a certain nod, or vibration, which manifested his pleasure and satisfaction. Without it, nice observers were certain that he was out of humour.

The wig was not the only thing about Handel that was enormous, according to William Coxe, who wrote a book of *Anecdotes* about Handel and emphasised Handel's sheer size:

> He was large in person, and his natural corpulency, which increased as he advanced in life, rendered his whole appearance of that bulky proportion, as to give rise to Quin's inelegant, but forcible expression; that his hands were feet, and his fingers toes. From a sedentary life, he had contracted a stiffness in his joints, which in addition to his great weight and weakness of body, rendered his gait awkward; still his countenance was open, manly, and animated; expressive of all that grandeur and benevolence, which were the prominent features of his character.

Burney also remembered Handel's imposing physical presence, but like Coxe and Hawkins, he was chiefly taken with his 'countenance':

> The figure of Handel was large, and he was somewhat corpulent, and unwieldy in his motions; but his countenance, which I remember as perfectly as that of any man I saw but yesterday, was full of fire and dignity; and such as impressed ideas of superiority and genius.

He was not always a good-natured genius, according to Burney:

> Handel's general look was somewhat heavy and sour; but when he did smile, it was his sire the sun, bursting out of a black cloud. There was a sudden flash of intelligence, wit, and good humour, beaming in his countenance, which I hardly ever saw in any other.

That 'heavy and sour look' was no doubt emphasised by the determined set of Handel's mouth, and it is this instantly recognisable feature that every authentic portrait of him has in common – even (and maybe especially) the later Hudson portrait, painted when Handel was blind. The early Denner portrait is especially compelling. It presents Handel in a particularly bold but complex manner. Handel was at the height of his powers, composing brilliant operas for London, when Denner – his exact contemporary – painted it. Handel has a knowing expression and you feel that he is scrutinising you, sizing you up, every bit as much as you are looking at him. He is self-confident, maybe a little arrogant; successful, and slightly supercilious; enigmatic, forever calculating and scheming; streetwise and crafty, clearly at ease with himself and the world; but also private, ironic, somewhat detached. No wonder that those who knew Handel often found him difficult to deal with – very much a larger-than-life character.

Meeting Handel

Halfway through the first biography of Handel, John Mainwaring slips in a brief sentence that passes almost unnoticed: 'The greatest talents are often accompanied with the greatest weaknesses.' It is a key to Handel's complex personality. As the music historian, John Hawkins, put it:

> Such as were but little acquainted with Handel are unable to characterize him otherwise than by his excellencies in his art, and certain foibles in his behaviour, which he was never studious to conceal: accordingly we are told that he had a great appetite, and that when he was provoked he would break out into profane expressions.

In other words, Handel was a disconcerting man: a genius, no doubt, but also somewhat vulgar. Mainwaring stresses his independence and obstinacy:

> In the sequel of his life he refused the highest offers from persons of the greatest distinction; nay, the highest favours from the fairest of the sex, only because he would not be cramped or confined by particular attachments . . . This noble spirit of independency, which possessed him almost from his childhood, was never known to forsake him, not even in the most distressing seasons of his life.

In 1737, when Handel became partially paralysed, 'Tho' he had the best advice, and tho' the necessity of following it was urged to him in the most friendly manner, it was with the utmost difficulty that he was prevailed on to do what was proper, when it was in any way disagreeable.' Eventually Handel did agree to go to Aix-la-Chapelle for a health cure, and charactistically he then spent three times longer in the vapour baths than was usual – 'his sweats were profuse beyond imagining' – made a miraculous recovery, and immediately took himself off to a nearby church to play the organ!

No doubt a very good dinner then followed, for Handel's appetite was prodigious. It was a source of some embarrassment to his biographers, who tried to justify it in various ways. Mainwaring did so on the grounds that everything about Handel was exceptional:

> Those who have blamed him for an excessive indulgence in this lowest of gratifications, ought to have considered, that the peculiarities of his constitution were as great as those of his character ... It would be as unreasonable to confine Handel to the fare and allowance of common men, as to expect that a London merchant should live like a Swiss mechanic. Not that I would absolve him from all blame on this article. He certainly paid more attention to it, than is becoming in any man: but it is some excuse, that Nature had given him so vigorous a constitution, so exquisite a palate, and so craving an appetite; and that fortune enabled him to obey these calls, to satisfy the demands of nature.

Burney argued that there were, after all, worse vices:

> Handel, with many virtues, was addicted to no vice that was injurious to society. Nature, indeed, required a great supply of sustenance to support such a huge mass, and he was rather epicurean in the choice of it; but this seems to have been the only appetite he allowed himself to gratify.

And William Coxe pointed out that whatever Handel's body was doing, his mind was always on higher things:

> His chief foible was a culpable indulgence in the sensual gratification of the table; but this foible was amply compensated by a sedulous attention to every religious duty, and moral obligation.

Mainwaring, meanwhile, found another excuse for this overeating, in the sheer amount of work Handel had to do:

> I mean his incessant and intense application to the studies of his profession. This rendered constant and large

supplies of nourishment the more necessary to recruit his exhausted spirits. Had he hurt his health or his fortune by indulgences of this kind, they would have been vicious: as he did not, they were at the most indecorous.

And according to Burney, if you dined with Handel, it might appear that he was never free from work:

The late Mr. Brown [sic], leader of his majesty's band, used to tell me several stories of Handel's love of good cheer, liquid and solid, as well as of his impatience. Of the former he gave an instance, which was accidentally discovered at his own house in Brook Street, where Brown, in the Oratorio season, among other principal performers, was at dinner. During the repast, Handel cried out – 'Oh – I have de taught,' [a thought, or inspiration] when the company, unwilling that, out of civility to them, the public should be robbed of any thing so valuable as his musical ideas, begged he would retire and write them down; with which request, however, he so frequently complied, that, at last, one of the most suspicious had the ill-bred curiosity to peep through the key-hole into the adjoining room; where he perceived that dese taughts, were only bestowed on a fresh hamper of Burgundy, which, as was afterwards discovered, he had received in a present from his friend, the late lord Radnor, while his company was regaled with more generous and spirited port.

Burney's first glimpse of Handel took place when he was only a boy of fourteen and Handel had stopped off at Chester on his way to Ireland for the premiere of *Messiah* in 1741:

I was at the Public School in that city and very well remember seeing him smoke a pipe, over a dish of coffee, at the Exchange Coffee House; for being extremely curious to see so extraordinary a man, I watched him narrowly as long as he remained in Chester, which, on account of the wind being unfavourable for his embarking at Parkgate, was several days. During this time, he applied to Mr. Baker, the Organist, my first music master, to know whether there were any choirmen in the cathedral who could sing at sight, as he wished to prove some books that had been hastily transcribed, by trying the choruses which he intended to perform in Ireland. Mr. Baker mentioned some of the most likely singers then in Chester, and, among the rest, a printer the name of Janson, who had a good bass voice and was one of the best musicians in the choir . . .

A time was fixed for this private rehearsal at the Golden Falcon, where Handel was quartered; but, alas! on trial of the chorus in the *Messiah*, 'And with his stripes we are healed,' poor Janson, after repeated attempts, failed so egregiously, that Handel let loose his great bear upon him; and after swearing in four or five languages, cried out in broken English: 'You shcauntrel! tit not you dell me dat you could sing at soite?' 'Yes, sir,' says the printer, 'and so I can, but not at first sight.'

Stories of Handel abound in quotations from him rendered phonetically by those who tried to catch the idiosyncrasies of his speech. And they had plenty of opportunity to listen to him: 'Handel was in the habit of talking to himself, so loud, that it was easy for persons not very near him, to hear the subject of his soliloquies.'

Hawkins had many conversations with him: 'The style of his discourse was very singular; he pronounced the English as the Germans do, but his phrase was exotic, and partook of the idiom of the different countries in which he had resided, a circumstance that rendered his conversation exceedingly entertaining.' Burney also remembered how entertaining Handel was:

His natural propensity to wit and humour, and happy manner of relating common occurrences in an uncommon way, enabled him to throw persons and things into very ridiculous attitudes. Had he been as great a master of the

English language as Swift, his *bons mots* would have been as frequent, and somewhat of the same kind.

But Coxe pointed out that in some areas Handel was a master of the English language:

> Though he was not able to pronounce the English with correctness, he thoroughly comprehended its nature and effects. In the funeral anthems, and the oratorios selected from the Scriptures, the words were principally chosen by himself; and the devotion of sounds, if the expression may be allowed, is in unison with the dignity, simple piety, and grandeur of the sacred writings.

You begin to suspect that maybe it suited Handel to cultivate his broken speech – he was, after all, far too intelligent not to have completely mastered spoken English had he wanted to, and he also knew Latin, French and Italian. So perhaps we are dealing here with an early example of a composer deliberately constructing an 'image', of interacting with people on his own terms. So what lay underneath the mask? According to Burney,

> Though he was so rough in his language, and in the habit of swearing, a vice much more in fashion than at present, he was truly pious, during the last years of his life, and constantly attended public prayers, twice a day, winter and summer, both in London and Tunbridge.

Hawkins was able to observe Handel at his devotions:

> For the last two or three years of his life he was used to attend divine service in his own parish church of St George, Hanover Square, where, during the prayers, the eyes that at this instant are employed in a faint portrayal of his excellencies, have seen him on his knees, expressing by his looks and gesticulations the utmost fervour of devotion.

But, for all this, Hawkins was clear that Handel's piety was anything but fanatical:

In his religion he was of the Lutheran profession; in which he was not such a bigot as to decline a general conformity with that of the country which he had chosen for his residence . . . and he would often speak of it as one of the great felicities of his life that he was settled in a country where no man suffers any molestation or inconvenience on account of his religious principles.

Coxe linked Handel's spirituality closely with his music:

His great delight was derived from his attachment to his own science, and he experienced particular satisfaction from religious principles, in presiding at the organ in the cathedral church of St Paul. He frequently declared in conversation, the high gratification he enjoyed in setting the Scriptures to music, and how greatly he was edified by contemplating the sublime passages abounding in the sacred writings . . . His pen . . . is sublime, affecting, animated, and devoted, without the gloom of superstition, to the service of God.

Coxe also pointed out that there were various practical sides to Handel's devotions:

Handel's religious disposition was not a mere display, it was amply productive of religion's best fruit, charity; and this liberal sentiment not only influenced him in the day of prosperity, but even when standing on the very brink of ruin. He performed *Acis and Galatea* (1740), for the benefit of the musical fund: the next year he gave them his *Epithalamium*, called 'Parnasso in Festa', and further extended his kindness by a legacy of one thousand pounds.

In the later years of his life Handel took a particular interest in the work of Thomas Coram's Foundling Hospital in London:

His early exertions in its favour were the principal support of that respectable establishment. He gave an organ to the chapel; and an annual benefit, by which seven thousand pounds was cleared in the course of a few years. He also presented the governors with the original score of the *Messiah*.

And there were more private displays of charity:

> He was equally attentive to the claims of friendship, affection and gratitude. The widow of his master Zackau [*sic*], being old and poor, received from him frequent remittances; and her son would have enjoyed the benefits of his liberality; but for his profligacy, and incurable drunkenness.

These acts of charity were made possible by Handel's careful managing of his finances. Although he was essentially a freelance musician, he benefited from royal patronage and three pensions from successive monarchs which eventually totalled six hundred pounds per year: two hundred from Queen Anne, a further two hundred from King George I, and two hundred from King George II in return for teaching music to the royal princesses. These sums apart, however,

> The rest was precarious; for some time it depended upon his engagement with the directors of the Academy, and afterwards upon the profits arising from the musical performances carried on by him on his own account. However, he had at all times the prudence to regulate his expense by his income.

This is Hawkins' elegant way of saying that Handel invested wisely and clawed himself back from the brink of bankruptcy several times. Occasionally he would also indulge one particular interest, which he had cultivated and refined since his early years spent in Italy: 'Like many of his profession, he had a great love for painting; and, till his sight failed him, among the few amusements he gave into, the going to view collections of pictures upon sale was the chief.'

So how did this maverick composer interact with people? If you were royalty you could expect deference, but also, as

Burney recalls, legendary displays of impatience if Handel had to wait for the royal party to arrive for a performance, or if anyone dared to talk during it. It was left to royalty to smooth things over: 'The Princess of Wales, with her accustomed mildness and benignity, used to say, "Hush! Hush! Handel's in a passion." ' And royalty remained loyal to the end: 'The King, and Prince and Princess of Wales, were ever fond of his music, and attended his Oratorios, even when they were so much deserted, that Lord Chesterfield wittily, but ill naturedly called attending an oratorio, "an intrusion on his Majesty's privacy".'

If you were a musician working with Handel, life was certainly never dull, as Coxe recalled:

> It is true, indeed, that the composer was not of a temper to treat singers with great respect; he considered them, perhaps too much, as mere instruments, which gave utterance to that harmony, of which he was so distinguished an Author. He possessed the impetuosity and inflexibility of genius . . . In temper he was irascible, impatient of contradiction, but not vindictive; jealous of his musical pre-eminence, and tenacious in all points, which regarded his professional honour.

But if you were compliant, you might expect sympathetic treatment, according to Burney: 'I acquired considerable knowledge of his private character and turn for humour. He was very fond of Mrs Cibber, whose voice and manners had softened his severity for her want of musical knowledge.'

And if Handel was in a good mood you would certainly be forgiven a little artistic license, as Matthew Dubourg, leader of the orchestra in Dublin, discovered to his relief:

> One night, while Handel was in Dublin, Dubourg having a solo part in a song, and a close to make, *ad libitum*, he wandered about in different keys a great while, and seemed indeed a little bewildered, and uncertain of his original key . . . but, at length, coming to the shake, which was to

terminate this long close, Handel, to the great delight of
the audience, and augmentation of applause, cried out loud
enough to be heard in the most remote parts of the theatre:
'You are welcome home, Mr Dubourg!'

Mainwaring, however, recounts a famous, fiery incident
with Francesca Cuzzoni, one of Handel's headstrong divas:

> Having one day some words with Cuzzoni on her refusing
> to sing 'False imagine' in *Ottone*; 'Oh! Madame' (said he)
> 'je sçais bien que vous êtes une veritable diablesse: mais je
> vous ferai sçavoir, moi, que je suis Beelzebub le Chef des
> Diables.' With this he took her up by the waist, and, if she
> made any more words, swore he would fling her out of the
> window.

And Burney recounts the time when the castrato Carestini
tried the same trick of refusing to sing an aria – one which
ironically turned out to be a great favourite:

> 'Verdi prati', which was constantly encored during the
> whole run of *Alcina*, was, at first, sent back to Handel by
> Carestini, as unfit for him to sing; upon which he [Handel]
> went, in a great rage, to his house, and in a way which
> few composers, except Handel, ever ventured to accost a
> first-singer, cries out: 'You toc! don't I know better as your
> seluf, vaat is pest for you to sing? If you vill not sing all de
> song I give you, I will not pay you ein stiver.'

Hawkins remembers Handel's disastrous falling out with his
principal castrato, the popular, but increasing arrogant
Francesco Bernadi, known as Senesino: 'Handel was not a
proud man, but he was capricious: in his comparison of the
merit of a composer and those of a singer, he estimated the
latter at a very low rate.' Exactly what went wrong is not clear,
but according to Mainwaring, Handel decided it was time for
Senesino to be taught a lesson:

> To manage him, he disdained; to control him with a
> high-hand, he in vain attempted. The one was perfectly

refractory; the other was equally outrageous. He remained inflexible in his resolution to punish Senesino for refusing him that submission, which he had been used to receive, and which he thought he had a right to demand: but a little pliability would have saved him abundance of trouble.

'Pliability', however, was not in Handel's nature, as Hawkins knew:

Such as are not acquainted with the personal character of Handel, will wonder at his seeming temerity, in continuing so long an opposition which tended but to impoverish him; but he was a man of firm and intrepid spirit, no way slave to the passion of avarice, and would have gone greater lengths than he did, rather than submit to those whom he had ever looked on as his inferiors.

As Mainwaring points out, all of this was just Handel's way of creating and maintaining his exacting high standards in an otherwise haphazard musical world:

The perfect authority which Handel maintained over the singers and the band, or rather the total subjection in which he held them, was of more consequence than can well be imagined. It was the chief means of preserving that order and decorum, that union and tranquillity, which seldom are found to subsist for any long continuance in musical societies.

In a word, Handel was totally uncompromising, and it could cost him dear, as Coxe points out:

He was averse to all restraint upon his freedom . . .
In England he was always well received and warmly patronised; but his general aversion to subscription engagements, and the resolute inflexibility of his temper, prevented the accession of some friends, and alienated others. With conscious pride, he was unwilling to be indebted but to his own abilities for his advancement, and they finally triumphed over all his opposers.

The same point is taken up by Mainwaring:

> It is a principal part of prudence, to command our temper
> on any trial we may chance to receive; a part of it which,
> to say the truth, he never practised or professed. This
> omission involved him in misfortunes, which taught him
> another part of prudence (if it must be called so) which he
> never ought to have practised, much less professed, that of
> consulting his interest at the expense of his art.

As for Handel's opinions of other composers, Burney recounts
an incident that took place one morning while Handel was at
the barber's. He was informed by a colleague, the violinist
Abraham Browne, that the Reverend Mr William Felton was
opening a subscription for a second set of his own organ
concertos and 'was extremely ambitious of the honour of his
[Handel's] name and acceptance of a book, merely to grace his
list, without involving him in any kind of expense':

> Handel, putting the barber's hand aside, got up in a fury,
> and with his face still in a lather, cries out with great
> vehemence: 'Tamn your seluf and go to der teiffel – a
> barson make Concerto! why he no make sarmon?' [Damn
> your self and go to the devil! A parson write a concerto!
> Why doesn't he write a sermon?] Brown[sic], seeing him
> in such a rage with razors in his reach, got out of the room
> as fast as he could.

Even a more distinguished composer than Felton could feel
the sharpness of Handel's tongue. Maurice Greene admired
Handel to the extent of often acting as his bellows-blower
when Handel first came to London, and liked to play the
organ at St Paul's Cathedral. Burney explains that Handel,
'after the three o'clock prayers, used frequently to get himself
and young Greene locked up in the church together; and, in
summer, often stript into his shirt, and played till eight or nine
o'clock at night'. But on being told later that Greene had set
one of Alexander Pope's lyrical odes, Handel replied dismis-
sively: 'It is de very ding vat my pellows-plower has set already

for ein tockter's tecree at Cambridge.' [It is the very thing that
my bellows-blower has already set for a Doctor's degree at
Cambridge.] And when Handel was asked his opinion of the
composer Gluck, 'his answer, prefaced by an oath **** was,
"he knows no more of contrapunto, as mein cook, Waltz." '
Yes, Handel's cook really did have the musical name of
Gustavus Waltz!

Away from the public arena, however, did Handel have a
close circle of friends? Coxe suggests not: 'Handel contracted
few intimacies, and when his early friends died, he was not
solicitous of acquiring new ones.' Burney accounts for this by
Handel's single-minded pursuit of music:

> He knew the value of time too well to spend it in frivolous
> pursuits, or with futile companions, however high in rank.
> Fond of his art, and diligent in its cultivation, and the
> exercise of it, as a profession, he spent so studious and
> sedentary a life, as seldom allowed him to mix in society,
> or partake of public amusements.

Hawkins agrees. Friends were at best a distraction:

> His social affections were not very strong; and to this
> may be imputed that he spent his whole life in a state of
> celibacy; that he had no female attachment of another kind
> may be ascribed to a better reason. His intimate friends
> were but few.

And what of Handel's sexuality? It is an ambiguous subject
that has been much debated in recent years. But the 'Handel
was gay' lobby has no real evidence to go on. So for the
moment we might as well accept Coxe's version of what
remain the mysteries of Handel's personal life:

> He was never married; but his celibacy must not be
> attributed to any deficiency of personal attractions . . . On
> the contrary, it was owing to the independence of his
> disposition, which feared degradation, and dreaded
> confinement. For when he was young, two of his scholars,

ladies of considerable fortune, were so much enamoured
of him, that each was desirous of a matrimonial alliance.
The first is said to have fallen a victim to her attachment.
Handel would have married her; but his pride was stung
by the coarse declaration of her mother, that she never
would consent to the marriage of her daughter with a
fiddler; and, indignant at the expression, he declined all
further intercourse. After the death of the mother, the
father renewed the acquaintance, and informed him that
all obstacles were removed; but he replied, that the time
was now past; and the young lady fell into decline, which
soon terminated her existence. The second attachment,
was a lady splendidly related, whose hand he might have
obtained by renouncing his profession. That condition he
resolutely refused, and laudably declined the connection
which was to prove a restriction on the great faculties
of his mind.

So what would it have been like to meet Mr Handel? What
would you have thought as you shook hands with this over-
weight, bow-legged autocrat who liked vast quantities of food,
talked to himself, swore in several languages, and conversed
with you in only broken and heavily inflected English? How
would you have reconciled what you had been told about his
piety and good works with all the other stories about his short
temper and high-handed treatment of colleagues and friends?
How would you have connected the all-too-human figure
standing before you with the composer of some of the most
sublime music you had ever heard?

Well maybe it is precisely the all-too-human aspects of
Handel that make him the composer of such sublime music. A
humanity as flawed, yet as all-embracing, as all-seeing as
Handel's, could be precisely what makes his music touch us so
deeply. That was very much the attitude of the film director,
Tony Palmer, and playwright, John Osborne, when they made
their controversial television film in 1985 to coincide with the
tercentenary of Handel's birth, *God Rot Tunbridge Wells*. It was

released for the first time on DVD in 2008 (Voiceprint, TPDVD 114), with booklet notes by Palmer looking back over the intervening years. 'I can quite see why the film . . . caused the purists to wet their pants,' writes Palmer. 'Not for the first (nor the last) time, John Osborne had taken aim at an icon of "British" culture, and come up with an altogether radical view of a national treasure, which treasures him for what he really was, a man who stood with his chin out, breast puffed up with bull-like stance, defiantly his own man.'

The film starred Trevor Howard as the aged Handel, alone and surveying his life in an extended monologue, illustrated with flashbacks. The specially recorded music was conducted with great brio by Charles Mackerras. 'The words put into Handel's mouth, although completely invented,' explains Tony Palmer, 'had derived from a clever reworking of those texts which Handel himself had used in his in his various operas and oratorios. Thus the King James Bible and the Book of Common Prayer, two books Osborne held in reverential awe, came singing onto the screen in unforgettable resonance, with the gin-soaked and pickled voice of Trevor Howard relishing every last syllable.' The film was made on a shoestring: it's brilliant, and flawed, and compelling. It makes you wonder if maybe you are meeting Handel.

Essential Handel

Handel said very little about his own works. He did however tell John Hawkins that he was particularly proud of two opera arias:

> Mr Handel looked upon the two airs, Cara Sposa, and Ombra Cara, as the two finest he ever made, and declared this his opinion to the author of this work.

'Cara sposa' comes from Act I of *Rinaldo* (1711), and 'Ombra cara' from Act II of *Radamisto* (1720). Both are indeed wonderful and they share a similar emotional intensity, with both heroes plunged in the deepest despair, and the orchestra weaving intricate lines around each voice.

Handel also told Thomas Morell, one of his librettists, that he thought *Theodora* (1750) was the best of his oratorios:

> And when I once asked him whether he did not look upon the Grand Chorus ['Hallelujah'] in the *Messiah* as his Master Piece? 'No', says he, 'I think the Chorus at the end of the second part in *Theodora* far beyond it.' ['He saw the lovely youth' etc.]

This chorus is another example of Handel at his most emotionally complex, moving from despair to hope as the persecuted Christians recall the story from St Luke's Gospel of the Widow of Nain mourning her lost son and rejoicing when he is restored to life. Winton Dean suggests that it 'embodies an intimate reflection of the composer's own spiritual preoccupations' in the latter years of his life.

So what would Handel's contemporaries have chosen? Well, none of Handel's top three choices featured in the first big music festival in London after his death, but the Handel Commemoration Concerts of 1784 give us a good idea of what was most popular at that time. The five concerts were held at Westminster Abbey and at the Pantheon in Oxford Street, and two of them were devoted to performances of *Messiah*. The other concerts were mixed programmes. Here are the complete details as reported in Charles Burney's book, *An Account of the Musical Performances in Westminster Abbey . . . in Commemoration of Handel*. (N.B. 'The Coronation Anthem' is *Zadok the Priest*, the 'Hautbois Concertos' refer to the Concerti Grossi, Op. 3, and 'Grand Concertos' refer to the Concerti Grossi, Op. 6, and some of the titles of the operas have been anglicised: e.g. 'Otho' instead of *Ottone*):

First Performance, Westminster Abbey, Wednesday, 26 May 1784
The Coronation Anthem
Part I
Overture – *Esther*
The *Dettingen Te Deum*
Part II
Overture, with the Dead March in *Saul*
Part of the Funeral Anthem
  When the ear heard him
  He delivered the poor that cried
  His body is buried in peace
'Gloria patri', from the *Jubilate*
Part III
Anthem – *O Sing unto the Lord*
Chorus – 'The Lord shall reign', from *Israel in Egypt*

Second Performance, Pantheon, Thursday Evening, 27 May 1784
Part I
Second Hautbois Concerto
'Sorge infausta', Air in *Orlando*
'Ye sons of Israel', Chorus in *Joshua*
'Rende il sereno', Air in *Sosarmes*
'Caro vieni', in *Richard the First*
'He smote all the first-born', Chorus from *Israel in Egypt*
'Va tacito e nascosto', Air in *Julius Caesar*

Sixth Grand Concerto
'M'allontano sdegnose pupille', Air in *Atalanta*
'He gave them hail-stones for rain', Chorus in *Israel in Egypt*
Part II
Fifth Grand Concerto
'Dite che fà', Air in *Ptolemy*
'Vi fida la sposo', in *Aetius*
'Fallen is the foe', Chorus in *Judas Maccabaeus*
Overture of *Ariadne*
'Alma del gran Pompeo', Accompanied recitative in
Julius Caesar
Followed by
'Affani del pensier', Air in *Otho*
'Nasco al bosco', Air in *Aetius*
'Io t'abbraccio', Duet in *Rodelinda*
Eleventh Grand Concerto
'Ah! Mio cor!', Air in *Alcina*
Anthem – *My heart is inditing of a good matter*

Third Performance, Westminster Abbey, Saturday, 29 May
1784
The Messiah

Fourth Performance, Westminster Abbey, 3 June 1784
By Command of His Majesty
Part I
Overture – *Esther*
The *Dettingen Te Deum*
Part II
Overture of *Tamerlane*, and Dead March in *Saul*
Part of the Funeral Anthem
  When the ear heard him
  He delivered the poor that cried
  His body is buried in peace
'Gloria patri', from the *Jubilate*
Part III
Air and Chorus – 'Jehovah crown'd with glory bright', in *Esther*
First Grand Concerto

Chorus – 'Gird on thy sword', in *Saul*
Fourth Hautbois Concerto
Anthem – *O sing unto the Lord all the whole earth*
Chorus – 'The Lord shall reign for ever and ever', *Israel in Egypt*
Coronation Anthem – *Zadok the Priest*

Fifth Performance
The Messiah
By Command of His Majesty
In Westminster Abbey
Saturday, 5 June 1784

How tastes change. There are a couple of pieces from 1784 that might still feature in a popular concert of Handel extracts, but a modern programme, or a 'Best of . . .' CD could well look more like this:

'Hallelujah' chorus (from *Messiah*)
'Arrival of the Queen of Sheba' (from *Solomon*)
Hornpipe (from the *Water Music*)
Largo (from *Serse*)
Sarabande (orchestrated from the Keyboard Suite in
D minor, HWV 437)
'Let the bright seraphim' (from *Samson*)
'See the conqu'ring hero comes' (from *Judas Maccabaeus*)
'Where'er you walk' (from *Semele*)
'Harmonious Blacksmith' (Keyboard Suite in E major,
HWV 430)
'Silent Worship' (adapted from *Tolomeo*)

Moving from extracts to complete works, what could make up a Handel Top Ten? The answer of course will vary from person to person, but here, as a guide to listening, is one suggestion from each of the main genres in which Handel composed. I have set aside Handel's two most iconic works – *Messiah* and the *Water Music* – on the *Desert Island Discs* principle that they are utterly essential: the equivalents of the Bible and Shakespeare which you miraculously always find waiting for you as a castaway!

So, with *Messiah* and the *Water Music* already in your pocket, here are ten other possible choices (see the various sections on Handel's music for commentaries on these works):

Opera: *Alcina*
Oratorio: *Israel in Egypt*
Ode: *Alexander's Feast*
Sacred vocal (Latin): *Dixit Dominus*
Sacred vocal (English): *Coronation Anthems*
Secular vocal: Italian Cantatas, beginning with *La Lucrezia*
Orchestral: Concerti Grossi, Op. 3
Concertos: Organ Concertos, Op. 4
Chamber: Trio Sonatas, Op. 2
Keyboard: The Eight Great Suites

HIP Handel

If you put 'HIP Handel' into www.google.co.uk on the Internet you get some curious results – try it! – but one of them is directly relevant: a page on the Handel and Haydn Society website. For HIP read 'Historically Informed Performance', the term that has grown up around the scholars and performers who have led the 'early music' revival, the movement that gathered momentum in the 1970s and gradually came to dominate the concert hall and especially the recording catalogue.

In broad terms, its aims were to return to the sources, consulting instrumental and vocal treatises of the period and rediscovering authentic instruments and radically different vocal styles. The results, although somewhat hit-and-miss at first (authentic did not always mean better!) have been far-reaching, and few composers have benefited more than Handel. For while Bach could survive the heavy-handed, albeit well-intentioned, approach of a conductor like Karl Richter – maybe because the aura of the study and the church made for an intellectual as well as an emotional experience – Handel just got trampled. Why? Because Handel is the supreme theatrical composer in whatever genre he is writing (a recurring theme of this book). Therefore he always needs light, space and air – and above all, he needs *gesture*. The notes – melody, harmony, counterpoint – are not enough on their own: they need *performance* to come alive. As this has been increasingly understood and demonstrated by the early music movement, Handel has been revealed as an ever greater composer.

I remember as a flute student what richness there seemed to be in the sonatas of J. S. Bach, and how pallid the Handel sonatas seemed in comparison. Well, the Bach sonatas are rich (and have been revealed to be even richer as players like Barthold Kuijken have explored them anew them on the baroque flute), but so are the Handel sonatas, only in a different way. Handel is always much more a visceral than intellectual composer. Hearing the baroque flautist Jed Wentz play this music as if he was one of Handel's operatic divas – alternately exultant, despairing, imploring, and with such flamboyant style – is a revelation. You suddenly realise that when you perform any Handel score, the curtain must always go up and the stage must fill with light.

You can also hear that very clearly in Andrew Manze's approach to Handel's violin sonatas. In Manze's hands, these works really are extraordinarily varied and eloquent, but they don't always look it on the page, or sound it in some other recordings. To release the real music you have to get behind and beyond the notes. For every composer, but for Handel especially, it's all in the performance. Just listen to Manze prove that with the Academy of Ancient Music in the Concerti Grossi, Op. 6, or John Eliot Gardiner with the English Baroque Soloists in the *Water Music* and *Fireworks Music*. As for Handel's operas and choral works, after William Christie's recording of *Acis and Galatea*, or Christopher Hogwood's *Rinaldo*, or René Jacobs' *Saul*, surely there is no going back. In fact the recording catalogue is well served at present with conductors who really understand Handel: among them are Harry Bicket, Ivor Bolton, Harry Christophers, Laurence Cummings, Christian Curnyn, Alan Curtis, Robert King, Paul McCreesh, Nicholas McGegan, Charles Mackerras, Marc Minkowski, Hervé Niquet, Trevor Pinnock and Christophe Rousset.

So this is very much a HIP Handel Guide and I hope you find the journey through the recordings as exhilarating as I have. Of course HIP Handel was not suddenly invented in the 1970s, it was just refocused, so by no means all of the recommended recordings are recent, or on authentic instruments. But wherever possible I have gone for those that have *life*, that really take the stage. For Handel you need heart, not just brains.

Handel the performer

Imagine Handel in 1710, a vigorous twenty-five-year-old who had learned his craft in Halle and Hamburg, perfected it in Florence, Rome and Venice, and was now returning to Germany, weighing up the options for where his career might take him next. In Handel's own words, related to John Hawkins, ' "When I first arrived at Hanover I was young man . . . I understood somewhat of music, and", putting forth both his broad hands, and extending his fingers, "could play pretty well on the organ".'

A disarming understatement! This, after all, was the young man who a few years earlier had been spotted in Venice at Carnival time. According to John Mainwaring, 'he was first discovered there at a Masquerade, while he was playing on a harpsichord in his visor. Domenico Scarlatti happened to be there and affirmed that it could be no one but the famous Saxon, or the devil.' That led to the often-told story of a competition between Handel and Scarlatti, arranged by Cardinal Ottoboni:

> As he [Scarlatti] was an exquisite player on the harpsichord, the Cardinal was resolved to bring him and Handel together for a trial of skill. The issue of the trial on the harpsichord hath been differently reported. It has been said that some gave the preference to Scarlatti. However, when they came to the organ there was not the least pretence for doubting to which of them it belonged. Scarlatti himself declared the superiority of his antagonist, and owned ingenuously, that till he had heard him upon this instrument, he had no conception of his powers.

Not surprisingly, when Handel came to London, his reputation as a performer had preceded him – but not everyone was prepared to be impressed. One 'principal performer', as Mainwaring called him:

... had affected to disbelieve the reports of his abilities before he came, was heard to say, from a too great confidence in his own, 'Let him come! We'll Handle him, I warrant ye!' There would be no excuse for recording so poor a pun, if any words could be found, capable of conveying the character of the speaker with equal force and clearness. But the moment he heard Handel on the organ, this great man in his own eye shrunk into nothing.

Handel's passion for the organ took him often to St Paul's Cathedral:

Handel was very fond of the St Paul's organ, built by Father Smith, and which was then almost a new instrument . . . the tone of the instrument delighted Handel; and a little intreaty was at any time sufficient to prevail on him to touch it, but after he had ascended the organ-loft, it was with reluctance that he left it; and he has been known, after evening service, to play to an audience as great as ever filled the choir.

And the story has been told in the previous chapter of how the composer Maurice Greene would often act as bellows-blower for these extended sessions which could last for four or five hours at a time!

So what was Handel actually like as a player? Mainwaring sums it up in a telling phrase: 'the wonderful force of his execution was as astonishing as the vast effort of his mind.' In other words, he brought the same elements of extraordinary vitality and variety to both his playing and his composing:

Handel had an uncommon brilliancy and command of finger: but what distinguished him from all other players who possessed these same qualities, was that amazing fullness, force, and energy, which he joined with them. And this observation may be applied with as much justness to his compositions, as to his playing.

Handel directed his own operas from the harpsichord, and on occasions he would play brilliantly improvised interludes during an aria – there is a notable example of this in *Agrippina*.

After he moved to the Covent Garden Theatre he had an organ installed and linked the two instruments together, and then when he turned to writing oratorios, he had the idea of writing organ concertos to play between the various parts. Once again, improvisation was a key element and the accompanying string players became used to working with only the bare bones of the score in front of them and taking their lead from Handel when it was time to play. (See the section on Handel's organ concertos in the chapter on Handel's music.) These concertos were keenly anticipated by audiences, as John Hawkins many times witnessed:

> Silence, the truest applause, succeeded the instant that he addressed himself to the instrument, and that so profound, that it checked respiration, and seemed to control the functions of nature, while the magic of his touch kept the attention of his hearers awake only to those enchanting sounds to which it gave utterance . . .
>
> His amazing command of the instrument, the fullness of his harmony, the grandeur and dignity of his style, the copiousness of his imagination, and the fertility of his invention were qualities that absorbed every inferior attainment. When he gave a concerto, his method in general was to introduce it with a voluntary movement on the diapasons, which stole on the ear in a slow and solemn progression; the harmony close wrought, and as full as could possibly be expressed; the passages concatenated with stupendous art, the whole at the same time being perfectly intelligible, and carrying the appearance of great simplicity. This kind of prelude was succeeded by the concerto itself, which he executed with a degree of spirit and firmness that no one ever pretended to equal.

Charles Burney remembers a more domestic scene later in Handel's life when he was present at a social evening at the home of the singer, Susannah Cibber. The actor, James Quin, was also present to hear Handel play the harpsichord:

Quin, after Handel was gone, being asked by Mrs Cibber, whether he did not think Mr Handel had a charming hand? replied – '*a hand*, madam! you mistake, it's a *foot*' – 'Poh! poh! says she, has he not a fine finger' '*Toes*, by G—, madam!' Indeed, his hand was then so fat, that the knuckles, which usually appear convex, were like those of a child, dinted or dimpled in, so as to be rendered concave; however, his touch was so smooth, and the tone of the instrument so much cherished, that his fingers seemed to grow to the keys. They were so curved and supple, when he played, that no motion, and scarcely the fingers themselves, could be discovered.

Those fingers, however, did not only make a musical impression, as Hawkins observed: 'He had a favourite Rucker harpsichord, the keys whereof, by incessant practice, were hollowed like the bowl of a spoon.' After Handel lost his sight, he relied more and more on his memory and powers of improvisation, but eventually decided that he could no longer continue. It must have been one of the great tragedies of his life, but William Coxe recounts Handel's characteristically bluff response to sympathy:

His surgeon, Mr Sharp, having asked him if he was able to continue playing the organ in public, for the performance of oratorios? Handel replied in the negative. Sharp recommended Stanley [a blind composer and organist], as a person whose memory never failed; upon which Handel burst into a loud laugh, and said: 'Mr. Sharp, have you never read the Scriptures? do you not remember, if the blind lead the blind, they will both fall in the ditch?'

Handel at work

25 Brook Street was the powerhouse of Handel's activities. He was the first occupant of this newly built property in London when he moved there in the summer of 1723 and he remained there for the next thirty-six years until his death. It was a modest house, on three floors but with quite small rooms, and it served as home, office, rehearsal space, and showroom for selling his music. Crucially, it was also the place where he composed, probably in the back room of the first floor. John Hawkins tells us that he worked constantly, quickly, and independently:

> His invention was for ever teeming with new ideas, and his impatience to be delivered of them kept him closely employed . . .
>
> He wrote very fast, but with a degree of impatience proportioned to the eagerness that possess men of genius, of seeing their conceptions rendered into form . . .
>
> His style was original and self-formed . . . for in a conversation with a very intelligent person now living, on the course of his studies, Mr Handel declared that, after he became master of the rudiments of his art, he forebore to study the works of others, and ever made it a rule to follow the suggestions of his own fancy.

Visitors were generally discouraged and when they ventured to interrupt him they got more than they bargained for, as the rather pompous Charles Jennens, Handel's librettist for his oratorio *Saul*, discovered in September 1738:

> Mr. Handel's head is more full of maggots than ever. I found yesterday in his room a very queer Instrument, which he calls carillon (Angelice, a Bell) and says some call it a Tubalcain, I suppose because it is both in the make and tone like a set of Hammers striking upon anvils. 'Tis

play'd upon with Keys like a Harpsichord, & with this Cyclopean Instrument he designs to make poor *Saul* stark mad. His second Maggot is an Organ of £500 price, which (because he is overstocked with money) he has bespoke of one Moss of Barnet. This Organ, he says, is so constructed that as he sits at it he has a better command of his performers than he used to have; and he is highly delighted to think with what exactness his Oratorio will be performed by the help of this Organ; so that for the future, instead of beating time at his oratorios, he is to sit at the organ all the time with his back to the Audience. His third Maggot is a Hallelujah which he has trump'd up at the end of his oratorio since I went into the Country, because he thought the conclusion of the oratorio not Grand enough; tho' if that were the case 'twas his own fault, for the words would have bore as Grand Musick as he could have set 'em to: but this Hallelujah, Grand as it is, comes in very nonsensically, having no manner of relation to what goes before. And this is more the extraordinary, because he refus'd to set a Hallelujah at the end of the first Chorus in the Oratorio, where I had placed one and where it was to be introduced with the utmost proprietary, upon a pretence that it would make the Entertainment too long. I could tell you more of his Maggots: but it grows late and I must defer the rest till I write next, by which time, I doubt not, more new ones will breed in his Brain.

When the Reverend Thomas Morell, another of Handel's librettists, arrived at Brook Street in July 1746, with the first act of *Judas Maccabaeus*, he also got more than he had bargained for, as Handel looked up from the text:

'Well', says he, 'and how are you to go on?' 'Why, we are to suppose an engagement, and that the Israelites have conquered, and so begin, with a chorus as "Fallen is the foe" or, something like it.' 'No, I will have this,' and began working it, as it is, upon the harpsichord. 'Well, go on.' 'I will bring you more tomorrow.' 'No, something now.'

'So fall thy foes, O Lord.'

'That will do', and immediately carried on the composition as we have it in that most admirable chorus.

So when Morell came back to Brook Street the following June, he was probably already on his guard as he handed over the text of a new oratorio, *Alexander Balus*. Handel leafed through it and arrived at Cleopatra's final aria in Act III:

When Mr Handel first read it, he cried out 'D— your Iambics'. 'Don't put yourself into a passion, they are easily Trochees.' 'Trochees, what are Trochees?' 'Why the very reverse of Iambics, by leaving out a syllable in every line, as instead of "Convey me to some peaceful shore", "Lead me to some peaceful shore".' 'That is what I want.' 'I will step into the parlour and alter them immediately.' I went down and returned with them altered in about 3 minutes; when he would have them as they were, and set them most delightfully, accompanied with only a quaver, and a rest of 3 quavers.

There is also a story that Handel took a carriage to Morell's house in Turnham Green in the early hours of one morning and got the poor man out of bed just to ask him the meaning of the word 'billows' in the same aria! True or not (and scholars think probably not), Morell eventually got a mention in Handel's will and a legacy of two hundred pounds for all his pains.

Handel's manuscripts

The amusing 'maggots' letter quoted in the previous chapter was written by Charles Jennens to his young relative Lord Guernsey, who later became Earl of Aylesford and, when Jennens died in 1773, inherited his collection of Handel scores. The Aylesford Collection, as it came to be known, was eventually sold at auction at Sotheby's in 1918. Much of it was bought by Newman Flower (who wrote an important biography of Handel) and is now in the Henry Watson Music Library in Manchester. Other manuscripts were bought by William Barclay Squire, music librarian at the British Museum, and are now in the extensive Handel Collection in the British Library, which houses over ninety per cent of known Handel manuscripts.

Another significant collection, mainly of extracts, fragments and sketches, plus one complete anthem, *O Praise the Lord with One Consent*, is at the Fitzwilliam Museum in Cambridge. It was donated to the University by Richard, Viscount Fitzwilliam, at his death in 1816, along with his works of art, his entire library, and a bequest to build the museum which now bears his name (see www.fitzmuseum.cam.ac.uk and follow links for Handel). Fitzwilliam, born in 1745, collected extensively and was part of the group of aristocratic music-lovers who devised the idea of the Handel Commemoration Concerts in 1784.

A book of essays on *Handel Collections and their History* was edited by Terence Best in 1993, and the definitive catalogue of the 'what' and 'where' of Handel's manuscripts and other music books was completed by Donald Burrows and Martha J. Ronish the following year (see 'Further reading' at the end of this book). Over 8,700 sheets of music are accounted for, and what could have been a very complicated story, given how prolific a composer Handel was, is made easier by the fact that he worked so fast. This meant that he generally used up his stocks of music paper very quickly, and so identifiable batches of paper followed each other throughout his career. Conveniently for future musicologists, Handel also often dated individual pages and kept his music quite carefully.

His 'Musick Books', as they were referred to in his will, comprised manuscripts and copies, including the scores that he conducted from. Handel left them to John Christopher Smith, the elder, who had been his copyist, secretary and concert manager for over forty years. When Smith died in 1763, the collection passed to his son, the younger John Christopher Smith, who in turn donated it to King George III, who had it catalogued and bound in eighty-eight volumes. These were housed first in Windsor Castle, then at Buckingham Palace, until in 1911 King George V donated the entire Royal Music Library to the British Museum on permanent loan. That loan was turned into a donation in 1957 by Queen Elizabeth II and the collection is now part of the British Library, housed in the new building in St Pancras (see www.bl.uk and follow links for Handel for a full description of the collection, and to view a signed draft of the 'Amen' chorus from *Messiah*).

Handel generally used good-quality paper for his manuscripts (no false economies for him, but maybe he also had a canny eye to posterity?), and most of them are still in good condition. Incidentally, all manuscript paper in the eighteenth century was manufactured plain, and then a five-pointed pen called a rastrum was used to draw the parallel lines of the stave – a time-consuming job, so not surprisingly, the impatient Handel generally bought paper that had been pre-ruled by someone else.

So what do Handel's manuscripts tell us about how he worked? According to Charles Burney, when he looked at the overture to the opera *Muzio Scevola*:

It is astonishing to see with what ease and certainty Handel wielded the pen on all occasions, and how clear and well arranged must have been his conceptions previous to committing them to paper. In the first foul [i.e. draft] copy of this excellent fugue of seven parts, written with the haste of a man whose thoughts flowed faster than his ink, scarce a single note has been altered, blotted, or erased!

That was not always so, however. Parts of the manuscript of *Saul*, for example, are thick with crossings-out, alterations and re-arrangements as Handel struggled towards realising his ideas. In general, however, there was a confidence and a boldness about his musical handwriting – as well there might be from someone who composed so quickly. Hawkins tells us that 'his overtures, excellent as they are, were composed as fast as he could write; and the most elaborate of them seldom cost him more than a morning's labour.' Handel wrote the 232 pages of the score of *Messiah* in twenty-five days and, working even faster, completed the combined total of six hundred pages for *Hercules* and *Belshazzar* between 19 July and 10 September 1744 – less than two months, making for an average of eleven pages per day!

Belshazzar, like many other Handel scores, has notes in the margin – in particular some stage directions for that crucial moment in Act II when the arrogant Belshazzar is challenged by God: 'As he is speaking a hand appears writing on the wall over against him: he sees it, turns pale with fear', etc. Elsewhere in Handel's manuscripts, as well as the dates of composition already referred to, he sometimes noted durations – '40 minutes' for Part II of *Solomon* – or gave performing instructions: 'the second time by french horns and hautbois and bassoons, without trumpet / the third time all together', for a movement of the *Fireworks Music*. Sometimes he even noted his age on finishing a work – '*aetatis* 63' at the end of *Susanna* in 1748, for example. Most poignantly, on page 91 of *Jephtha*, he wrote in German on 13 February 1751 that this was where he had had to stop 'on account of the weakening of the sight of my left eye'.

These points are described and illustrated by Alec Hyatt King in his booklet, *Handel and his Autographs* (1967), unfortunately long out of print, but worth searching for second-hand. Earlier biographers of Handel, Victor Schoelcher (1857) and William S. Rockstro (1883), made particular studies of the evolution of Handel's musical handwriting, among other things noting how he developed a style that allowed him to work carefully and confidently at speed. Hyatt King sums it all up by applying to Handel a quotation from Thomas Carlyle: 'genius, which means transcendent capacity for taking trouble, first of all'. But did this particular genius also have something to hide?

Handel's borrowings

The comments from John Hawkins quoted at the start of the chapter on 'Handel at work' seem to establish three things about Handel's compositional habits: that he worked constantly, quickly, and independently. The first two of these claims are manifestly appropriate, but the truth of the third must be challenged. Charles Burney alluded delicately to the subject of Handel's borrowings in his essay at the time of the Handel Commemoration Concerts in 1784:

> I know it has been said that Handel was not the original and immediate inventor of several species of Music, for which his name has been celebrated; but, with respect to originality, it is a term to which proper limits should be set, before it is applied to the productions of any artist.

The truth of the matter was that Handel borrowed musical material regularly and freely throughout his career, both from himself and (despite what he told Hawkins) from other composers. And it was not just a case of a theme here, or an idea there: Handel's borrowings can be of complete pieces or movements. He was by no means alone in this in the eighteenth century, but he did so much borrowing that even his broad-minded contemporaries remarked on it. No other composer of his time seems to have borrowed nearly as much. For later generations, particularly in the nineteenth century, this posed a real dilemma, becoming regarded as a moral issue, and the word 'plagiarism' began to be used as the moralists lined up against the apologists. The beginning of the twentieth century saw two significant books: Sedley Taylor's *The Indebtedness of Handel to Works by Other Composers* (1906), and Percy Robinson's *Handel and His Orbit* (1908). Taylor came out for the moralists, demonstrating systematically for the first time the extent of Handel's borrowings from other composers and concluding that this was 'wrong'. Robinson took the side of the apologists, advancing any number of reasons why Handel might have done something which was not at all unusual in his own time: to honour another composer, for example; to demonstrate skill in reworking; to make a musical connection that might be appreciated by a patron or the audience; or even just to solve the problem of lack of time.

Even as recently as the Handel Bicentenary in 1985, however, Handel's borrowings could still disturb and alarm. Nicholas Kenyon's editorial in *Early Music* that August reported on a recent conference:

> Sleepless nights were caused for Handel scholars, we were told, by John Roberts's newly announced discoveries, about the extent of Handel's borrowings . . . the fear that Handel might turn out, in the fullness of time, to be a wholly unoriginal composer, seemed to be the disturbing factor in these discoveries; this feeling even overbalanced that expressed by George Buelow that the historical perspective of three centuries had removed any opprobrium from the borrowings.

Essays by Buelow and Roberts were subsequently published in the *Handel Tercentenary Collection*, edited by Stanley Sadie and Anthony Hicks. In 'The case for Handel's borrowings: the judgement of three centuries', Buelow argues for the apologists, while in 'Why did Handel borrow?', Roberts takes up a new position (post-moralist, perhaps?) and declares outright:

> I would like to suggest another explanation for Handel's borrowing, one that has never been seriously proposed, though often hastily discounted: that he had a basic lack of facility in inventing original ideas. That after all is the obvious answer.

It's an extreme position – and you may well prefer to go with Winton Dean's broader picture of Handel's psyche, advanced in the second volume of his study of the operas:

> The elucidation of the process that generated music in Handel's subconscious mind, if possible at all, would seem

to require the services of a psychoanalyst, a computer, and perhaps the equivalent of an Enigma machine, as a well as a corps of musicians.

Dean also has a theory, proposed in his earlier book about the oratorios, that Handel sometimes needed something 'to give his imagination a boost before the engine would start', and relates this tendency to his love of improvisation. Roberts's dismissal of this is not entirely convincing, and no doubt the debate will continue.

What can be said, and agreed on by apologists, moralists and others, is that the net result of Handel's borrowings was nearly always positive. 'What is borrowed must be repaid with interest,' wrote Handel's friend, Johann Mattheson, and fellow composer William Boyce summed up Handel's position succinctly: 'He takes other men's pebbles and polishes them into diamonds.' Roberts, too, believes that 'Handel tended to transform as he composed.' Whether the sources are his own or others, these transformations are a fascinating and integral part of Handel's greatness.

Various borrowings are referred to throughout this book, but one particular 'polished pebble' is worth mentioning here to demonstrate William Boyce's point. One of Handel's most famous pieces, the 'Arrival of the Queen of Sheba' (the orchestral interlude that begins Part III of the oratorio *Solomon*) turns out to be derived from ideas found in the first movement of the F major Concerto for three violins in Part III of Telemann's *Tafelmusik*. But if you go back to Telemann's original, it actually sounds like a poor imitation of Handel!

Handel's life

> The life of so great a Genius as the late Mr Handel, who
> was, in truth, the very Shakespeare of Music, cannot be
> altogether an indifferent subject . . .
> *The Monthly Review*, JUNE 1760

When John Mainwaring set out to write Handel's biography,
almost immediately after the composer's death, he wrote: 'All
that is here intended, is to give a plain, artless account of such
particulars as we have been able to learn, and such only as we
have reason to believe authentic.' In fact Mainwaring's
account is anything but artless – he knew how to tell a good
story – and so I have interleaved the following chronology of
Handel's life with extracts from Mainwaring, supplemented
with contributions from the three other main contemporary
chroniclers of Handel's life: William Coxe, John Hawkins and
Charles Burney (see the Introduction for details of their
books).

What is missing is anything significant from Handel himself. Burney relates that when Handel was requested several
times by his friend, Johann Mattheson, to furnish some biographical details – the first time in 1735 – he had a ready
excuse: 'As for drawing up memoirs concerning myself, I find
it utterly impossible, on account of my being continually
occupied in the service of the court and nobility, which puts it
out of my power to think of anything else.' Burney goes on to
remark that Mattheson generally asked at the wrong time,
when things were not going well for Handel, and that 'as
Handel was unfortunate, unhappy, and "too proud to be
vain", the request that he would become his own biographer
was not likely to be granted'.

Early years

1685

23 February Born in Halle, Saxony

> . . . by a second wife of his father, who was an eminent
> surgeon and physician of the same place, and above sixty
> when his son was born.
>
> MAINWARING

24 February Christened Georg Friederich Händel.

1689 (AGE 4)

> From his very childhood Handel had discovered such a
> strong propensity to Music, that his father, who had
> always intended him for the study of the Civil Law,
> had reason to be alarmed.
>
> MAINWARING

1690 (AGE 5)

> Perceiving that this inclination still increased, he [Handel's
> father] took every method to oppose it. He strictly forbade
> him to meddle with any musical instrument . . .
>
> MAINWARING

1691 (AGE 6)

> He [Handel] had found means to get a little clavichord
> privately convey'd to a room at the top of the house.
> To this room he constantly stole when the family was
> asleep.
>
> MAINWARING

1692 (AGE 7)

> He had made some progress before Music had been
> prohibited, and by his assiduous practice at the hours of
> rest, had made such farther advances, as, tho' not attended

to at that time, were no slight prognostics of his future
greatness.

MAINWARING

Visits the court at Weissenfels with his father.
Plays the organ for Duke Johann who advises tuition for him.

But he [Handel's father] begged leave humbly to represent
to his Highness that though Music was an elegant art, and
a fine amusement, yet if considered as an occupation, it
had little dignity . . . The Prince could not agree with him
in his notions of Music as a profession, which were much
too low and disparaging, as great excellence in any kind
entitled men to great honour.

MAINWARING

Begins music lessons in Halle with Friedrich Zachow,
organist of the Marienkirche.

An excellent performer on the organ and other
instruments . . . he composed many pieces for the
church, and some lessons for the clavier or harpsichord.
His eminence in his faculty occasioned a great resort of
young persons to him for instruction; and it is no small
addition to his reputation that he was the master of
Mr Handel.

HAWKINS

The first object of his [Zachow's] attention was to ground
him thoroughly in the principles of harmony. His next was
to cultivate his imagination, and form his taste.

MAINWARING

After having taught him the principles of the science,
Zachow put into the hands of his young pupil the works
of the greatest among the Italian and German composers,
and, without directing his attention to any of them, left
him to form a style of his own.

HAWKINS

1694 (AGE 9)

Handel had now been under the tuition of Zachow about two years, during which time he had frequently supplied his place, and performed the cathedral duty.

HAWKINS

By the time he was nine he began to compose the church services for voices and instruments, and from that time did actually compose a service every week for three years successively.

MAINWARING

1696 (AGE 11)

Plays at the Prussian court in Berlin and meets the composers Bononcini and Ariosti, who ran the opera there.

The former of these, a most admirable musician, was yet a haughty and insolent man; the other, his inferior, was of a modest and placid disposition, a proof whereof he gave in the the affection shewn by him to this young stranger, whom he would frequently set upon his knee, and listen with delight while he played on the harpsichord.

HAWKINS

Many and great were the compliments and civilities which he received on his leaving Berlin. As yet he had been but twice from home, and both times had received such marks of honour and distinction, as are seldom, if ever, paid to one of his age and condition.

MAINWARING

1697 (AGE 12)

11 February Death of his father.
18 February Writes a poem mourning his father.

Ah! Bitter grief! My dearest father's heart
From me by cruel death is torn away.

Ah! Misery! And ah! The bitter smart
Which seizes me, poor orphan from this day . . .
. . . God, who bereaves me of a father's care
By that dear father's death, yet liveth still;
And henceforth, in mine anguish and despair,
I find my help and guidance in his Will.

1698 (AGE 13)

By the time he was arrived at the age of thirteen, Handel
began to look upon Halle as a place not likely to afford
him opportunities of much farther improvement.

HAWKINS

1699 (AGE 14)

Composes his earliest dateable work: the Trio Sonata in
G minor, Op. 2 No. 2 (HWV 387).

1701 (AGE 16)

Begins a lifelong friendship with Telemann in Leipzig.

Handel and I were continually exercising our fancy, and
reciprocally communicating our thoughts, both by letter
and conversation, in the frequent visits we made to each
other.

TELEMANN, QUOTED BY BURNEY

Handel, speaking of his [Telemann's] uncommon skill and
readiness, was used to say that he could write a piece of
church music of eight parts with the same expedition as
another would write a letter.

HAWKINS

1702 (AGE 17)

10 February Enrols at the University of Halle.
13 March Becomes organist at the Calvinist Cathedral
in Halle.

He had heard so high a character of the singers and
composers of Italy, that his thoughts ran much on a
journey into that country. But this project required
a longer purse than he was as yet provided with, and
was therefore suspended until such time as it could be
compassed without hazard or inconvenience.

MAINWARING

Apprenticeship in Hamburg

1703 (AGE 18)

June–July Moves to Hamburg.

As his fortune was to depend on his skill in his profession,
it was necessary to consider of some place less distant
where he might employ his time to advantage . . . Next to
the Opera of Berlin, that of Hamburg was in the highest
request. It was resolved to send him thither on his own
bottom, and chiefly with a view to improvement.

MAINWARING

July Makes friends with the composer and performer Johann
Mattheson.

Mathyson [*sic*] was no great singer . . . but he was a good
actor, a good composer of lessons, and a good player on
the harpsichord.

MAINWARING

Mattheson was very well acquainted with Handel. Before
the latter came to settle in England they were in some sort
rivals, and solicited with equal ardour the favour of the
public. Mattheson relates that he had often vied with him
on the organ both at Hamburgh and Lubec . . . Handel
approved so highly of the compositions of Mattheson,
particularly his [harpsichord] lessons, that he was used to
play them for his private amusement.

HAWKINS

Mattheson was a vain and pompous man, whose first
wish in all his writings was to impress the reader with due
reverence for his own abilities and importance . . . he
sometimes appears as a friend, companion, and admirer
of Handel's genius and abilities, and at others assumes the
critic, discovering manifest signs of rivalry, envy, and
discontent, at his superior success.

BURNEY

August Visits Buxtehude at Lübeck with Mattheson.

There was a vacancy for the organist's place. They
performed this journey in the public caravan, with all the
thoughtless hilarity of youth, singing extempore duets,
and amusing themselves with all imaginable frolics on the
road; to which the affected simplicity and archness of
Handel gave an exquisite zest. Finding the acceptance of a
place coupled with a condition, that the organist was to take
a wife, who was to be chosen for him by the magistrates,
they each of them declined offering themselves on such
conditions, and returned together to Hamburg.

COXE

Joins the Hamburg Opera orchestra as a violinist and
harpsichordist. Reinhard Keiser is the director.

He [Keiser] was a most voluminous writer, and is said to
have exceeded Scarlatti in the number of operas composed
by him . . . such was the native ease and elegance of his
style, and such his command over the passions of his
hearers, that all became susceptible of their effects . . . he
had the direction of the opera at Hamburg from the time
when it was first established, till, being a man of gaiety and
expense, he was necessitated to quit it . . .

HAWKINS

Though he [Handel] pretended to know nothing, yet he
used to be very arch, for he had always a dry way of
making the gravest people laugh, without laughing

himself. But his superior abilities were soon discovered, when, upon occasion of the harpsichord-player at the opera being absent, he was first persuaded to take his place; for he then shewed himself to be a great master, to the astonishment of every one, except myself, who had frequently heard him before, upon keyed-instruments.

MATTHESON, QUOTED BY BURNEY

Composes various arias and cantatas.

1704 (AGE 19)

Composes his first opera, *Almira*.
5 December Quarrels with Mattheson over who should play harpsichord in one of Mattheson's operas.

As they were coming out of the orchestra, he [Mattheson] made a push at him [Handel] with a sword, which being aimed full at his heart, would forever have removed him from the office he had usurped, but for the friendly Score, which he accidentally carried in his bosom; and through which to have forced it, would have demanded all the might of Ajax himself.

MAINWARING

Handel, at the time of the quarrel, was twenty years of age [*sic*]; tall, strong, broad-shouldered, and muscular; consequently, well able to defend himself.

MATTHESON, QUOTED BY BURNEY

30 December Reconciled with Mattheson.

They had been in habits of intimacy, which they soon resumed; and were rejoiced at the lucky conclusion of so serious an incident, arising from so trifling a cause.

COXE

1705 (AGE 20)

8 January Premiere of *Almira* at the Hamburg Opera.

The success of it was so great that it ran for thirty nights without interruption.

MAINWARING

25 February Premiere of his second opera *Nero*.

Italian interlude

1706 (AGE 21)

Composes two more operas, *Florindo* and *Daphne*.
August Leaves Hamburg for Italy, at the recommendation of the Prince of Tuscany, probably going first to Florence, and then on to Rome by January 1707.

It never was his intention to settle at Hamburg . . . he came thither only as a traveller, and with a view to improvement . . . he was willing to be employed, but was resolved to see more of the world before he entered into any engagements which would confine him long to any particular place.

MAINWARING

Composes many chamber cantatas while living in Italy up to 1710.

1707 (AGE 22)

February Composes *Il delirio amoroso*, on a text by Cardinal Pamphili, one of his Italian patrons.

He [Handel] was compared to Orpheus, and exalted above the rank of mortals. Whether his eminence chose this subject as most likely to inspire him with fine conceptions, or with a view to discover how far so great an Artist was proof against the assaults of vanity it is not material to determine.

MAINWARING

April Composes *Dixit Dominus*.

May–October Enters the employment of the Marquis Francesco Ruspoli. Composes cantatas and motets.

> Handel was desired to furnish his quota; and there was always such a greatness and superiority in the pieces composed by him, as rendered those of the best masters comparatively little and insignificant.
>
> MAINWARING

June Premiere of *Il trionfo del Tempo e del Disinganno* at the palace of Cardinal Ottoboni.
July Composes *Laudate pueri Dominum*, *Nisi Dominus* and other liturgical works commissioned by Cardinal Colonna.
November Returns to Florence. Premiere of *Rodrigo*.

> . . . for which he was presented with 100 sequins, and a service of plate. This may serve for a sufficient testimony of its favourable reception.
>
> MAINWARING

Travels to Venice for the Carnival season.

> He was first discovered there at a Masquerade, while he was playing on a harpsichord in his visor. Scarlatti happened to be there, and affirmed that it could be no one but the famous Saxon, or the devil.
>
> MAINWARING

> He was distinguished, according to the custom of his country, by the appellation of *Il Sassone*; and had he remained in Italy, that distinction would have superseded his patronimic.
>
> COXE

1708 (AGE 23)

January *Florindo* and *Daphne* performed in Hamburg in his absence.
3 March Returns to Rome by this date.

8 April *La Resurrezione* is performed on Easter Sunday.
Corelli leads the orchestra.
May Travels to Naples.

> As at most other places, he had a palazzo at command,
> and was provided with table, coach, and all other
> accommodation . . . he received invitations from most of
> the principal persons who lived within reach of that
> capital; and lucky was he esteemed, who could engage
> him soonest, and detain him longest.
>
> MAINWARING

16 June Completes *Aci, Galatea e Polifemo*, probably intended
for the wedding of the Duke of Alvito on 16 July.
July Returns to Rome
August Composes *La Lucrezia*.

1709 (AGE 24)

Takes part in a keyboard competition with Domenico
Scarlatti, organised by Cardinal Ottoboni.

> The issue of the trial on the harpsichord hath been
> differently reported. It has been said that some gave the
> preference to Scarlatti. However, when they came to the
> Organ there was not the least pretence for doubting to
> which of them it belonged. Scarlatti himself declared the
> superiority of his antagonist, and owned ingenuously, that
> till he had heard him upon this instrument, he had no
> conception of his powers.
>
> MAINWARING

16 July Death of his sister, Johanna.
Returns to Florence in the autumn.
9 November Prince Ferdinand de Medici provides him with
a letter of recommendation to Prince Carl von Neuburg,
Governor of the Tyrol, in Innsbruck.
Returns to Venice and is invited to visit London by the Duke
of Manchester, the English ambassador.

26 December Premiere of *Agrippina* in Venice.

> The audience was so enchanted with this performance,
> that . . . the theatre, at almost every pause, resounded
> with shouts and acclamations of *viva il caro Sassone!* and
> other expressions of approbation too extravagant to be
> mentioned. They were thunderstruck with the grandeur
> and sublimity of his style.
>
> MAINWARING

Hanover and London

1710 (AGE 25)

10 January Orchestral extracts from *Rodrigo* are played
in London.
Leaves Venice and travels via Innsbruck to Hanover.

> The whole time of his abode in Italy was six years. During
> this interval he had made an abundance of Music, and
> some in almost every species of composition. These early
> fruits of his studies would doubtless be vast curiosities
> could they now be met with. The lovers of the art would
> regard them with something of the same veneration,
> which the Literati would pay to the precious remains of a
> Livy, a Cæsar, or a Tacitus! Indeed the few fragments of
> those pieces which have come to our hands, serve only to
> increase our concern for the parts which have perished.
>
> MAINWARING

16 June Appointed Kapellmeister to Georg Ludwig, Elector
of Hanover.

> The Elector . . . struck with his merit, proposed to retain
> him in his service, with a salary of fifteen hundred crowns
> per annum. This liberal offer Handel accepted; but on
> condition, that he should be permitted to visit England,
> whither he had been invited by many persons of high rank,
> whom he had seen in Italy, and at Hanover.
>
> COXE

Handel loved liberty . . . he had leave to be absent for
a twelve-month, or more, if he chose it; and to go
wheresoever he pleased.

MAINWARING

Completes *Apollo e Dafne*.
August Travels to Halle to see his mother.

Her extreme old-age, and total blindness; tho' they
promised him but a melancholy interview, rendered this
instance of his duty and regard the more necessary.

MAINWARING

Continues on to Düsseldorf and the court of the
Elector Palatine.

The Elector Palatine was much pleased . . . but as much
disappointed to find that he was engaged elsewhere. At
parting he made him a present of a fine set of wrought
plate for a desert, and in such a manner as added greatly
to its value.

MAINWARING

November Travels to London via the Netherlands.

It was in the winter of 1710, when he arrived in London,
one of the most memorable years of that longest, but most
prosperous war . . . which England has ever waged with a
foreign power. . . . Nothing indeed seemed wanting to
compleat the national felicity, but a person capable of
charming down, by the magic of his melody, that evil spirit
of faction and party, which fortune seems, at this time, to
have conjured up.

MAINWARING

Excepting a few good compositions in the church style,
and of a very old date, I am afraid there was very little to
boast of, which we could call our own . . . the best composer could hardly be distinguished from the worst. The
arrival of Handel put an end to this reign of nonsense.

MAINWARING

To the wit, poetry, literature, and science, which marked this period of our history, Handel added all the blandishments of a nervous and learned music, which he first brought hither, planted, and lived to see grow to a very flourishing state.

COXE

1711 (AGE 26)

6 February Performs for Queen Anne at St James's Palace.

The report of his uncommon abilities had been conveyed to England before his arrival, and through various channels. Some persons had seen him in Italy, and others during his residence at Hanover. He was soon introduced at Court, and honoured with marks of the Queen's favour.

MAINWARING

24 February Premiere of *Rinaldo*.

Many of the nobility were impatient for an opera of his composing. To gratify this eagerness, *Rinaldo*, the first he made in England, was finished in a fortnight's time. . . . Its success was very great, and his engagements at Hanover the subject of much concern with the lovers of Music. For when he could return to England, or whether he could at all, was yet very uncertain.

MAINWARING

Mr Handel had gotten possession of the public ear, and the whole kingdom were forming their taste for harmony and melody by the standard of his compositions.

HAWKINS

June Returns to Germany, visiting Düsseldorf on the way to Hanover.

When he took leave of the Queen at her court, and expressed his sense of the favours bestowed upon him, her Majesty was pleased to add to them by large presents, and

to intimate her desire of seeing him again. Not a little
flattered . . . he promised to return, the moment he could
obtain permission from the Prince, in whose service he
was retained.

MAINWARING

17 June The Elector Palatine writes to the Elector of
Hanover apologising for detaining Handel.

Soon after his return to Hanover he made twelve chamber
Duettos for the practice of the late Queen, then electoral
Princess. The character of these is well known to the
judges in music . . . Besides these Duettos (a species of
composition of which the Princess and court were
particularly fond) he composed [a] variety of other things
for voices and instruments.

MAINWARING

23 November Visits Halle for the baptism of his niece
Johanna Michaelsen and becomes her godfather.
Returns to London.

1712 (AGE 27)

23 January *Rinaldo* is revived in London in his absence.
Autumn Given permission from the Elector of Hanover to
return to London for the next opera season. Stays mainly with
the Earl of Burlington in Piccadilly.

His return to London was hailed by the musical world as
a national acquisition, and every measure was adopted to
render his abode pleasant and permanent.

COXE

He was chiefly, if not constantly, at the Earl of Burlington's.
The character of this nobleman, as a scholar and virtuoso,
is universally known.

MAINWARING

The course of his life was regular and uniform . . . his time
was divided between study and practice, that is to say, in

composing for the opera, and in conducting concerts at
the Duke of Rutland's, the Earl of Burlington's, and the
houses of others of the nobility who were patrons of his
music, and his friends.

HAWKINS

He remained three years with Lord Burlington, during
which time he became acquainted with Pope, Gay, and
Arbuthnot. Pope . . . had no knowledge of the science of
music . . . he heard the performances of Handel with
perfect indifference, if not impatience. Gay was pleased
with music without understanding it, but forgot the
performance when the notes ceased to vibrate. Arbuthnot,
on the contrary, who was a judge of music, and a composer, felt the merits of Handel, and conceived an esteem
for him.

COXE

22 November Premiere of *Il pastor fido*.

1713 (AGE 28)

10 January Premiere of *Teseo*.
13 January Completes the *Utrecht Te Deum*.

Handel was preferred to all others, seemingly without
a murmur from native musicians, to compose the Hymn
of Gratitude and Triumph on the occasion. Envy, though
outrageous and noisy at the success of comparative
abilities, is struck dumb and blind by excess of superiority.

BURNEY

In that composition he acquitted himself with all that
wonderful effect of sublimity and judgement, for which
he was remarkable.

COXE

January Composes the *Ode for the Birthday of Queen Anne* for
6 February, but it was possibly not performed.
6 May Revival of *Rinaldo*.

The time had again elapsed to which the leave he had obtained, could in reason be extended. But whether he was afraid of repassing the sea, or whether he had contracted an affection for the diet of the land he was in; so it was, that the promise he had given at his coming away, had somehow slipt out of his memory.

MAINWARING

May Dismissed from his post at Hanover.
2 June Possible premiere of *Silla*.
7 July *Utrecht Te Deum* is performed at the Thanksgiving Service at St Paul's Cathedral.

No performance can be thoroughly excellent, unless it is wrought *con amore*, as the Italians express it. Handel, it must be owned, had all these advantages. And it is not too much, perhaps it is too little to say, the work was answerable to them. But let the grand *Te Deum* and *Jubilate* speak for themselves!

MAINWARING

28 December Granted a pension of £200 per year by Queen Anne.

This act of the royal bounty was the more extraordinary, as his foreign engagements were not unknown.

MAINWARING

1714 (AGE 29)

1 August Death of Queen Anne. The Elector of Hanover becomes King George I.
26 September *'Caroline' Te Deum* is performed at St James's Palace at a service to mark the arrival of the Hanoverian Royal Family.
30 December Revival of *Rinaldo*.

1715 (AGE 30)

25 May Premiere of *Amadigi di Gaula*. Composes no more operas until 1720.

25 June Further revival of *Rinaldo*.
10 October Paid the arrears of his Hanover salary.

1716 (AGE 31)

Composes *Brockes Passion*.
16 February Revival of *Amadigi di Gaula*.
20 June Premiere of the Concerto Grosso in F major, Op. 3
No. 4, between the acts of *Amadigi di Gaula*.
Later in the year travels to Germany, visiting Halle then
proceeding to Ansbach where he persuades his friend, Johann
Christoph Schmidt, to return to England with him. Schmidt
later changes his name to John Christopher Smith and
becomes Handel's business assistant and copyist.

1717 (AGE 32)

5 January Revival of *Rinaldo*.
16 February Revival of *Amadigi di Gaula*.
17 July King George travels by barge on the River Thames
from Whitehall to Chelsea. The *Water Music* is performed
three times during the trip.
August Becomes composer in residence to James Brydges,
Earl of Carnarvon (later Duke of Chandos) at Cannons in
Edgware. Begins to compose the *Chandos Anthems*.

> Cannons, a place which was then in all its glory, but
> remarkable for having much more of art than nature, and
> much more cost than art . . . Whether Handel was *provided*
> as a mere implement of grandeur, or *chosen* from motives
> of a superior kind, it is not for us to determine. This one
> may venture to assert, that the having such a Composer,
> was an instance of *real* magnificence.
>
> MAINWARING

> The Duke of Chandos . . . among other splendid and
> princely kinds of magnificence, established a chapel, in
> which the cathedral service was daily performed by a choir
> of voices and instruments, superior, at that time, perhaps

in number and excellence, to that of any sovereign prince in Europe. Here Handel produced, besides his anthems, the chief part of his hautbois concertos, sonatas, lessons, and organ fugues.

BURNEY

1718 (AGE 33)

Completes the eleven *Chandos Anthems* and also a *Te Deum*. They are performed at the Church of St Lawrence in the Cannons Estate.
Composes *Esther* and *Acis and Galatea* – both are probably performed at Cannons.
8 August Death of his sister, Dorothea.

Opera and the Royal Academy
1719 (AGE 34)

February Formation of the Royal Academy of Music.

During the last year of his residence at Cannons, a project was formed by the Nobility for erecting an academy at the Haymarket. The intention of this musical society was to secure themselves a constant supply of operas to be composed by Handel, and performed under his direction. For this end a subscription was set on foot: and as his late Majesty was pleased to let his name appear at the head of it, the Society was dignified with the title of the Royal Academy.

MAINWARING

14 May Commissioned by the Royal Academy of Music to travel abroad and engage singers for the opera. Visits his family in Halle during the trip.

J. S. Bach, who at the time was in the service of the Prince of Anhalt-Cöthen, hearing that his great contemporary was only a matter of about twenty miles away, journeyed

from Cöthen to Halle, in the hope of seeing him.
Unfortunately, however, Handel had left for England
before Bach's arrival at Halle.

BURNEY

July Negotiates for singers in Dresden, securing in particular
the services of the soprano, Margherita Durastanti, the alto
castrato, Francesco Bernardi, known as Senesino, and the
bass, Giuseppe Boschi.

30 November Appointed 'Master of the Orchestra' at the
Royal Academy of Music. Returns to London late 1719 or
early 1720.

1720 (AGE 35)

2 April Opening of the first opera season of the Royal
Academy of Music at the King's Theatre, Haymarket.

At this time Bononcini and Attilio [Ariosti] composed for
the opera, and had a strong party in their favour. Great
reason they saw to be jealous of such a rival as Handel,
and all the interest they had was employed to decry his
music, and hinder him from coming to the Haymarket:
but these attempts were defeated by the powerful
association above-mentioned, at whose desire he had just
been to Dresden for singers.

MAINWARING

It was hardly possible that men possessed of talents so
different as were those of Handel and Bononcini, should
be equally admired and patronised by the same persons.
The style of Bononcini was tender, elegant, and pathetic;
Handel's possessed all these qualities, and numberless
others, and his invention was inexhaustible.

HAWKINS

27 April Premiere of *Radamisto*, attended by King George I
and the Prince of Wales.

He first produced for the Academy the opera of
Radamisto; the great success of which evinced his talents
as a composer, and a happy power of adapting airs to the
abilities of the respective singers.

COXE

If persons who are now living, and who were present at
that performance may be credited, the applause it received
was almost as extravagant as his *Agrippina* had excited: the
crowds and tumults of the house at Venice were hardly
equal to those at London . . . there was no shadow of
form, or ceremony, scarce any appearance of order or
regularity, politeness or decency.

MAINWARING

14 June Granted a royal warrant for the sole right to publish
his music for fourteen years.
14 November Publication of the first volume of keyboard
music: *Suites de pièces pour le clavecin*.
19 November Opening of the second season of the Royal
Academy of Music
28 December Premiere of the revised version of *Radamisto*
and the first appearance of the castrato Senesino in a Handel
opera.

I am as far from asserting, as I am from believing that
any other composer could have shown such a singer to
equal advantage. Let any impartial and competent judge
consider, whether it is likely that the whole musical world
could have afforded a composer beside himself, capable of
furnishing Senesino with such a song, as that of 'Ombra
cara' in the very opera before us.

MAINWARING

This opera, however, with all its merits and success, did
not obtain for Handel a victory sufficiently decisive, to
oblige the enemy to quit the field.

BURNEY

1721 (AGE 36)

23 March Completes the composition of Act III of *Muzio Scevola*, an opera possibly intended to settle the rivalry between Handel and Bononcini, who composed Act II. A third composer, Filippo Amadei, wrote Act I.

> Some say, compar'd to Buononcinny
> That Mynheer Handel's but a Ninny.
> Others aver, that he to Handel
> Is scarcely fit to hold a Candel:
> Strange that this difference there should be
> 'Twixt Tweedle-dum and Tweedle-dee!
> JOHN BYROM

15 April Premiere of *Muzio Scevola*.

> His act was the last, and the superiority of it so very
> manifest, that there was not the least pretence for any
> further doubts or disputes . . . The Academy being now
> firmly established, and Handel appointed composer to it,
> all things went on prosperously for a course of between
> nine and ten years. And this may justly be called the
> period of musical glory . . . most certainly not to be
> surpassed, if equalled, in any age or country.
> MAINWARING

5 July Premiere of a new cantata, probably *Crudel tiranno amor*, sung by the soprano Durastanti at her benefit concert.
25 November Revival of *Radamisto*.
9 December Premiere of *Floridante*.

1722 (AGE 37)

9 February First recorded concert performance of the *Water Music*, at the Stationers' Hall.
7 November Revival of *Muzio Scevola* opens the Royal Academy opera season.
4 December Revival of *Floridante*.

1723 (AGE 38)

12 January Premiere of *Ottone*.
25 February Appointed 'Composer of Musick' to the Chapel Royal and granted an annual royal pension.
14 May Premiere of *Flavio*.
June Appointed Master of Music to the Princesses Anne and Caroline.
July Moves to a new house at 25 Brook Street, built in 1722.
11 December Revival of *Ottone*.

1724 (AGE 39)

20 February Premiere of *Giulio Cesare*.
24 August Plays the organ at St Paul's Cathedral for the royal princesses.
31 October Premiere of *Tamerlano* opens the Royal Academy opera season.
Around this time composes various solo sonatas and a series of German arias.

1725 (AGE 40)

2 January Revival of *Giulio Cesare*.
13 February Premiere of *Rodelinda*.
1 May Revival of *Tamerlano*.
6 May Publication of *Rodelinda*, his first score issued by subscription.
18 December Revival of *Rodelinda*.

1726 (AGE 41)

8 February Revival of *Ottone*.
12 March Premiere of *Scipione*.
5 May Premiere of *Alessandro*. It marks the arrival in Handel's company of the soprano Faustina Bordoni. She and the reigning soprano, Francesca Cuzzoni, became bitter rivals.

1727 (AGE 42)

31 January Premiere of *Admeto*.
20 February Becomes a British citizen by royal assent to an act of naturalisation.
11 April Revival of *Ottone*.
29 April Revival of *Floridante*.
11 June Death of King George I.
30 September Revival of *Admeto* opens the Royal Academy opera season.
11 October First performance of the *Coronation Anthems* at the Coronation of King George II and Queen Caroline.
11 November Premiere of *Riccardo Primo*.
30 December Revival of *Alessandro*.

1728 (AGE 43)

17 February Premiere of *Siroe*.
30 April Premiere of *Tolomeo*.
25 May Revival of *Admeto*.
1 June Performance of *Admeto* closes the last season of the Royal Academy of Music.

> Senesino . . . began to feel his strength and importance . . .
> Handel . . . resolved to subdue these Italian humours . . .
> The one was perfectly refractory; the other was equally
> outrageous . . . The merits of the quarrel I know nothing
> of. Whatever they were, the nobility would not consent
> to his design of parting with Senesino, and Handel was
> determined to have no further concerns with him.
> Faustina and Cuzzoni, as if seized with the contagion of
> discord, started questions of superiority, and urged their
> respective claims to it with an eagerness and acrimony,
> which occasioned a total dis-union betwixt them. And
> thus the Academy, after it had continued in the most
> flourishing state for upwards of nine years, was at once
> dissolved.
> MAINWARING

Perhaps, if Handel's temper had at all resembled his finger, in flexibility, a reconciliation might have been effected on no very mortifying or dishonourable terms. It is painful to dwell on this part of his life, which was one continued tissue of losses and misfortunes . . . after the dissolution of the Academy, in 1729, none [of his operas] were attended with the success that was due to their intrinsic and superior merit, though some of the best were posterior to that period.

BURNEY

The Second Royal Academy

1729 (AGE 44)

18 January Enters into an agreement with the impresario John James Heidegger to continue operas at the King's Theatre under their own management for five years.
4 February Travels to Italy to look for singers. Visits Venice, Bologna, Rome, and Naples.

The umbrage which he had given to many of the nobility, by his implacable resentments against a person whose talents they so much admired, was likely to create him a dangerous opposition . . . New singers must be sought, and could not be had any nearer than Italy. The business of choosing, and engaging them, could not be dispatched by a deputy.

MAINWARING

June Visits Hamburg, Hanover, and Halle. Sees his mother for the last time. Declines an invitation from W. F. Bach to meet J. S. Bach.
29 June Returns to London, having engaged seven singers, among them the soprano Anna Maria Strada del Pò.
10 October Performs with the new singers for the King and Queen at Kensington.
2 December Premiere of *Lotario* opens the first season of the new opera company.

Being thus embarked on a new bottom, he went on in conjunction with Heidegger, but not with that even and prosperous gale which had wafted him so smoothly and pleasantly through the nine preceding years.

MAINWARING

1730 (AGE 45)

17 January Revival of *Giulio Cesare*.
24 February Premiere of *Partenope*.
19 May Revival of *Tolomeo*.
8 August Plays the new organ at Westminster Abbey.
Senesino returns to London by October and rejoins Handel's company.
3 November Revival of *Scipione* opens the second opera season.
12 December Revival of *Partenope*.
16 December Death of his mother.

1731 (AGE 46)

2 February Premiere of *Poro*.
6 April Revival of *Rinaldo*.
4 May Revival of *Rodelinda*.
July/August Sends jewellery to his niece in Halle as a wedding present.
13 November Revival of *Tamerlano* opens the third opera season.
23 November Revival of *Poro*.
7 December Revival of *Admeto*.

1732 (AGE 47)

15 January Premicrc of *Ezio*.
1 February Revival of *Giulio Cesare*.
15 February Premiere of *Sosarme*.
23 February Performance of the oratorio *Esther* by the Chapel Royal at the Crown and Anchor tavern on his birthday.

Esther was made originally for the Duke of Chandos . . . after it had been performed at Cannons, it was played at the Crown and Anchor; and this indeed is said to have first furnished the hint for bringing oratorios on the stage.

MAINWARING

This novel species of entertainment was . . . greatly approved.

COXE

18 April Revival of *Flavio*.
May Performance of a pirated production of *Acis and Galatea* at the New Theatre, Haymarket.
2 May Premiere of a new, expanded version of *Esther*.
25 November Revival of *Alessandro*.
2 December Revival of *Acis and Galatea*.
5 December Receives a letter from Aaron Hill asking him to write English operas.

. . . deliver us from our *Italian bondage*; and demonstrate, that *English* is soft enough for opera, when compos'd by poets, who know how to distinguish the *sweetness* of our tongue, from the *strength* of it.

AARON HILL

7 December Opening of John Rich's new theatre in Covent Garden.
John Walsh publishes editions of the Solo Sonatas, Op. 1 and Trio Sonatas, Op. 2.

1733 (AGE 48)

2 January Revival of *Tolomeo*.
27 January Premiere of *Orlando*.
3 March Revival of *Floridante*.
17 March Premiere of *Deborah*.
14 April Revival of *Esther*.
July Visits Oxford for performances of his music, but declines an honorary degree.

5 and 7 July Performances of *Esther* at the Sheldonian Theatre, Oxford.

10 July Premiere of *Athalia* at the Sheldonian Theatre, Oxford.

11 July Performance of *Acis and Galatea* in the Hall of Christ Church, Oxford.

12 July Performance of *Deborah* at the Sheldonian Theatre, Oxford.

27 October An announcement appears that he will compose the wedding music for Princess Anne, instead of Maurice Greene, but the wedding is postponed when the Prince of Orange is taken ill.

30 October Premiere of the pasticcio *Semiramide* opens the fifth opera season.

Some of his singers defect to a rival company, the Opera of the Nobility, newly established at Lincoln's Inn Fields Theatre.

> About the time of the separation at the Haymarket, occasioned by the disagreement between Handel and his singers, many of the nobility raised a new subscription in order to carry on another Opera at Lincoln's-Inn-Fields, in which they could have singers and composers of their own choosing. With this view they sent for Porpora, Farinelli, and others . . . Tho' Handel bore up with great spirit and firmness against this opposition, he soon felt the effects of it.
>
> MAINWARING

> He fought manfully, changed alternately to the Haymarket, Lincoln's Inn Fields, and Covent Garden Theatre, varying his performers, and even his style of music. Yet such was the inveteracy of the opposing party, that though his operas were most admirable compositions, and those of his adversaries far inferior in merit, the tide of fashion set decidedly against him.
>
> COXE

13 November Revival of *Ottone*.

John Walsh publishes a second volume of *Suites de pièces pour le clavecin*.

Opera and oratorio together

1734 (AGE 49)

26 January Premiere of *Arianna in Creta*.

13 March Premiere of *Il Parnasso in festa*.

14 March First performance of *This is the Day which the Lord Hath Made* at the wedding of Princess Anne and the Prince of Orange at St James's Palace.

2 April Revival of *Deborah*.

27 April Revival of *Sosarme*.

7 May Revival of *Acis and Galatea*.

18 May Revival of *Il pastor fido*.

6 July End of his last opera season at the King's Theatre.

27 August Makes an agreement with John Rich to hold the next opera season at Covent Garden.

9 November Revival of *Il pastor fido* opens the new opera season at Covent Garden.

27 November Revival of *Arianna in Creta*.

His publishing privilege expires.

December Publication by John Walsh of the Concerti Grossi, Op. 3

10 December Revival of *Ottone* by the Opera of the Nobility, at the King's Theatre.

19 December Receives a Royal Bounty of £1000.

1735 (AGE 50)

8 January Premiere of *Ariodante*.

5 March Introduces organ concertos during performances of oratorios during Lent. Revival of *Esther*, with the Organ Concertos Op. 4 Nos. 2 and 3.

It was during these early performances of oratorios, that Handel first gratified the public by the performance of concertos on the organ, a species of music wholly of his own invention, in which he usually introduced an extempore fugue, a diapason piece, or an adagio, manifesting not only the wonderful fertility and readiness of his invention, but the most perfect accuracy and neatness of execution.

BURNEY

26 March Revival of *Deborah*, with the Organ Concerto, Op. 4 No. 5.
1 April Revival of *Athalia*, with the Organ Concerto, Op. 4 No. 4.
16 April Premiere of *Alcina*.
John Walsh publishes Six Keyboard Fugues.

1736 (AGE 51)

19 February Premiere of *Alexander's Feast*, with the cantata *Cecilia volgi un sguardo*, the Concerto Grosso, HWV 318, the Harp Concerto, Op. 4 No. 6, and the Organ Concerto, Op. 4 No. 1.

Handel could not complain of neglect. Though Farinelli and the nobility at that time opposed him; though he had no capital singer except Strada, and laboured under other disadvantages, his *Alexander's Feast* (19th February, 1736) was attended by an audience uncommonly numerous. Thirteen hundred persons were assembled at the Theatre of Covent Garden, and the receipt of the house amounted to four hundred and fifty pounds.

COXE

The success of this performance determined him in his resolution to addict himself for the future to this species of composition [i.e. oratorio], and accordingly he persisted in it, with a few occasional deviations, for the remainder of his life.

HAWKINS

24 March Revival of *Acis and Galatea*.
7 April Revival of *Esther*.

27 April First performance of *Sing unto God* at the wedding of the Prince of Wales to the Princess of Saxe-Gotha at the Chapel Royal.

5 May Revival of *Ariodante*.

12 May Premiere of *Atalanta*.

6 November Revival of *Alcina* opens the new opera season.

20 November Revival of *Atalanta*.

8 December Revival of *Poro*.

1737 (AGE 52)

12 January Premiere of *Arminio*.

29 January Revival of *Partenope*.

16 February Premiere of *Giustino*.

9 March Revival of *Il Parnasso in festa*.

16 March Revival of *Alexander's Feast*.

23 March Premiere of *Il trionfo del Tempo e della Verità*.

6 April Revival of *Esther*.

13 April Has an attack of 'rheumatism' and temporarily loses the use of his right arm.

> In this arduous situation, which lasted near eleven years, he displayed great superiority and force of mind . . . but so long a contest, with such expensive exertions, and such unfavourable consequences, could not fail alike to injure the body and the mind. Handel evinced, in the course of the struggle, occasional symptoms of mental derangement, and lost the use of his right arm by a stroke of the palsy.
>
> COXE

> Neglect and opposition conspired to rob him at once of health, fame and fortune!
>
> BURNEY

14 May Reported to be ill with a 'paralytic disorder'.

> The observation that misfortunes rarely come single, was verified in Handel. His fortune was not more impaired, than his health and his understanding. His right-arm was

become useless to him, from a stroke of the palsy; and how greatly his senses were disordered at intervals, for a long time, appeared from an hundred instances, which are better forgotten than recorded. The most violent deviations from reason, are usually seen when the strongest faculties happen to be thrown out of course.

MAINWARING

18 May Premiere of *Berenice*.
10 June Revival of *Alcina*.
11 June Final performance of the Opera of the Nobility.
25 June A performance of *Alexander's Feast* closes his last Covent Garden season.

Though Handel had some good singers, none of them could be compared to Farinelli . . . and it soon appeared that the relish of the English for music, was not strong enough to support two operas at a time . . . his expenses in providing singers, and in other preparations, had been very large; and his profits were in no way proportionate to such charges . . . Had he been disposed to make any concessions, his friends might easily have effected a reconciliation between him and his opponents . . . nothing was wanting to insure his future prosperity, excepting a spirit which know how to yield on proper occasions.

MAINWARING

Nor had his enemies any cause to exult. Though Handel gave up the contest, no victory was gained by them; though he was impoverished, they were not enriched.

COXE

September Travels to Aix-la-Chapelle for a health cure. Returns late October.

It was thought best for him to have recourse to the vapor-baths of Aix-la-Chapelle, over which he sat near three times as long as hath ever been the practice . . . his sweats were profuse beyond what can well be imagined. His cure,

from the manner as well as from the quickness, with which
it was wrought, passed with the nuns for a miracle. When,
but a few hours from the time of his quitting the bath,
they heard him at the organ in the principal church as well
as the convent, playing in a manner so much beyond any
they had ever been used to, such a conclusion in such
persons was natural enough.

MAINWARING

October Moves back to the King's Theatre, Haymarket and
manages to engage some of the singers of the Opera of the
Nobility, but the opening of the season is delayed by the death
of Queen Caroline.

17 December First performance of *The Ways of Zion do Mourn*
at the funeral for Queen Caroline in Westminster Abbey.

It is not the least astonishing part of his character, that his
promptitude of invention, and brilliancy of ideas, in all
this time did not forsake him. At the moment of his recovery (1737) from a violent illness, and even attended with
fits of lunacy, his faculties were exerted with their full
vigour in bringing forward the opera of *Faramondo*; and
in composing the funeral anthem on the death of his
lamented patroness, Queen Caroline, equal in pathos and
sublimity to his best compositions.

COXE

1738 (AGE 53)

3 January Premiere of *Faramondo* opens the opera season at
the King's Theatre.

25 February Premiere of the pasticcio *Alessandro Severo*.

8 March Publication of the full score of *Alexander's Feast* by
subscription.

28 March Given a benefit night at the King's Theatre.

Handel's affairs were at this time so deranged that he was
under constant apprehension of being arrested by Del Pò,
the husband of Strada. This stimulated his friends to

persuade him to have a benefit; and, in following their advice, he received such testimonies of public favour at the opera house, in the Haymarket . . . as proved extremely lucrative.

BURNEY

From a single benefit . . . from which he is said to have received £1500 it is easy to guess what might have been done to recover his affairs. But he was so averse to subscription-engagements, that he resolved to be for the future on a quite different footing. No prospects of advantage could tempt him to court those by whom he thought he had been injured and oppressed. Full of lofty sentiment he returned to Covent-Garden, where he performed a few more operas . . .

MAINWARING

15 April Premiere of *Serse*.
23 April Becomes a founder member of the Fund for the Support of Decay'd Musicians, now the Royal Society of Musicians.
1 May His statue by Louis-François Roubiliac is unveiled at Vauxhall Gardens.

He received an honourable mark of distinction from the liberality of an individual, seldom conferred on any man during his life. His statue, admirably sculptured by Roubillac [*sic*], was placed by Mr. Jonathan Tyers in the gardens at Vauxhall (1738); and the public coincided in the justice and propriety of the compliment paid to his merit.

COXE

23 July Begins to compose the first draft score of *Saul*.
18 September Visited by Charles Jennens who finds him 'full of maggots' [wild schemes] and makes various suggestions for revising *Saul*.
October Works on *Israel in Egypt*.
4 October Publication by John Walsh, the younger, of the Organ Concerti, Op. 4.

1739 (AGE 54)

22 January Premiere of *Saul*.

17 February Revival of *Alexander's Feast*.

28 February Publication by John Walsh of the Trio Sonatas, Op. 5.

3 March Revival of *Il trionfo del Tempo e della Verità*.

28 March Benefit performance of *Alexander's Feast* for the Decay'd Musicians Fund.

4 April Premiere of *Israel in Egypt*, including a new Organ Concerto, HWV 295.

September Begins to compose the Concerti Grossi, Op. 6. Completes them by the end of October.

19 October Great Britain declares war on Spain.

31 October Granted a second copyright privilege, for fourteen years.

22 November Premiere of *Ode for St Cecilia's Day* opens a season of oratorios and odes.

> He performed a few more operas . . . [but] finding that the taste of his audience was naturally averse to this species of composition, he now introduced another, more suited to the natural gravity and solidity of the English, tho' borrowed from the *concert spirituel* of their volatile neighbours on the continent.
>
> MAINWARING

> He continued every year the same style of composition, and generally with the greatest success; though with occasional failures, owing to the latent seeds of former animosity.
>
> COXE

13 December Revival of *Acis and Galatea*, with two of the new Concerti Grossi, Op. 6.

1740 (AGE 55)

27 February Premiere of *L'Allegro, il Penseroso ed il Moderato*, with a new Organ Concerto, Op. 7 No. 1.

21 March Revival of *Saul*, with the premiere of another Op. 7 Organ Concerto.

26 March Revival of *Esther*.

1 April Revival of *Israel in Egypt*, with the premiere of another Op. 7 Organ Concerto.

21 April Publication by John Walsh of the Concerti Grossi, Op. 6.

23 April Performance of *L'Allegro, il Penseroso ed il Moderato*, with the premieres of two more Op. 7 Organ Concerti.

July Travels to Europe, visiting Haarlem and probably Hanover, Berlin and Halle.

October Returns to London. Begins the composition of *Deidamia*.

8 November Revival of *Il Parnasso in festa* opens the new season of operas, odes, and oratorios at Lincoln's Inn Fields.

> Too much accustomed to disappointments to be easily
> dispirited, he continued these new entertainments,
> so excellently adapted to the season of the year in
> which they are exhibited, till the beginning of the
> year 1741.
>
> MAINWARING

22 November Premiere of *Imeneo*.

The oratorio years

1741 (AGE 56)

10 January Premiere of *Deidamia*.

31 January Revival of *L'Allegro, il Penseroso ed il Moderato*.

10 February Performance of *Deidamia* – the last performance of any Italian opera directed by him in London.

> The public always sided with Handel; but the public,
> except of the higher class of society, are not sufficiently
> attached to the Italian Opera, to give celebrity and profit
> to the undertaking . . . His last opera was *Deidamia*;

which, although abounding in beauties, was received with indifference, and performed but three nights.

COXE

Handel had been so unfortunate in all his attempts to carry on operas . . . in opposition to his former protectors, the members of the Royal Academy, that he was reduced to the necessity of drawing out of funds ten thousand pounds, which he had lodged there in his more prosperous days; and still Strada, Montagnana, and other singers employed in his last operas were unpaid, and obliged to quit this country with promissory notes instead of cash. Handel, however, who was a man of strict probity, and accustomed to pay his performers not only honestly, but generously, discharged these debts very honourably, as soon as he was able.

BURNEY

28 February Revival of *Acis and Galatea*.
18 March Revival of *Saul*.
4 April A letter in a newspaper fuels rumours that he plans to leave England.
8 April The end of his second and last Lincoln's Inn Fields season.
August Invited by the Lord Lieutenant of Ireland to visit Dublin for the winter season.

At that time his affairs again carried so ill an aspect, that he found it necessary to try the event of another peregrination. He hoped to find that favour and encouragement in a distant capital, which London seemed to refuse him.

MAINWARING

22 August Begins to compose *Messiah*.
28 August Completes the draft of Part I of *Messiah*.
6 September Completes the draft of Part II of *Messiah*. After writing out the 'Hallelujah' Chorus, he is reported to have exclaimed to his servant with tears in his eyes, 'I did think

I did see all Heaven before me, and the great God Himself seated on His throne, with his Company of Angels.'

12 September Completes the draft of Part III of *Messiah*.

November Leaves London for Dublin. On the way he is observed by the young Charles Burney in Chester.

> I was at the Public School in that city, and very well remember seeing him smoke a pipe, over a dish of coffee, at the Exchange-Coffee-House; for being extremely curious to see so extraordinary a man, I watched him narrowly as long as he remained in Chester, which, on account of the wind being unfavourable for his embarking at Parkgate, was several days.
>
> BURNEY

18 November Arrives in Dublin and takes lodging in Abbey Street.

> He was received at Dublin with such strong marks of approbation, as did no less honour to him, than to the taste of the nation.
>
> SMITH

> Dublin has always been famous for the gaiety and splendour of its court, the opulence and spirit of its principal inhabitants, the valour of its military, and the genius of its learned men. Where such things were held in esteem he rightly reckoned, that he could not better pave the way to his success, than by setting out with a striking instance and public act of generosity and benevolence.
>
> MAINWARING

10 December Plays the organ at a service at St Andrew's Church, Dublin, during which his *Utrecht Te Deum, Jubilate*, and a *Coronation Anthem* are performed to benefit the Mercer's Hospital.

23 December Opens a subscription series of six concerts at the New Music Hall, Fishamble Street, with a revival of *L'Allegro, il Penseroso ed il Moderato*, two *concerti grossi*, and an organ concerto.

1742 (AGE 57)

20 January Revival of *Acis and Galatea* and *Ode for St Cecilia's Day*.

3 February Revival of *Esther*.

17 February Revival of *Alexander's Feast* opens a second subscription series of six concerts at the New Music Hall, Fishamble Street.

17 March Revival of *L'Allegro, il Penseroso ed il Moderato*.

24 March Revival of *Imeneo* as *Hymen, a Serenata*.

27 March Announces a performance of *Messiah* for the benefit of three charities.

> Such a design drew together not only all the lovers of music, but all the friends of humanity. There was a particular propriety in this design from the subject of the oratorio itself; and there was a particular grace in it from the situation of Handel's affairs. They were brought into a better posture by his journey to Dublin.
>
> MAINWARING

7 April Revival of *Esther* ends the second subscription series.

9 April Public rehearsal of *Messiah*.

13 April Premiere of *Messiah*.

> His *Messiah* . . . was applauded with all the enthusiasm due to claims of such uncommon excellence.
>
> COXE

> The reception that he met with, at the same time that it shewed the strong sense which the Irish had of his extraordinary merit, conveyed a kind of tacit reproach on all those on the other side of the water, who had enlisted in the opposition against him.
>
> MAINWARING

25 May Revival of *Saul*.

3 June Performance of *Messiah* – his last public concert in Dublin.

13 August Leaves Dublin and returns to England.

> The public in his absence had become fully sensible of
> his merits . . . and Handel no longer had to contend with
> prejudices, or combat the malignancy of inveterate
> opposition.
>
> COXE

1743 (AGE 58)

18 February Premiere of *Samson* and probably of the Organ
Concerto, Op. 7 No. 2, at Covent Garden.

> At his return to London . . . the minds of most men were
> much more disposed in his favour . . . Fortune seemed
> rather to court and caress, than to countenance and
> support him. This return was the era of his prosperity.
>
> MAINWARING

18 March Revival of *L'Allegro, il Penseroso ed il Moderato*, with
Ode for St Cecilia's Day.
19 March Announces the London premiere of 'A New
Sacred Oratorio', not mentioning *Messiah* by name.
23 March First London performance of *Messiah* at
Covent Garden.

> His *Messiah* . . . met with a cold reception. Either the sense
> of musical excellence was become so weak, or the power of
> prejudice so strong, that all the efforts of his unparalleled
> genius and industry proved ineffectual.
>
> MAINWARING

31 March A performance of *Samson* closes the oratorio
season.
April Suffers more health problems with a return of paralysis.
27 June Troops led by King George II gain victory over the
French at Dettingen.
27 November First performances of the *Dettingen Te
Deum* and *Dettingen Anthem* at a service at the Chapel Royal
celebrating George II's safe and victorious return to England.

1744 (AGE 59)

10 February Premiere of *Semele* begins a second Lenten season at Covent Garden.
24 February Revival of *Samson*.
2 March Premiere of *Joseph and his Brethren*.
16 March Revival of *Saul*.
3 November Revival of *Deborah* opens the new subscription series.
1 December Revival of *Semele*.

1745 (AGE 60)

5 January Premiere of *Hercules*.
17 January Announces his intention to return most of the subscription money as his concerts do not seem to please the public.

> Though the oratorio of the *Messiah* increased in reputation . . . yet, to some of his other oratorios, the houses were so thin, as not nearly to defray his expenses; which, as he always employed a very numerous band, and paid his performers liberally, so deranged his affairs, that in the year 1745 . . . he stopped payment.
> BURNEY

21 January Publication of an anonymous poem supporting him and blaming his problems on a conspiracy of a society lady.

> He fell under the heavy displeasure of a certain fashionable lady. She exerted all her influence to spirit up a new opposition against him. But the world could not long be made to believe that her card-assemblies were such proper entertainments for Lent, as his oratorios.
> MAINWARING

25 January Announces that he will resume his concerts.

> But I perfectly remember, that none were well attended, except *Samson* and the *Messiah*. His majesty King George

the Second, was a steady patron of Handel during these times, and constantly attended his oratorios, when they were abandoned by the rest of his court.

BURNEY

1 March Revival of *Samson*.
13 March Revival of *Saul*
15 March Revival of *Joseph and his Brethren*.
27 March Premiere of *Belshazzar*.
9 April Revival of *Messiah*.
23 April Performance of *Messiah* closes the subscription oratorio season after sixteen of the planned twenty-four concerts.

From that time to the present, this great work has been heard in all parts of the kingdom with increasing reverence and delight; it has fed the hungry, clothed the naked, fostered the orphan, and enriched succeeding managers of oratorios, more than any single musical production in this or any country.

BURNEY

April to June Leaves London and visits various spa towns on account of ill health.
21 July Prince Charles Edward Stuart, the Young Pretender, begins the second Jacobite rebellion.
24 October Lord Shaftesbury describes him in a letter:

Poor Handel looks something better. I hope he will entirely recover in due time though he has been a good deal disordered in his head.

1746 (AGE 61)

14 February Premiere of *The Occasional Oratorio*.
16 April Jacobite forces are defeated by the Duke of Cumberland at Culloden.

1747 (AGE 62)

6 March Revival of *The Occasional Oratorio* opens a new non-subscription series of Lenten concerts at Covent Garden.

20 March Revival of *Joseph and his Brethren*.

1 April Premiere of *Judas Maccabaeus*, in honour of the Duke of Cumberland, 'upon his returning victorious from Scotland', along with a new concerto, probably the Concerto a Due Cori, No. 3.

1748 (AGE 63)

26 February Revival of *Judas Maccabaeus* opens a new series of Lenten concerts.

9 March Premiere of *Joshua*, with the Concerto a Due Cori, No. 1.

23 March Premiere of *Alexander Balus*, with the Concerto a Due Cori, No. 2.

7 April Performance of *Judas Maccabaeus* closes the oratorio season.

7 October The Peace of Aix-la-Chapelle ends the War of Austrian Succession.

1749 (AGE 64)

10 February Premiere of *Susanna* opens the series of Lenten concerts at Covent Garden.

3 March Revival of *Samson*.

17 March Premiere of *Solomon*.

23 March Revival of *Messiah* closes the oratorio season.

27 April First performance of the *Music for the Royal Fireworks*, at Green Park, in celebration of the Peace of Aix-la-Chapelle.

4 May Offers the General Committee of the Foundling Hospital a performance to benefit the charity at the newly built Chapel.

27 May Premiere of the *Foundling Hospital Anthem* at the first benefit concert at the Foundling Hospital, attended by the Prince and Princess of Wales. The programme also includes the *Music for the Royal Fireworks*, the *Dettingen Anthem*, and selections from *Solomon*.

August Travels to Bath and returns to London in September.

1750 (AGE 65)

2 March Revival of *Saul* opens a new Lenten concert series.
9 March Revival of *Judas Maccabaeus*.
16 March Premiere of *Theodora*, with the new Organ Concerto, Op. 7 No. 5.
4 April Revival of *Samson*.
12 April Revival of *Messiah* ends the oratorio season.
1 May Performance of *Messiah* to benefit the Foundling Hospital charity.

> His *Messiah* which had before been received with so
> much indifference, became from this time the favourite
> oratorio . . . consecrated to the service of the most
> innocent, most helpless, and most distressed part of the
> human species.
> MAINWARING

9 May Elected a Governor of the Foundling Hospital.
15 May Second benefit performance of *Messiah* for the Foundling Hospital charity.

> The Foundling Hospital originally rested on the slender
> foundations of private benefactions . . . Handel formed the
> noble resolution to lend his assistance, and perform his
> *Messiah* annually for its benefit. The sums raised by each
> performance were very considerable, and certainly of great
> consequence in such a crisis of affairs. But what was of
> much greater, was the magic of his name, and the universal
> character of his sacred drama . . . The very successful
> application of this wonderful production of his genius to
> so beneficent a purpose, reflected equal honour on the
> artist and the art.
> MAINWARING

> The organ in the chapel of this hospital was likewise a
> present from Handel; and he bequeathed, as a legacy to
> this charity, a fair copy of the original score of the *Messiah*.
> BURNEY

1 June Makes his will, leaving most of his estate to his niece Johanna Flörcke (née Michaelsen), but also some bequests to his friend John Christopher Smith.

August Travels to Germany for the last time.

21 August Newspaper reports that he was injured in a coach accident between The Hague and Haarlem, but that he is now recovering.

27 August Visits Haarlem.

December Returns to London.

14 December Writes to Telemann, discussing various musical matters and enclosing a gift of rare plants, as Telemann was an amateur botanist.

1751 (AGE 66)

4 January Completes the Organ Concerto, Op. 7 No. 3, his final instrumental work.

21 January Begins to compose *Jephtha*.

13 February Suffers loss of sight in his left eye while working on a chorus in *Jephtha*: 'How dark, O Lord, are thy decrees'.

> This misfortune sunk him for a time into the deepest despondency. He could not rest until he had undergone some operations as fruitless as they were painful.
>
> MAINWARING

22 February Revival of *Belshazzar* opens a new series of Lenten concerts.

23 February Continues work on *Jephtha*.

1 March Revival of *Alexander's Feast* and premieres of *The Choice of Hercules* and the Organ Concerto, Op. 7 No. 3.

15 March Revival of *Esther*.

20 March Revival of *Judas Maccabaeus*.

20 March Death of the Prince of Wales. The rest of the concert season is cancelled.

3 June Visits Bath and Cheltenham to take the waters and returns to London later that month.

30 August Completes *Jephtha*.

John Christopher Smith, the younger, returns to London from France to assist him with the management and conducting of the oratorio seasons.

> It was a most affecting spectacle to see the venerable musician, whose efforts had charmed the ear of a discerning public, led by the hand of friendship to the front of the stage, to make an obeisance of acknowledgement to his enraptured audience.
>
> COXE

1752 (AGE 67)

14 February Revival of *Joshua* opens a new series of Lenten concerts at Covent Garden.

21 February Revival of *Hercules*.

26 February Premiere of *Jephtha*.

6 March Revival of *Samson*.

18 March Revival of *Judas Maccabaeus*.

26 March Revival of *Messiah* closes the oratorio season.

9 April Benefit performance of *Messiah* for the Foundling Hospital charity.

17 August The *General Advertiser* reports that Handel has lost his sight.

3 November Undergoes a partially successful eye operation, performed by William Bromfield, Surgeon to the Princess of Wales.

> He was afflicted with the misfortune of blindness, which, great as it was, did not totally incapacitate him from study, or the power of entertaining his public.
>
> HAWKINS

1753 (AGE 68)

9 March Revivals of *Alexander's Feast* and *The Choice of Hercules* open a new season of Lenten concerts at Covent Garden. Lady Shaftesbury reports:

It was such a melancholy pleasure, as drew tears of sorrow, to see the great though unhappy Handel, dejected, wan and dark, sitting by, not playing on the harpsichord, and to think how his light had been spent by being overplied in music's cause. I was sorry to find the audience so insipid and tasteless (I may add unkind) not to give the poor man the comfort of applause; but affectation and conceit cannot discern or attend to merit.

16 March Revival of *Jephtha*.
23 March Revival of *Judas Maccabaeus*.
4 April Revival of *Samson*.
13 April Revival of *Messiah* closes the oratorio season.
16 April Performance of the *Foundling Hospital Anthem* at the official opening of the Foundling Hospital Chapel.
1 May Plays an organ concerto and voluntary for the last time in public at a benefit performance of *Messiah* for the Foundling Hospital charity.

When Handel became blind, though he no longer presided over the oratorios, he still introduced concertos on the organ between the acts. At first he relied on his memory, but the exertion becoming painful to him, he had recourse to the inexhaustible stores of his rich and fertile imagination. He gave to the band, only such parts of his intended compositions, as were to be filled up by their accompaniment; and relied on his own powers of invention to produce, at the impulse of the moment, those captivating passages, which arrested attention, and enchanted his auditors.

COXE

To see him, however, led to the organ . . . at upwards of seventy years of age, and then conducted towards the audience to make his accustomed obeisance, was a sight so truly afflicting and deplorable to persons of sensibility, as greatly diminished their pleasure, in hearing him perform.

BURNEY

1754 (AGE 69)

1 March Revival of *Alexander Balus* opens a new season of Lenten concerts at Covent Garden.
8 March Revival of *Deborah*.
17 March Revival of *Saul*.
22 March Revival of *Joshua*.
27 March Revival of *Judas Maccabaeus*.
29 March Revival of *Samson*.

> He was always much disturbed and agitated by the similar circumstances of Samson, whenever the affecting air in that oratorio of 'Total eclipse, no sun, no moon' etc. was performed.
>
> BURNEY

5 April Revival of *Messiah* closes the oratorio season.
6 April Final performance of *Admeto* – the last staged performance of any Handel opera until the twentieth century.
15 May Benefit performance of *Messiah* for the Foundling Hospital charity. This was the final one he conducted.
23 May Revivals of *L'Allegro, il Penseroso ed il Moderato* and *Ode for St Cecilia's Day*.
25 June John Christopher Smith, the younger, is appointed organist at the Foundling Hospital.
20 September Dictates and signs a letter to Telemann, rejoicing that rumours of Telemann's death are false and promising to send him another gift of exotic plants.

1755 (AGE 70)

14 February Revivals of *Alexander's Feast* and *The Choice of Hercules* open the new season of Lenten concerts at Covent Garden.
21 February Revivals of *L'Allegro, il Penseroso ed il Moderato* and the *Ode for St Cecilia's Day*.
26 February Revival of *Samson*.
28 February Revival of *Joseph and his Brethren*.
5 March Revival of *Theodora*.

12 March Revival of *Judas Maccabaeus*.
19 March Revival of *Messiah*.
21 March Performance of *Messiah* closes the oratorio season.
1 May Benefit performance of *Messiah* for the Foundling Hospital charity.

1756 (AGE 71)

5 March Revival of *Athalia* opens a new season of Lenten concerts.
17 March Revival of *Israel in Egypt* with a new version of Part I.
19 March Revival of *Deborah*.
26 March Revival of *Judas Maccabaeus*.
2 April Revival of *Jephtha*.
9 April Revival of *Messiah* closes the oratorio season.
19 May Benefit performance of *Messiah* for the Foundling Hospital charity.
6 August Modifies his will, adding bequests to Thomas Morrell and Newburgh Hamilton, and increasing John Christopher Smith's bequest by £1,500.

1757 (AGE 72)

25 February Revival of *Esther* opens a new season of Lenten concerts at Covent Garden. It includes a new addition, 'Sion now her head shall raise', which is probably the last chorus he composes.
7 March Revival of *Israel in Egypt*.
9 March Revival of *Joseph and his Brethren*.
11 March Premiere of *The Triumph of Time and Truth*.

His faculties remained in their full vigour almost to the hour of his dissolution, as appeared from songs and choruses, and other compositions, which from the date of them, may almost be considered as his parting words, his last accents! This must appear the more surprising, when it is remembered to how great a degree his mind was disordered, at times, towards the latter part of his life.

MAINWARING

22 March Modifies his will again, adding bequests to two servants.

25 March Revival of *Judas Maccabaeus*.

30 March Revival of *Messiah*.

1 April Performance of *Messiah* closes the oratorio season.

5 May Benefit performance of *Messiah* for the Foundling Hospital charity.

4 August Modifies his will for a third time, adding bequests to John Rich, Charles Jennens, and Bernard Granville, and bequeathing a copy of the score and parts of *Messiah* to the Foundling Hospital.

1758 (AGE 73)

10 February Revival of *The Triumph of Time and Truth* opens a new series of Lenten concerts at Covent Garden.

22 February Revival of *Belshazzar*.

24 February Revival of *Israel in Egypt*.

1 March Revival of *Jephtha*.

3 March Revival of *Judas Maccabaeus*.

10 March Revival of *Messiah*.

17 March Revival of *Messiah* closes the oratorio concert series.

27 April Benefit performance of *Messiah* for the Foundling Hospital charity.

August Travels to Tunbridge Wells for more eye treatment by the oculist John Taylor, but it is unsuccessful.

1759 (AGE 74)

2 March Revival of *Solomon*, revised by John Christopher Smith, the younger, opens the Lenten concert series at Covent Garden.

9 March Revival of *Susanna*.

14 March Revival of *Samson*.
23 March Revival of *Judas Maccabaeus*.
30 March Revival of *Messiah*.
6 April Revival of *Messiah* closes the oratorio concert series.

> He continued his oratorios with uninterrupted success,
> and unrivaled glory, till within eight days of his death . . .
>
> MAINWARING

> His merit and perseverance were amply rewarded; he
> retained a firm hold of the public favour and patronage to
> the end of his life; and he was not only enabled to clear
> himself from all incumbrances, but to realize a fortune of
> twenty thousand pounds.
>
> COXE

> Handel . . . manifested his powers of invention in extem-
> porous flights of fancy to be as rich and rapid, a week
> before his decease, as they had for many years.
>
> BURNEY

7 April Intends to travel to Bath but is too ill to do so.

> His health had been declining apace for several months
> before his death. He was very sensible of its approach, and
> refused to be flattered by any hopes of recovery. One
> circumstance was very ominous, I mean the total lack of
> appetite, which was come upon him, and which must
> prove more pernicious to a person always habituated,
> as he had been, to an uncommon portion of food and
> nourishment.
>
> MAINWARING

> Nature at last became exhausted, he exhibited evident
> symptoms of decay; his appetite failed him, and he saw
> without dismay his disolution approaching.
>
> COXE

11 April Modifies his will for the fourth time, bequeathing
£1,000 to the Society for the Support of Decay'd Musicians,

requesting burial in Westminster Abbey, and providing £600
for a monument of himself to be erected there.

> He was sensible of his approaching dissolution; and having
> always been impressed with a profound reverence for the
> doctrines and duties of the Christian religion . . . he had
> most seriously and devoutly wished, for several days before
> his death, that he might breathe his last on Good Friday,
> 'in hopes', he said, 'of meeting his Good God, his sweet
> Lord and Saviour, on the day of his resurrection', meaning
> the third day, or the Easter Sunday following.
>
> BURNEY

14 April Dies at his home in Brook Street on Easter Saturday
at about 8 a.m.

17 April His death is reported by a friend, James Smyth, in a
letter to another friend, Bernard Granville:

> According to your request to me when you left London,
> that I would let you know when our good friend departed
> this life, on Saturday last at 8 o'clock in the morn died the
> great and good Mr Handel. He was sensible to the last
> moment; made a codicil to his will on Tuesday, ordered to
> be buried privately in Westminster Abbey, and a monu-
> ment not to exceed £600 for him. I had the pleasure to
> reconcile him to his old friends; he saw them and forgave
> them, and let all their legacies stand! In the codicil he left
> many legacies to his friends, and among the rest he left me
> £500 and has left you the two pictures you formerly gave
> him. He took leave of all his friends on Friday morning,
> and desired to see nobody but the Doctor and Apothecary
> and myself. At 7 o'clock in the evening he took leave of
> me, and told me we 'should meet again'; as soon as I was
> gone he told his servant 'not to let me come to him any
> more, for that he had now done with the world'. He died
> as he lived – a good Christian, with a true sense of his duty
> to God and man, and he lived in perfect charity with all
> the world. If there is anything I can be of further service to

you please let me know. I was to have set out for Bath tomorrow, but must attend the funeral, and shall then go next week . . . He has left *Messiah* to the Foundling Hospital, and one thousand pounds to the decayed musicians and their children, and the residue of his fortune to his niece and relations in Germany. He has died worth £20,000, and left legacies with his charities to nearly £6,000. He has got by his Oratorios this year £1,952 12s 8d.

20 April Buried in the South Transept of Westminster Abbey. Some three thousand people attend his funeral.

His funeral service was preached by Dr. Pearce, Bishop of Rochester; and at his own expence a marble monument was erected to his memory, by the sculpture of Roubillac [*sic*]. His figure is represented standing before the organ, and listening to the harp of an Angel. On a scroll are recorded his own divine notes, set to those emphatical words, comprising the sum of Christian hope, 'I know that my Redeemer liveth'.

COXE

21 April The *Universal Chronicle* publishes 'An Attempt towards an Epitaph':

Beneath this Place
Are reposited the Remains of
GEORGE FREDERICK HANDEL
The most Excellent Musician
Any Age ever produced:
Whose Compositions were a
Sentimental Language
Rather than mere Sounds;
And surpassed the Power of Words
In expressing the various Passions
Of the Human Heart.

Handel's music

Operas

> The prodigious number of his compositions will account
> for a much greater proportion of time than any man could
> well be supposed to spare from sleep and the necessary
> recruits of nature.
>
> JOHN HAWKINS

Handel's output was vast and covered many different genres
of composition, but none was more important than opera. He
was first and foremost a man of the theatre, and his passion for
opera provides the key to understanding and appreciating
all of his music. Whenever you hear a routine or a dull
performance of anything by Handel, you can be sure that the
performers have overlooked this vital fact. Opera for Handel
was drama and colour and gesture – and above all, emotion –
and he wrote in the spirit of his operas even when he was
composing something else. Handel produced operas nearly all
of his life, and he would have carried on to the end if only the
English public had continued to support him. As it was, he
cleverly reinvented opera to make oratorios – and the English
loved them, even though some of them at least were arguably
operas by another name. Various of the oratorios have indeed
been staged by opera companies in recent years, which just
underlines the sense of continuity in Handel's output.
So beware reverential performances of the oratorios in the
concert hall – *Belshazzar* is related to *Giulio Cesare*, at least
musically!

The complete operas surveyed here are listed chronologi-
cally, with information about the dates of composition
(Handel often noted these in his scores), the libretto, and the
date and place of the premiere, followed by a brief synopsis,
some notes putting each opera in context, pointers to some of
the musical highlights, and finally a recommendation of a CD

recording, or recordings. Where available, there are also recommendations of DVDs of staged productions.

In addition to the operas, there are a number of *pasticcios*, or pastiche operas. These were works put together, either by Handel, or by others, using material almost exclusively from existing works. The most significant pasticcios are *Genserico* (1728), *Tito* (1731), *Oreste* (1734), *Alessandro Severo* (1738), and *Giove in Argo* (1739). Of these, the only recordings available at the time of writing were of *Oreste* and *Giove in Argo*:

🎧 *Oreste*: Nesi/Mitsopoulu/Katsuli/Koroneos/Magoulas/
Spanos
Camerata Stuttgart/Petrou
MDG 609 1273-2 (2 CDs). Recorded 2004.
🎧 *Giove in Argo*: Aspelemeier/Tjalve/Nelles/Haller/Auerbach/
Spogis
Kammerchor Würzburg/Concert Royal Köln/Kraus/Beckert
Musicaphon M56891 (2SACDs). Recorded 2006 and 2007.

The genial companion on my own journey through all these operas was Handel's younger contemporary, Charles Burney, who wrote about most of them in the second volume of his *A General History of Music* (1789). Burney was too young to have seen the operas at the time they were first produced, but he talked to people who were there, and studied the scores, beginning with *Rinaldo*, Handel's first opera for London. Burney is an entertaining and outspoken guide, so I have tagged the recommended highlights of each opera with some of his comments. He is passionate when he likes something, but also not afraid to criticise. By the 1780s he thought much of Handel's music was 'old-fashioned' (and Christopher Hogwood points out in his biography of Handel that Burney's unpublished notebooks reveal more criticism than he was prepared to put into print), but Burney knew that Handel 'burned' at times with a special 'fire' that transcended everything; he was 'grand, masterly, full and flowing'. Burney's own style of writing now seems, of course, old-fashioned, but that is part of his charm – an authentic voice from Handel's time. You should note that one of

Burney's favourite adjectives, 'pathetic', relates to pathos and means 'sad and deeply expressive', not 'contemptible' as in the modern usage of the word.

One of the things you soon realise when reading Burney is the extent to which writing operas really was a 'business' in the eighteenth century, owing at least as much to practical considerations as to inspiration. Wagner – with his 'art for art's sake' and his idealistic and integrated concept of music drama – was still a long way off. Handel took a cool (though also on occasions quite heated) look at the singers he had available and tailored his music accordingly. It is by no means easy, therefore, to establish a definitive version of many of these operas, as Handel made many practical changes for subsequent revivals. So, when talking of Handel's operas, the 'work' has to be viewed as the 'performance', rather than as the 'score' – a challenge and frustration to all subsequent commentators.

Handel's operas are by no means uniformly good, but they do all contain much glorious music, and are all imbued with what Winton Dean called 'one of Handel's supreme virtues, the range, depth and subtlety of his insight into human character'. That is what makes them so endlessly fascinating. And to quote Dean again, a good performance of a Handel opera should demonstrate that 'music and drama go hand in hand in continuous motion'. From first to last Handel held faith with the form of the *opera seria*, characterised by a succession of alternating recitatives and arias, with libretti based on mythological subjects. The recitatives (a form of speech-related singing) were either *secco* – accompanied by just continuo instruments (e.g. harpsichord and cello) – or *accompagnato* – accompanied by the orchestra. The arias were mainly *da capo* – in three parts with the opening section repeated after a contrasting middle section – and offered many opportunities for elaborate vocal display and imaginative interplay between the voice and orchestra. Most were also 'exit arias' – a dramatic convention which required the character to leave the stage at the end. In essence, therefore, the recitatives contain the maximum amount of action in the minimum of time, moving the plot quickly forward, while the arias do exactly the opposite, pausing to muse on a situation or a state of mind. There are many more solo arias than duets or ensembles in Handel's operas, and he makes only limited use of the chorus (an element that would come into its own later in his oratorios).

The wonder is that the potentially restrictive conventions of *opera seria* clearly fuelled Handel's genius time and time again. His recitatives reflect all the subtlety of human speech and dialogue – be it amorous, defiant, or despairing – while his best arias have you on the edge of your seat, breathless, as he accelerates the high-wire drama and excitement of the music, or as he seems to suspend time itself, spinning something infinitely magical and touching. Take *Ariodante*, for example, and compare the rapt desolation of 'Scherza infida' in Act II, with the vocal fireworks of 'Dopo notte' in Act III. If Handel had only written operas, without any of the other works on which his reputation has rested for most of the 250 years since his death, he would still deserve his place among the greatest of composers.

The information given below is necessarily brief. If you want to immerse yourself completely in Handel's operas, then Winton Dean's monumental but eminently readable two-volume study, *Handel's Operas 1704–1726* and *Handel's Operas 1726–1741*, is indispensable.

The Hamburg operas 1705–8

Almira, HWV 1
Composition Not known.
Libretto Friedrich Christian Feustking.
Premiere 8 January 1705, Theater am Gänsemarkt, Hamburg.
Synopsis A medieval tale of love and intrigue at the court of Almira, the newly crowned Queen of Castile in Valladolid. Three couples – Almira and her secretary Fernando (eventually revealed to be a prince), Prince Osman and Princess Bellante, and King Raymondo and Princess Edilia, undergo a series of misunderstandings and other complications before they are finally united in marriage.

Notes This was a brilliant debut for Handel and a great success – it ran for twenty performances. Full of marvellous, inventive music (the running time is three hours forty-five minutes), it begins with a French-style overture that could almost have been by Lully, and continues in the Hamburg tradition with a mixture of German and Italian arias, plus various dance movements. Some of the music, however, is unfortunately lost. In the orchestra, Handel makes prominent use of the bassoon, an instrument that recurs as an obbligato instrument throughout his operas. *Almira* is Handel's only surviving opera without any parts for a castrato voice. It is indebted in style to the Hamburg court composer, Reinhard Keiser, but already demonstrates that Handel was the greater composer, and refutes the claim made by his friend and rival Johann Mattheson to have taught him all he knew! It contains much music which Handel would reuse in subsequent operas, and absolutely deserves a modern stage revival.

Highlights Act I: 'Schönste Rosen' (Edilia) – an early example of Handel's artistry in writing a simple, tuneful and memorable aria. 'Proverai di che fiere saette' (Edilia) – bustling orchestral writing and vocal gymnastics. 'Geloso tormento' (Almira) – a plaintive vocal line and oboe obbligato, with dramatic orchestral interjections. Act II: 'Scepter und Kron' (Osman) – a prosaic vocal line, but a joyously beguiling ritornello. 'Mi dà speranza al core' (Raymondo) – imaginative orchestral counterpoint to the voice, a forerunner of many similar moments in later operas. 'Move i passi a le ruine' (Almira) – like 'Schönste Rosen', a gently flowing and affecting aria. Act III: 'Quillt, ihr überhäuften Zähren' (Edilia) – a beautiful vocal line for the soprano, with the emotion heightened by the bass viol obbligato.

🎧 Monoyios/Rozario/Gerrard/Thomas/Nasrawi/
MacDougall/Haye/Elsner
Fiori Musicali/Lawrence-King
CPO 999 275-2 (3 CDs). Recorded 1994.

Nero, HWV 2

Composition Not known.

Libretto Friedrich Christian Feustking.

Premiere 25 February 1705, Theater am Gänsemarkt, Hamburg.

Notes The music is lost.

Florindo, HWV 3

Composition Not known.

Libretto Heinrich Hinsch.

Premiere Probably January 1708, Theater am Gänsemarkt, Hamburg.

Notes Most of the music is lost. There is no recording.

Daphne, HWV 4

Composition Not known.

Libretto Heinrich Hinsch.

Premiere Probably January 1708, Theater am Gänsemarkt, Hamburg.

Notes Most of the music is lost. *Florindo* and *Daphne* were originally conceived as a single opera, but separated before their first performances. There is no recording.

The Florence and Venice operas 1707–9

Rodrigo, HWV 5

Composition 1707.

Libretto Francesco Silvani.

Premiere Late October or early November 1707, Teatro Civico Accademico, Florence.

Synopsis The plot is based on the historical figure of Rodrigo, the last Visigothic King of Spain, whose disloyalty to both his wife, Esilena, and mistress, Florinda, fuels the drama and nearly costs him his life. Plot and counterplot multiply, with deception, siege and imprisonment, until all ends happily – a victory of love over revenge – as Rodrigo, reconciled to Esilena, abdicates in favour of the King of Aragon, who marries Florinda. The moral is in the opera's subtitle: 'self-conquest is the greatest victory'.

Notes This was Handel's first exclusively Italian opera. Unfortunately there is no contemporary account of how the Florentine audience received it. The opening section of the overture is identical to that of *Almira*, initiating the ongoing story of Handel's self-borrowings throughout his operatic career. Some of the music was missing until fairly recently. The reconstructed edition by Alan Curtis is persuasive evidence that this is a significant and satisfying work.

Highlights Act I: 'Pugneran con noi le stelle' (Florinda) – a brilliant display for both the singer and orchestra. 'Per dar pregio all'amor mio' (Esilena) – an extended declaration of fidelity (almost eight minutes). Handel borrowed the music from the cantata *Il delirio amoroso*, composed earlier in 1707, but it is much more effective in the slower version here. The infinitely expressive vocal line is partnered by a violin obbligato, with extensive and eloquent *ritornelli* from strings and oboe, particularly the recurring, falling motif that closes each section – a characteristic Handel fingerprint. Act II: 'Dolce amor che mi consola' (Rodrigo) – a brief, strophic song, with pauses between each phrase and the strings doubling the voice. A perfect miniature. Haunting. Act III: 'Addio! mio caro bene' and 'Prendi l'alma et prendi il core' (Rodrigo and Esilena) – two lyrical and touching duets.

♠ Banditelli/Piau/Cecchi Fedi/Müller/Invernizzi/Calvi
Il Complesso Barocco/Curtis
Virgin Veritas 7243 5 45897 2 (2 CDs). Recorded 1999.

Agrippina, HWV 6

Composition 1709.
Libretto Cardinal Vincenzo Grimani.
Premiere 26 December 1709, Teatro San Giovanni Grisostomo, Venice.
Synopsis This is ancient Roman history retold with a scintillating mix of drama and satirical comedy. The scheming Agrippina, wife of the supposedly dead Emperor Claudio, is determined to gain the throne for her son, Nerone. When Claudio inconveniently reappears and declares that Ottone,

Commander of the Imperial Army, should succeed him, Agrippina spins a web of confusion and intrigue, involving, among others, two of her would-be lovers, Pallante and Narciso, and the equally devious Roman lady, Poppea, before finally achieving her goal.

Notes Handel's biographer, John Mainwaring, said that Handel had initially been reluctant to write an opera for Venice – and then he finished it in three weeks! He borrowed widely from his Italian cantatas, composed while he was in Rome. *Agrippina* is a brilliant demonstration of Handel's skill at characterisation in music and it was a popular success, running for twenty-seven successive performances. Ecstatic audiences were said to have hailed Handel with '*Viva il caro Sassone*' – 'Long live the dear Saxon' (it sounds better in the original Italian than in translation). The cast included four singers who would later appear in Handel's operas in London: Margherita Durastanti, Giuseppe Maria Boschi, Francesca Vanini-Boschi and Valeriano Pellegrini. For some performances Handel included an aria with interludes which he brilliantly improvised on the harpsichord – something incorporated into the recent modern dress, political power-play production at English National Opera.

Highlights Act I: 'L'alma mia fra le tempeste' (Agrippina) – a brilliantly virtuosic first aria for the scheming heroine. 'Lusinghiera mia speranza' (Ottone) – the vocal line is memorably accompanied by troubled, leaping counterpoint in the orchestra. 'Vaghe perle, eletti fiori' (Poppea) – mellifluous orchestral accompaniment for the giddy Poppea. Act II: 'Otton', qual portentoso fulmine' and 'Voi che udite il mio lamento' (Ottone) – accompanied recitative and aria: a profound appeal for sympathy, with a plaintive oboe and piercing suspensions in the strings. 'Pensieri, voi mi tormentate!' (Agrippina) – a dramatic *scena* with powerful interplay between the voice and orchestra. Act III: 'Come nube che fugge dal vento' (Nerone) – high-wire coloratura, and pathos in the central section.

🎧 Jones/Miles/Ragin/Brown/Chance/Mosley/Kenny/
Clarkson/von Otter
English Baroque Soloists/Gardiner
Philips 438 009-2 (3 CDs). Recorded 1997.
📺 Kremer/Arends/Hart-Davis/de Lang/Micinski/van der
Linde/Muuse/Alofs
Combattimento Consort Amsterdam/de Vriend
Buchmann (stage director)
Challenge Classics CCDVD 72143 (1 DVD). Filmed 2004.

The first London operas: 1711–15

Rinaldo, HWV 7
Composition 1710–11.
Libretto Giacomo Rossi and Aaron Hill, from Tasso.
Premiere 24 February 1711, Queen's Theatre, Haymarket.
Synopsis A story of heroism and love during the First Crusade
in the eleventh century. The knight Rodrigo's plans to capture
Jerusalem and win the hand of Almirena are initially thwarted
by the deceptions of the sorceress Armida, but virtue and
Christianity triumph, and in the end all are rewarded.
Notes The music historian John Hawkins wrote: 'We are told
that Mr Handel composed this opera in a fortnight . . . the
applause it met with was greater than had been given to any
musical performance in this kingdom: in a word it established
Mr Handel's character on a firm and solid basis.' The librettist
Aaron Hill was a young writer and would-be impresario who
had taken over the management of the Queen's Theatre for the
1710–11 season. He was hoping to establish Italian opera with
newly composed works, rather than the *pasticcio* that had previously been put together with music from various different
works. Handel borrowed some of the music for *Rinaldo* from
his Italian works, including *Aci, Galatea e Polifemo*, *Il Trionfo del
Tempo edel Disinganno*, *Agrippina*, and various of his Italian
cantatas – which perhaps explains how he was able to complete
it in only two weeks. The orchestra displays a wide range of
inventive instrumental colour, as Handel takes advantage of the

greater number of skilled players available in London, compared with either Florence or Venice. Sparrows were released to fly onstage at one point in Act I, but ended up in the auditorium as well, as various London papers reported, pointing out with wry amusement 'the inconveniences which the heads of the audience may sometimes suffer from them'. *Rinaldo* contains one great number after another. It was the first Handel opera that Charles Burney wrote about in his *A History of Music*. Despite it being an early work, he declared it 'peculiarly compact and forcible in the style' and was keen to expound on its 'beauties'. He pointed out that Handel himself and others subsequently 'pillaged' it for music to use in other works, concluding that 'it is, however, so superior in composition to any opera of that period which had ever been performed in England, that its great success does honour to our nation'. From this point onwards, the quoted comments accompanying my selections of highlights from the various operas all come from Burney.

Highlights Act I: 'Furie terribili' (Armida) – 'full of genius and fire, and truly dramatic'. 'Cara sposa, amante cara, dove sei?' (Rinaldo) – 'one of the best airs in that style that was ever composed by himself or any other master; and by many degrees the most pathetic song, and with the richest accompaniment, which had been then heard in England'. 'Venti, turbini, prestate le vostre ali a questo piè' (Rinaldo) – a brilliant showcase aria for the castrato Nicolo Grimaldi, known as Nicolini. Act II: 'Il Tricerbero umiliato' (Rinaldo) – 'a passionate aria . . . had English Bacchanalian words set to it: "Let the waiter bring clean glasses", to which it was sung at merry and convivial meetings all over the kingdom'. 'Lascia ch'io pianga mia cruda sorte' (Almirena) – Burney was curiously silent about this tragically beautiful aria, but it is surely one of the most moving Handel wrote. 'Fermati – No, crudel' (Rinaldo and Armida) – 'a duet of infinite genius, spirit, and originality'. 'Vo' far guerra, e vincer voglio' (Armida) – 'with an accompaniment for the harpsichord . . . and which Handel played himself, during the run of the opera, must have captivated by the lightness and elasticity of his finger'. Act III: 'È' un incendio fra due venti' (Rinaldo) – 'spirited and pleasing. The violin part reminds us of the accompaniment to a movement in the coronation anthem.' Burney was right: the angular orchestral opening sounds like 'Exceeding glad shall he be', from *The King Shall Rejoice*. 'Bel piacere è godere fido amor' (Almirena) – 'a light natural air' which Handel supports with a gossamer-light orchestral accompaniment. Enchanting! 'Ora la tromba in suon festante mi richiamo a trionfar' (Rinaldo) – 'an excellent air of spirit for Nicolini, with a trumpet accompaniment, and bold and new effects'.

𝆓 Fink/Bartoli/Daniels/Taylor/Finley/Orgonasova/Mehta/ Rincón/Bott/Padmore
Academy of Ancient Music/Hogwood
Decca 467 087-2 (3 CDs). Recorded 1999.
𝆓 Genaux/Persson/Kalna/Zazzo/Rutherford/Dumaux/ Visse/Freiberger
Barockorchester/Jacobs
Harmonia Mundi HMC 901796.98 (3 CDs). Recorded 2002.
▯ Walker/York/Daniels/Köhler/Silins/Nadelmann/Maxwell
Bavarian State Orchestra/Bicket
D. Alden (stage director)
Arthaus Musik 100 388 (2 DVDs). Filmed 2001.

Il pastor fido, HWV 8

Composition Completed 24 October 1712.
Libretto Giacomo Rossi, after Giovanni Battista Guarini.
Premiere 22 November 1712, Queen's Theatre, Haymarket.
Synopsis Love and jealousy in Arcadia. The nymph Amarilli loves the faithful shepherd Mirtillo – as does the scheming Eurilla – but Amarilli is betrothed to another shepherd, Silvio, who is in turn loved by Dorinda. Overcoming various obstacles, and narrowly avoiding human sacrifice, the right couples are eventually brought together and Eurilla repents so that all can have a happy ending.
Notes Handel returned to London in 1712 to find Aaron Hill no longer in charge of the Queen's Theatre, and the castrato

Nicolini no longer singing in the city. He stayed with the Earl of Burlington, a great admirer of his music, from 1712 to 1715, and composed four operas during this time. *Rinaldo* had been staged with great splendour, but *Il pastor fido* was put on as cheaply as possible. There were basically two types of Italian opera: the heroic and the pastoral. *Rinaldo* had been heroic, and the English loved it; *Il pastor fido* was pastoral and they didn't – it seemed monotonous, drab, and too short. It was a miscalculation on Handel's part and only received seven performances. Everything is indeed scaled down in this opera: it is shorter than *Rinaldo*, with fewer characters, simpler accompaniments to the arias, and a reduced range of orchestral colour. All that ran counter to English taste and when Handel revised the opera in 1734 he introduced choruses (borrowing music from *Il Parnasso in festa*, composed earlier the same year) and increased the role of the orchestra. The second version ran for thirteen performances, and then Handel produced a third version later in 1734. He had moved to Covent Garden Theatre, which had a ballet troupe led by Marie Sallé, so he added dance movements and a prologue along the lines of a French *opéra-ballet*, combining singing and dancing. Handel also made changes to many of the arias, using more material borrowed from earlier works. So *Il pastor fido* was now completely transformed from the original, and had ended up virtually as a *pasticcio*. Such changes were largely due to the new and different singers Handel had at his disposal – writing operas was both a pragmatic and an opportunistic business! The entire role of Silvio, for example, was changed from castrato in 1712 to tenor in 1734. Happily, all these changes were for the good and the final version is full of great music – vintage Handel! Burney excused the 1712 version as being very much of the style of the time, and made the point that in pastoral drama 'simplicity was propriety', but he concluded that it contains 'proofs of genius' nonetheless.

Highlights These refer to the final 1734 version. Act I: 'Lontan del mio tesoro' (Mirtillo) – a gently sustained slow air: 'This purity and simplicity, when the melody and the voice which delivers it are exquisite, would be always pleasing to an audience, as a contrast to rich harmony and contrivance.' 'Finchè un zeffiro soave' (Amarilli) – mellifluous warblings of the voice with flutes added to the strings. 'Oh! Quanto bella gloria' – an imaginative, extended chorus, with colourful orchestration composed in 1734 to end the act. An unexpected gem! Act II: 'Caro amor' (Mirtillo) – one of those atmospheric moments when Handel suspends time with a slow, yearning air. 'Sol nel mezzo risona del core' (Silvio) – 'in jig time, *alla caccia*, and perfectly adapted to the character . . . a gay and frolicksome swain, much fonder of field-sports than the society of females'. 'Scherza in mar la navicella' (Amarilli) – exciting vocal virtuosity and scurrying orchestral writing. Act III: 'Sciogliete quelle mani' / 'Per te, mio dolce bene' / 'Si unisce al tuo martir' (Mirtillo, Amarilli, and Chorus) – a flowing sequence of three brief movements – expressive recitative, duet, and chorus – demonstrating the suppleness of Handel's art. 'Caro / Cara' (Amarilli and Mirtillo) – a joyous love duet to herald the happy ending.

🎧 Esswood/Farkas/Lukin/Kállay/Flohr/Gregor
Savaria Vocal Ensemble/Capella Savaria/McGegan
Hungaraton HCD 129112/13 (2 CDs). Recorded 1988.

Teseo, HWV 9
Composition Completed 19 December 1712.
Libretto Nicola Haym, after Philippe Quinault.
Premiere 10 January 1713, Queen's Theatre, Haymarket.
Synopsis A retelling of the ancient Greek legend of the warrior Theseus (Teseo) who loves Agilea, but has to compete with King Egeo (who is eventually revealed to be Teseo's father) and the enchantress Medea (who is betrothed to Egeo) to win her.
Notes Dedicated to the Earl of Burlington, *Teseo* was a return to the heroic opera formula that had made *Rinaldo* such a success. The soprano castrato Valeriano Pellegrini sang the title role. The libretto was an adaption of the one that Lully had used for his lyric tragedy, *Thésée*, and is unique in Handel's

operas in being cast in the five-act French form and removing many of the exit arias. *Teseo* was a great success, running for thirteen performances, although after the second, the theatre manager, Owen Swiney, absconded with the box-office takings! He was immediately replaced by John Heidegger who continued to work with Handel for many years.

Highlights Act I: Overture – on a grand scale, like a *concerto grosso*. 'In the first movement . . . there is something bold and piquant in the harmony, which must have been very new at this time.' 'M'adora l'idol' mio' (Agilea) – a brilliant aria with a virtuoso oboe obbligato. Act II: 'Dolce riposo, ed innocente pace!' (Medea) – 'rich in harmony and pleasing in effects'. 'Si ti lascio, altro amore io chiudo' (Medea and Egeo) – 'very ingenious and original . . . sung by two lovers who have quarrelled . . . as their inclinations move different ways, so do the notes they sing'. 'O stringerò nel' sen' (Medea) – 'full of fire and dramatic effects'. Act III: 'S'armi il fato, s'armi amore!' (Teseo) – 'a sprightly air of an original cast for the hero of the piece, who seems, however, to have drawn from Handel's pen no testimony of uncommon powers as a singer; though the composition has, in the accompaniment, some of the author's own fire'. Act IV: 'Cara/Caro, ti dono in pegno il cor' (Teseo and Agilea) – 'a most admirable duet . . . equal if not superior to any one of the kind that Handel ever composed . . . there still remains such fire and originality, as can be found perhaps in no other duet of the same period.'

🎧 James/Jones/Gooding/Ragin/Napoli/Gall
Musiciens du Louvre/Minkowski
Erato 2292-458062-2 (2 CDs). Recorded 1992.
📺 Laszczkowski/Wesseling/Meyer/Rostorf-Zamir/Wölfel/Diestler
Lauen Compagney Berlin/Katschner
Köhler (stage director)
Arthaus Musik 100708 (1 DVD). Filmed 2004.

Silla, HWV 10
Composition 1713.

Libretto Giacomo Rossi, from Plutarch.

Premiere ?2 June 1713, Queen's Theatre, Haymarket, or Burlington House.

Synopsis The Ancient Roman dictator Lucius Cornelius Sulla (Handel's librettist changed his name to Silla) exercises his absolute and lascivious power, to the despair of his wife, Metella. Encouraged at first by the gods, he is finally shipwrecked, yields up his sword, and is reconciled to all whom he has wronged.

Notes Unusually for Handel, this is a relatively short and uncomplicated opera. There was probably only ever one, private performance – for the new French Ambassador, the duc d'Aumont, to whom the work was dedicated. Burney made no mention of *Silla*. Some of the music reappears in the following two operas, *Amadigi di Gaula* and *Radamisto*.

Highlights Act I: 'Con tromba guerriera' (Claudio) – a thrilling, warlike aria with trumpet obbligato. Act II: 'Dolce nume' (Silla) – sensuous music for the sleep scene. 'Sol per te bell'idol mio' (Flavia and Lepido) – a touching duet of love reaffirmed. 'La vendetta è un cibo' (Silla) – a character portrait of the cruel hero. 'Sei già morto' (Celia) – a moving plea in the face of loss.

⌒ Bowman/Lunn/Baker/Nicholls/Marsh/Cragg/Dixon
London Handel Orchestra/Darlow
Somm SOMMCD 227-8 (2 CDs). Recorded 2000.

Amadigi di Gaula, HWV 11

Composition 1715.

Libretto Nicola Haym, or Giacomo Rossi, after Antoine Houdar de la Motte.

Premiere 25 May 1715, King's Theatre, Haymarket.

Synopsis A tale of chivalry and magic. The knight, Amadigi, has to overcome the jealous machinations of his faithless friend, Dardano, and the sorceress, Melissa, in order to win the hand of his beloved Oriana.

Notes Another heroic opera, in the style of *Rinaldo* and *Teseo*. Handel borrowed music for it from *Silla* (see above). It was given a lavish production and scored a great success, running for six performances, and it was revived in 1716 and 1717. The castrato Nicolini had returned to London and sang the title role. *Amadigi* is the masterly culmination of Handel's first period of operas for London. Burney declared there was 'more invention, variety, and good composition, than in any one of the musical dramas of Handel which I have yet carefully and critically examined'.

Highlights Act I: 'Ah! Spietato!' (Melissa) – 'slow, pathetic, and still new. There is a fine solo part for the hautbois, which is in dialogue with the voice . . . the second part is quick, and full of agitation and fury'. 'Gioie, venite in sen' (Oriana) – 'one of the most graceful and pleasing [airs] that has ever been composed in the Siciliano style . . . the voice, wholly undisturbed, is left to expand in all the tenderness and expression which the air itself excites'. Act II: 'S'estinto è l'idol mio' (Oriana) – 'the pathetic subject, the natural and pleasing imitations in the instrumental parts, the richness of the harmony, the affecting modulation . . . but above all, the strain of sorrow which runs through every page of the voice-part, all conspire to render it one of the most perfect compositions of the kind'. 'T'amai, quant'il mio cor' (Amadigi) – 'begins in a sublime style of cantabile, and in the second part is painted all the rage and fury which could be excited in an offended knight'. 'Crudel, tu no ferai' (Amadigi and Melissa) – 'a quarrel supported with great spirit between the hero Amadigi and the slighted Enchantress, à grand orchestra'. 'Desterò dall'empia Dite' (Melissa) – 'a capital *aria d'abilità*, accompanied by a trumpet and hautbois . . . very masterly and fine'.

☊ Stutzmann/Smith/Harrhy/Fink/Bertin
Musiciens du Louvre/Minkowski
Erato 2292-45490-2 (2 CDs). Recorded 1989.
☊ Wesseling/De La Merced/Rostorf-Zamir/Domènech
Al Ayre Español/López Banzo
Ambroisie AM 133 (2 CDs). Recorded 2006.

The First Royal Academy Operas 1720–8

Radamisto, HWV 12
Composition 1720.
Libretto Nicola Haym, after Domenico Lalli.
Premiere First version: 27 April 1720, King's Theatre, Haymarket.
Second version: 28 December 1720, King's Theatre, Haymarket.
Synopsis Lust, tyranny and noble love in Armenia *c*.AD 50, loosely based on Tacitus's *Annals of Imperial Rome*. King Tiridate wages war on King Farasmane and his son Radamisto in order to possess Zenobia, Radamisto's wife. Zenobia resists, and all are saved by a revolt and the overthrow of Tiridate.
Notes This was Handel's first production for the newly formed opera company called the Royal Academy of Music. It was lavishly produced and well received. Handel produced two versions of *Radamisto*, tailored to two different star singers he had recently engaged for the company. The soprano Margherita Durastanti sang the title role in April, and the alto castrato Senesino (Francesco Bernardi) in December, when Durastanti moved to the role of Radamisto's loving wife, Zenobia. Burney declared: 'The composition of this opera is more solid, ingenious, and full of fire than any drama which Handel had yet produced in this country.'
Highlights Act I: 'Cara sposa' (Radamisto) – 'always admired, and so elegantly simple and pathetic, that it must always please when well sung'. 'Dopo torbide procelle' (Polissena) – a lilting and gently syncopated aria: 'one of the most agreeable *arie fugate* that I know'. Act II: 'Ombra cara di mia sposa' (Radamisto) – one of the greatest of all Handel's arias: 'Indeed, too much praise cannot be given to that song, in which, though the composition is so artful, an inverted chromatic imitation being carried on in the accompaniments, yet the cantilena is simply pathetic throughout.' Act III: 'Deggio dunque, oh Dio, lasciarti' (Zenobia) – 'a pathetic and fine air, which a great singer could always make modern'. 'Un

dì più felice' (*tutti*) – an unusually extended final chorus, full
of brilliant effects.

␁ DiDonato/Beaumont/Ciofi/Cherici/Labelle/Stains/Lepore
Il Complesso Barocco/Curtis
Virgin Classics 5 4573 2 (3 CDs). Recorded 2003. The first
version, April 1720.
␁ Baker/King/Jones/Hill/Harrhy/Russell/Kwella
ECO/Norrington
Ponton PO-1054 (3 CDs). Recorded 1984.The first version,
April 1720. An uneven performance and dry recording, but
worth considering for the singing of Janet Baker in the title
role. Her 'Ombra cara', in particular, is not to be missed!
␁ Popken/Gondek/Saffer/Hanchard/Frimmer/Dean/Cavallier/
Freiburger Barockorchester/McGegan
Harmonia Mundi HMU 907111.13 (3 CDs). Recorded 1993.
The second version, December 1720.

Muzio Scevola (Act III), HWV 13
Composition Completed 23 March 1721.
Libretto Paolo Rolli, after Livy.
Premiere 15 April 1721, King's Theatre, Haymarket.
Synopsis Porsenna, King of Tuscany, enlists the help of his
officer, Muzio, to win the hand of Clelia, not knowing that the
two are already secretly betrothed. After various acts of
valour, the king discovers the truth and the lovers are united.
Notes Shared between three composers, this opera may have
been intended to settle the rivalry between Handel and
Giovanni Bononcini, who wrote Act II, and had quite a following with London audiences. He was admired for his slow,
expressive arias. A minor composer, Filippo Amadei, wrote Act
I. *Muzio Scevola* ran for ten performances and was revived the
following season. Burney disputed the idea of an open competition, but concluded: 'Upon the whole, this one act of an
opera must have evinced the enlightened public, of Handel's
great powers of invention and knowledge of harmony as effec-
tually as a hundred entire operas could have done.' Handel
later borrowed music from it for *Scipione*, *Admeto*, and *Ottone*.

Highlights Act III: 'Lungo pensar' (Clelia) – 'very pleasing and graceful, with a violin accompaniment of a different character . . . being more frequently in dialogue, than unison, with the voice'. 'Io d'altro Regno' (Clelia) – 'a piece of such impassioned recitative . . . in the year 1720 this species of dramatic painting, was somewhat new, at least in England.' 'Ma come amar e come mai fidar' (Muzio and Clelia) – 'the harmony, contrivance and texture of the parts, at a time when this kind of duet was highly reverenced . . . must have greatly extended the composer's reputation.'

☾ Fortunato/Baird/Ostendorf/Mills/Urrey/Lane/
Matthews/Brewer
Baroque Chamber Orchestra/Palmer
Newport Classic NPD 85540/2 (2 CDs). Recorded 1991.

Floridante, HWV 14

Composition Completed 28 November 1721.
Libretto Paolo Rolli, after Francesco Silvani.
Premiere 9 December 1721, King's Theatre, Haymarket.
Synopsis Deception, jealousy and betrayal beset the path of true love. Two pairs of noble lovers, Floridante and Elmira, and Timante and Rossane, have to overcome the machinations of the false King Oronte before they can be united in marriage and rule the kingdoms of Persia and Tyre in justice and peace.
Notes After an initial run of nine performances, *Floridante* had three revivals up to 1733, with various revisions depending on the singers available. There are more slow arias than usual – as if Handel was continuing to prove that he was superior to Bononcini (see *Muzio Scevola*). Burney commented: 'I mention the slow songs in this opera particularly, as superior in every respect to those of Bononcini . . . the spirit, invention, and science of Handel, has never been disputed.'
Highlights Act I: Overture – although this was not at all to Burney's taste, 'the fugue being upon a convulsive and unpleasant theme', it actually has great verve – perhaps it was too modern-sounding for Burney? 'Mà pria vedrò le stelle precipitarsi in mar' (Elmira) – 'the words are admirably

expressed, particularly "precipitarsi in mar," to which the sounds given are true echoes to the sense; and the symphonies of this air are characteristic of Handel's fire and thunder.' 'Ah, mia cara, se tu resti' (Floridante and Elmira) – 'an exquisite duet in a grand style of pathetic'. Act II: 'Fuor di periglio di fiero artiglio' (Rosanne and Timente) – 'in which the cooing of the dove is attempted to be expressed, must have had a new and pleasing effect.' 'Notte cara . . . Parmi ascoltare' (Elmira) – 'the solemn air . . . with the accompanied recitative after it, is in Handel's finest style of majestic pathos'. Act III: 'Se dolce m'era già viver' (Floridante) – an eloquent lament, 'of a pathetic kind, and admirable'.

🎧 Minter/Zádori/Gáti/Moldvay/Makert/Farkas
Capella Savaria/McGegan
Hungaraton HCD 31304-06 (3 CDs). Recorded 1990.
🎧 Mijanovic/DiDonato/Priante/Invernizzi/Novaro/
Rostorf-Zamir
Il Complesso Barocco/Curtis
Archiv 477 6566 (3 CDs). Recorded 2005.

***Ottone*, HWV 15**
Composition Completed 10 August 1722.
Libretto Nicola Haym, after Stefano Pallavicino.
Premiere 12 January 1723, King's Theatre, Haymarket.
Synopsis The scheming Gismonda and her son Adalberto try to prevent King Ottone of Germany from assuming the throne of Italy and marrying the Princess Teofane. Meanwhile, Matilda, who loves Adalberto, and Emireno, who is Teofane's brother Basilio in disguise, add further twists to the complex plot, involving deception, imprisonment, escape, a storm at sea, a host of misunderstandings, and finally repentance and reconciliation.
Notes One of Handel's most popular operas – only *Rinaldo* had more performances. It marked the London debut of the soprano Francesca Cuzzoni, as well as featuring various others of Handel's star singers: sopranos Margherita Durastanti and Anastasia Robinson, alto castrati Senesino and Gaetano

Berenstadt, and bass Giuseppe Boschi. The Act I aria 'Falsa imagine' became a popular hit, although Cuzzoni originally didn't want to sing it, thus incurring Handel's wrath and a threat to throw her out of the window! The Concerto in Act I, for the arrival of Ottone in Rome, later reappeared as the opening movement of the Concerto Grosso, Op. 3 No. 6.

Highlights Burney was justifiably enthusiastic: 'The number of songs in this opera that became national favourites, is perhaps greater than in any other that was ever performed in England. The slow air, "Falsa imagine" [Act I], the first which Cuzzoni [Teofane] sung in this country, fixed her reputation as an expressive and pathetic singer; as "Affanni del pensier" [Act I] did Handel . . . The accompanied recitative for Cuzzoni, "O grati orrori", with the subsequent air, "S'io dir potessi" [Act II], had a great effect in the performance . . . The airs sung by Senesino [Ottone], "Ritorna, o dolce amor" [Act I], "Doppo l'orrore" [Act II], "Dove sei?" [Act III], "Tanti affani" [Act III], all in different styles, have severally some peculiar merit of melody, harmony, or contrivance. The airs for Durastanti [Gismonda], "La speranza" [Act I], "Pensa ad amare" [Act I], long after they had done their duty at the opera house, were favourites with all the performers on the German flute in the kingdom, which about this time superseded the common flute, and became the fashionable gentleman's instrument . . . "Vieni, o figlio" [Act II], in the style of Steffani, is a fine composition; and the light and gay duet, "A' teneri affetti" [Ottone and Teofane, Act III], was long a favourite with flute players . . . "Del minacciar del vento" [Act I], and "No, non temere" [Act III], two arias for Boschi [Emireno] in different styles are admirable. Indeed there is scarce a song in the opera, that did not become a general favourite, either vocally or instrumentally. And the passages in this and the other operas which Handel composed about this time, became the musical language of the nation.' Burney could also have mentioned another show-stopper for Senesino as Ottone, 'Deh! non dir', in Act II, with cooing recorders and strings representing bird calls.

∩ Bowman/McFadden/Smith/Visse/George/Denley
King's Consort/King
Hyperion CDA 66751/2/3 (3 CDs). Recorded 1993.

Flavio, HWV 16

Composition Completed 7 May 1723.
Libretto Nicola Haym, after Matteo Noris.
Premiere 14 May 1723, King's Theatre, Haymarket.
Synopsis A gentle satire on human foibles and fantasies. Flavio,
King of Lombardy and England, desires Teodata, daughter of
his counsellor, Ugone, but Teodata has a secret lover, Vitige,
who is Flavio's adjutant. Meanwhile, Ugone's son, Guido, is all
set to marry Emilia, daughter of Flavio's other counsellor,
Lotario, until the two counsellors fall out and fight a duel to
avenge the family honour. Lotario is killed by Guido, the plot
thickens impossibly, and in the end Flavio saves the day by
dealing out a series of supposed punishments that turn out to
be what each of the characters wanted in the first place.
Notes One of Handel's shorter operas, *Flavio* had the same
star casting as *Ottone*, but enjoyed none of its success. It had
just eight performances and only one later revival. Maybe the
mix of comedy and tragedy was bemusing to audiences used to
Handel's predominantly heroic operas.
Highlights Burney thought that 'though this opera is less
renowned than many other of Handel's dramatic compositions
. . . yet there are innumerable fine and masterly strokes in it.' He
cited the skill and mastery of 'S'egli ti chiede affetto' (Lotario,
Act II), 'Con un vezzo' (Teodata, Act II), the pathos of 'Amor,
nel mio penar' (Guido, Act III), and the gracefulness of the duet
'Deh perdona' (Emilia and Guido, Act III). He might also have
noted, among other gems in this engaging score, the love duet
for Teodata and Vitige, 'Ricordati mio ben', which, unusually for
Handel, opens the opera, and two touching laments in Act II for
the much misused Emilia, 'Parte, si', and 'Mà chi punir desio'.

∩ Gall/Ragin/Lootens/Fink/Högman/Fagotto/Messthaler
Ensemble 415/Jacobs
Harmonia Mundi HMC 901312/3 (2 CDs). Recorded 1989.

Giulio Cesare, HWV 17

Composition Completed 1724.

Libretto Nicola Haym, after Giacomo Bussani.

Premiere 20 February 1724, King's Theatre, Haymarket.

Synopsis A part-historical, part-fictional retelling of the love story of Caesar and Cleopatra. Cesare has defeated his rival Pompeo and pursued him to Egypt, where Cleopatra and her brother, Tolomeo, rule. Tolomeo executes Pompeo and arrests his widow Cornelia and her son, Sesto. Cleopatra seduces Cesare, but Tolomeo, helped by his henchman, Achilla, schemes to assassinate him and seize the crown. Achilla double-crosses Tolomeo, and Sesto kills the latter in a duel. Cesare crowns Cleopatra and the two swear undying love.

Notes One of the greatest Handel operas – the first, with *Tamerlano* and *Rodelinda*, of a trilogy of outstanding works from the mid-1720s. Possibly composed after he moved to his new house in Brook Street in July 1723, it was an immediate success, with thirteen performances in the first season and a further twenty-one in subsequent revivals. Handel's star line-up of singers again appeared, led by Senesino (Cesare) and Cuzzoni (Cleopatra). The score was published by Handel soon after the premiere – a measure of his own high opinion of it.

Highlights Burney called *Giulio Cesare* 'an opera abounding with beauties of various kinds, but in which both the composer and performers seem to have acquired even more reputation from the recitatives than the airs . . . there are three accompanied recitatives superior to those of any that I have seen in his other operas, or in any operas of contemporary composers: these are the celebrated "Alma del gran Pompeo" [Act I], and "Dall'ondoso periglio" (Act III) . . . in which Senesino [Cesare] gained so much reputation as an actor, as well as singer; and one that is equally beautiful and pathetic, for Cuzzoni [Cleopatra] . . . "Voi, che mie fide ancelle" [Act III]'. Burney also commented on many of the arias – and indeed it is difficult to pick out just a few from this rich score, but absolutely not to be missed are 'Svegliatevi nel core' (Act I, Sesto), 'Non disperar, chi sa' (Act I, Cleopatra), 'Va tacito e nascosto' (Act I, Cesare) with its haunting horn obbligato, 'V'adoro pupille' (Act II, Cleopatra), 'Se in fiorito ameno prato' (Act II, Cesare), 'Se pietà di me non senti' (Act II, Cleopatra), 'Piangerò la sorte mia' (Act III, Cleopatra), 'Aure, deh, per pietà' (Act III, Cesare), 'Da tempeste il legno infranto' (Act III, Cleopatra), and 'Caro/Bella! Più amabile beltà' (Act III, Cesare and Cleopatra).

ᛒ Baker/Booth-Jones/Walker/Jones/Masterson/Bowman/ Tomlinson/James
ENO Chorus and Orchestra/Mackerras
Chandos 30193 (3 CDs). Recorded 1984.
ᛒ Mijanovic/Kožená/von Otter/Hellekant/Mehta/Ewing/ Bertin/Ankaoua
Les Musiciens du Louvre/Minkowski
Archiv 474 210-2 (3 CDs). Recorded 2002.
▢ Baker/Masterson/Walker/Jones/Bowman/Tomlinson
ENO Chorus and Orchestra/Mackerras
Copley (stage director)
Arthaus Musik 100 308 (1 DVD). Filmed 1984.
▢ Connolly/Kirchschlager/De Niese/Dumaux/Bardon/ Maltman/Abdeslam
Glyndebourne Chorus/Orchestra of the Age of Enlightenment/Christie
McVicar (stage director)
Opus Arte OA 0950 D (3 DVDs). Filmed 2006.

Tamerlano, HWV 18
Composition 3 to 23 July 1724.
Libretto Nicola Haym, after Agostino Piovene, after Jacques Pradon.
Premiere 31 October 1724, King's Theatre, Haymarket.
Synopsis Tamerlano, the cruel Emperor of the Tartars, has vanquished the Turkish Sultan, Bazajet, and fallen in love with his daughter, Asteria. He enlists the help of the Greek general, Andronico, to win her, promising him the hand of Irene, Princess of Trebizond, whom Tamerlano himself is meant to marry. But Andronico loves Asteria, and she him, so she

pretends to give in to Tamerlano and then tries to poison him.
Irene, in disguise, prevents her, and when Asteria is sentenced
to death, Bazajet is driven to commit suicide. Tamerlano then
repents, unites the lovers, and honours his own promise to
marry Irene.

Notes The manuscript of *Tamerlano* is the first on which
Handel recorded the dates he started and completed the
composition of one of his operas – 3 and 23 July 1724 –
demonstrating the astonishing speed at which he worked.
Handel then made major revisions before the premiere, partly
due to the arrival of a new singer and changes in the libretto,
but also to tighten the dramatic impact of the work – London
audiences would already have known the exotic *Tamerlano*
story from a popular play by Nicholas Rowe. Tenor Francesco
Borosini (Bazajet) was the new singer who joined Handel's
regular troupe, led by Senesino (Andronico) and Cuzzoni
(Asteria).

Highlights Act I: 'Forte e lieto a morte' (Bazajet) – a swaggering aria of defiance. 'Bella Asteria' (Andronico) – a gently
affecting love song, 'one in which Senesino, according to the
idea with which tradition has furnished us of his powers, must
have greatly distinguished himself'. The same could also be
said of the beautiful 'Benchè mi sprezzi' (Andronico). 'Deh,
lasciatemi il nemico' (Asteria) – a yearning aria, 'original and
totally different from all the other songs in the opera'. Act II.
'Non è più tempo no' (Asteria) – 'gay and pleasing'. 'Par che
mi nasca' (Irene) – 'a beautiful melody and beautifully accompanied'. 'Voglio strage' (Tamerlano, Asteria, Bazajet) – a rare
dramatic trio in a Handel opera. 'Cor di padre' (Asteria) – an
extended, impassioned aria with effective orchestral interjections. Act III: 'Su la sponda' and 'Figlia mia, non pianger'
(Bazajet) – resignation in the face of death, the emotional
heart of the opera. 'Vivo in te, mio caro bene' (Asteria and
Andronico) – a radiant love duet, with recorders gently
colouring the orchestral strings. 'D'atra notte già mirasi a
scorno' – Handel's crowning masterstroke: an ambiguous
final chorus, the music tinged with a melancholy that belies

the optimism of the text hailing 'the splendour of a fine new day'.

🎧 Bacelli/Randle/Norberg-Schulz/Pushee/Bonitatibus/Abete
English Concert/Pinnock
Avie AV 0001 (3 CDs). Recorded 2001.
📺 Bacelli/Randle/Norberg-Schulz/Pushee/Bonitatibus/Abete
English Concert/Pinnock
Miller (stage director)
Arthaus Musik 100 702 (2 DVDs). Filmed 2001.

Rodelinda, HWV 19
Composition Completed 20 January 1725.
Libretto Nicola Haym, after Antonio Salvi, from Pierre Corneille.
Premiere 13 February 1725, King's Theatre, Haymarket.
Synopsis A highly moral tale of marital fidelity rewarded. Rodelinda, Queen of Lombardy, believing her husband, Bertarido, to be dead, reluctantly agrees to consider marrying his usurper, Grimoaldo, to save the life of her young son. Grimoaldo is urged on by the evil Duke of Turin, Garibaldo, who secretly wants him dead so that he can marry Bertarido's sister, Eduige, and gain the throne. Bertarido returns in disguise, but is discovered, and with the help of Unolfo, supposedly Grimoaldo's faithful adviser, manages to escape prison, save Grimoaldo from death at the hand of Garibaldo, and reclaim his faithful wife and the throne.
Notes The trilogy of great Handel operas of the mid-1720s was completed by *Rodelinda*. It scored a great success, with an initial run of thirteen performances and a further sixteen during revivals in 1725 and 1731. The cast was again led by Senesino (Bertarido) and Cuzzoni (Rodelinda), with Francesco Borosini (Grimoaldo) and Giuseppe Boschi (Garibaldo). It was the first Handel opera to be revived in the twentieth century (albeit in a heavily cut version), on 26 June 1920 at Göttingen.
Highlights Burney provided a commentary on most of the opera, which 'contains such a number of capital and pleasing airs, as entitles it to one of the first places in Handel's dramatic

productions'. Writing of Bertarido's Act I aria, 'Dove sei, amato bene', which became a popular favourite, he remembered being taught to sing it, 'without knowing how to construe, or even pronounce the words', as a boy of fourteen by the organist of Chester Cathedral. Here are the absolute highlights: Act I: 'Pompe vane di morte' and 'Dove sei, amato bene?' (Bertarido) – 'a solemn and beautiful symphony to introduce a fine accompanied recitative . . . previous to a beautiful and always favourite air, 'Ombre, piante, urne funeste' (Rodelinda) – in a grand theatrical style of pathetic'. Act II: 'Ritorna, o caro e dolce mio tesoro' (Rodelinda) – 'a very pleasing Siciliana' (somewhat of an understatement for this radiantly beautiful aria). 'Io t'abbraccio' (Rodelinda and Bertarido) – 'which may be ranked among Handel's finest compositions'. Burney returned to this wonderful, transcendent duet when it was performed at the 1784 Handel Commemoration celebrations: 'it seems of a kind that must be immortal, or at least an evergreen; which, however times and seasons vary, remains fresh and blooming as long as it exists'. Act III: 'Chi di voi fù più infedele' (Bertarido) – 'one of the finest pathetic airs that can be found in all his works . . . rendered affecting by new and curious modulation, as well as by the general cast of the melody. It is followed by a fine soliloquy ['Ma non so che dal remoto balcon'] . . . in an accompanied recitative, a tempo, or measured, which if not the first, was at least a very early attempt at such a dramatic effect'. 'Se il mio duol non è si forte' (Rodelinda) 'in the highest style of pathetic . . . of which the melody, harmony, and accompaniment . . . are in Handel's best style of cantabile. This air can never be old-fashioned'. 'Pastorello d'un povero armento' (Grimoaldo) – 'a pastoral air of the most elegantly simple kind'. Finally, there is also 'Vivi, tiranno!' (Bertarido) – one of Handel's thrilling, virtuosic set pieces for the castrato, Senesino.

🎧 Kermes/Mijanovic/Davislim/Prina/Lemieux/Prainte
Il Complesso Barocco/Curtis
Archiv 00289 477 5391 (3 CDs). Recorded 2004.

Antonacci/Streit/Chiummo/Winter/Scholl/Stefanowicz/
Siese
Glyndebourne Festival Opera/Christie
Villégier (stage director)
NVC Arts 3984-23024-2 (1 DVD). Filmed 1998.

Scipione, HWV 20
Composition Completed 2 March 1726.
Libretto Paolo Rolli, after Antonio Salvi.
Premiere 12 March 1726, King's Theatre, Haymarket.
Synopsis The Roman general, Scipione, conquers Carthaginia
and falls in love with one of the prisoners, Berenice, offered to
him by one of his officers, Lelio, who in turn loves another
prisoner, Armira. Berenice's father, Ernando, offers a ransom
to Scipione and begs him to honour Berenice's betrothal to the
Spanish prince, Lucejo, who, incidentally, has been travelling
in disguise with the army. Lucejo is unmasked and condemned
to be sent as a prisoner to Rome, but Scipione eventually
relents, setting aside his own desires and uniting the lovers.
Notes Handel composed this opera in haste early in 1726,
laying aside the unfinished *Alessandro* because of the delayed
arrival from Venice of a new soprano, Faustina Bordoni.
Nevertheless, *Scipione* was musically strong and achieved considerable success, with thirteen performances and a revival in
1730. Burney summed it up as 'a work worthy of its great
author in his meridian splendour'. The cast was headed by
Senesino (Lucejo) and Cuzzoni (Berenice).
Highlights Act I: March – 'played on the drawing up of the
curtain, for Scipione's triumph . . . a general favourite, and
adopted by His Majesty's Lifeguards, and constantly played
on the parade for near forty years'. 'Un caro amante'
(Berenice) – 'a very pleasing pastoral'. 'Dimmi, cara' (Lucejo) –
'was long in favour throughout the nation. The melody is natural, elegant, and pleasing'. Act II: 'Braccio si valoroso'
(Ernando) – 'admirable', a heroic bass aria with a spirited
orchestral accompaniment'. 'Com'onda incalza' (Berenice) –
'it is all tenderness and expression, and written in Handel's

never-failing Sicilian style, of which this aria may be placed at the head, for the beauty of the melody and richness of the accompaniment'. 'Scioglio d'immota fronte' (Berenice) – 'bold, fanciful, and elegant', one of Handel's most thrilling coloratura arias. 'This second act of *Scipione* is equal in excellence to that of any of Handel's most celebrated operas.' Act III: 'Il poter quel che brami' (Scipione) – an eloquent accompanied recitative. 'Se mormora' (Lucejo) – 'a *cantabile* in a very pathetic style, and in which many bold and new effects are produced'. 'Come al nazio boschetto' (Lucejo) – 'one of the most agreeable of all Handel's gay opera songs; the melody itself is natural and pleasing, and each of the instrumental parts has a distinct character, which is preserved in an ingenious and masterly manner.'

🎧 Ragin/Piau/Lamprecht/Lallouette/Tabery/Fletcher
Les Talens Lyriques/Rousset
Fnac 592245 (3 CDs). Recorded 1993.

Alessandro, HWV 21
Composition Completed 11 April 1726.
Libretto Paolo Rolli, after Ortensio Mauro.
Premiere 5 May 1726, King's Theatre, Haymarket.
Synopsis A heroic-comic tale, loosely based on historical characters, notably Alexander the Great (Alessandro) who is loved by both the Scythian Princess Lisaura and the Persian Princess Rossane. Lisaura in turn is loved by the Indian King Tassile. Alessandro is unable to choose between the two princesses and becomes increasingly arrogant, despite the good counsel of the Macedonian Prince Clito, and insists on being worshipped as divine. General Leonato plots to depose him, but Alessandro escapes an assassination attempt, chooses Rossane, and allies himself with Tassile by promising him the hand of Lisaura. The conspirators are thus defeated and magnanimously pardoned by Alessandro.
Notes This was the first Handel opera to feature his new leading lady, the soprano Faustina Bordoni (who later married the composer, Johann Hasse). She appeared as Rossane,

alongside Cuzzoni as Lisaura, and the two immediately became deadly rivals. The score is notable for the extent and brilliance of the writing for these two characters – including the only duet Handel ever dared to compose for them! – and for Senesino who played Alessandro. It was well received, with thirteen initial performances, and revivals in 1727 and 1732.

Highlights Act I: 'There is no passing by the overture of this opera without remarking its excellence . . . written with uncommon force . . . masterly and happy'. 'Frà le stragi' (Alessandro) – 'full of fire and contrivance'. 'Lusinghe più care' (Rossane) – 'became a national favourite . . . it is light and airy'. 'Placa l'alma, quieta il petto!' (Lisaura and Rossane) – 'the duet between two rival singers *passibus equis*, ambitious of fame and supremacy'. Act II: 'Vano amore, lusinga, diletto' (Alessandro) – an emotional *tour de force* with a dramatic interplay between the voice and the orchestra. 'Che tirannia d'Amor' (Lisaura) – 'is in Handel's never-failing style of *Siciliana* pathetic'. 'Il cor mio' (Alessandro) – 'is, and ever must be, pleasing to lovers of elegant simplicity'. Act III: 'Sfortunato è il mio valore' (Clito) – 'a very fine slow cavatina'. 'Brilla nell'alma un non intenso ancor' (Rossane) – 'it is manifest that Handel intended to display the uncommon talents of a great singer. It is *bravura* of the first class'. 'In generoso onor' (Alessandro, Lisaura, and Rossane) – proceeding from duet (with Alessandro and each of the leading ladies in turn), to trio, to final chorus, 'is graceful and pleasing; and this may be said of the whole opera'.

♫ Jacobs/Boulin/Poulenard/Nirouët/Varcoe/De Mey/Bollen
La Petite Bande/S. Kuijiken
Deutsche Harmonia Mundi GD 77110 (3 CDs). Recorded 1984.

Admeto, HWV 22
Composition Completed 10 November 1726.
Libretto ?Nicola Haym, after Aurelio Aureli, after Ortensio Mauro.

Premiere 31 January 1727, King's Theatre, Haymarket.

Synopsis King Admeto of Thessaly is mortally ill and can only be saved if someone else dies in his place. His wife, Alceste, sacrifices herself for him, and the distraught Admeto sends Ercole (Hercules) to Hades to rescue her. Meanwhile Admeto's former love, the Trojan Princess Antigona, arrives in disguise, hoping to win him back, but she also has to contend with the unwelcome attentions of Trasimede, Admeto's brother. Ercole reports that he could not find Alceste in Hades, and Admeto, torn between his love for two women, eventually resolves to marry Antigona. However, Alceste has in fact returned, also in disguise, and although fiercely jealous, she prevents Trasimede from killing Admeto. Antigona graciously concedes her place to Alceste and all is resolved.

Notes An immediate success, with nineteen performances on its first run – more than for any other Handel opera – *Admeto*'s final revival in April 1754 marked the last stage performance of any Handel opera until the twentieth century. The story-line, suitably modified from the original Greek myth, gave Handel great opportunities to display the vocal talents of his two leading ladies. Faustina played Alceste, and Cuzzoni was Antigona, with Senesino in the title role of Admeto. Burney was impressed by the opera's 'passion, tenderness, and marvellous circumstances and situations for machinery and decoration'. In Handel's hands, he felt, music had grown up: 'it was no longer regarded as a mere soother of affliction, or incitement to hilarity; it could now paint the passions in all their various attitudes.' He concluded: 'Upon the whole, this opera contains many of Handel's best dramatic productions.'

Highlights Act I: 'Orride larve! . . . Chiudetevi miei lumi' (Admeto) – 'an impassionated [*sic*] and admirable accompanied recitative, followed by one of the finest pathetic airs that can be found in all Handel's works'. 'Luci care, addio, posate' (Alceste) – a tragic and noble aria of farewell, with a magical entry for solo flute at bar 45. 'Se l'arco avessi, e i strali' (Trasimede) – 'one of the best and most agreeable hunting songs . . . the French-horn parts are remarkably well written.'

Act II: 'Di tanti affanni oppressa' (Antigona) – 'a pathetic Siciliana in Handel's best manner'. 'Ah, sì, morrò' (Admeto) – 'a very pathetic air, accompanied in a rich and masterly manner'. 'Vedrò fra poco' (Alceste) – an exultant aria in lively counterpoint with the orchestra: 'excellent composition'. Act III: 'A languire ed a penar' (Admeto) – 'a very fine slow air of an original cast . . . there is but one violin accompaniment, but this preserves a particular character of complaint from the beginning to the end.' 'Là dove gli occhi io giro' (Alceste) – 'for Faustina . . . a very agreeable song for the display of her execution, which . . . in the year 1727, was imagined to be supernatural'. 'Alma mia, dolce ristoro' (Admeto and Antigona) – 'an admirable duet . . . the voice parts have traits of beautiful melody totally different from the subject of the accompaniment. I can recall no duet of Handel's that is more pleasing or ingenious than this.' 'Sì, caro, sì' (Alceste) – 'is so natural and pleasing . . . this song was the delight of all lovers of music throughout the kingdom many years after the opera was laid aside'.

🎧 Lehane/Armstrong/Baker/Kitchener/Lenski/Temperley/Welsby
Baroque Opera Orchestra/Lewis
Ponto PO-1029 (3 CDs). Recorded 1968.
🎧 Jacobs/Yakar/Cold/Dams/Bowman/Gomez/Van Egmond
Il Complesso Barocco/Curtis
Virgin Veritas 5 61369 2 (3 CDs). Recorded 1997.
🎧 📺 Rexroth/Lichtenstein/Bach/Mead/Nolte/Hirsch/Vogel
Händelfestspielorchester Halle/Arman
Köhler (stage director)
Arthaus Musik 101 257 (2 DVDs + 2 CDs). Recorded and filmed 2006.

Riccardo Primo, HWV 23
Composition Completed 16 May 1727.
Libretto Paolo Rolli, after Francesco Briani.
Premiere 11 November 1727, King's Theatre, Haymarket.
Synopsis Riccardo (Richard I, King of England) is ship-

wrecked off the coast of Cyprus on his way to meet his bride, Costanza, Princess of Navarre, whom he has never seen. Costanza and her guardian Berardo are taken in by the tyrannical Governor of Cyprus, Isacio, his daughter Pulcheria, and her lover Prince Oronte. Isacio determines to marry Costanza himself, and orders his daughter to masquerade as Costanza to deceive Riccardo. Oronte discovers this plan and allies himself with Riccardo to help him defeat Isacio. In the end, Riccardo pardons Isacio, claims Costanza, appoints Oronte governor and unites him with Pulcheria.

Notes This opera was probably intended for the end of the previous season, but Faustina and Cuzzoni had come to blows on stage during a Bonnoncini opera and the theatre had closed early on 6 June. The royal subject of *Riccardo Primo* was a happy coincidence, as it allowed the work to be dedicated to the new King George II, who had acceded on 15 June and was crowned on 11 October. However, it was only a reasonable success, with eleven performances, and was never revived. It is richly scored, with more use of wind instruments than usual. Senesino, Cuzzoni and Faustina took the three main roles of Riccardo, Costanza and Pulcheria.

Highlights Act I: 'Vado per obberdirti' (Pulcheria) – 'for Faustina . . . the most agreeable song of execution of the times. I have been told that the brilliancy of her voice made its way through the busy accompaniment of this song in a manner which filled the whole theatre.' 'V'adoro, o luci belle' (Orente) – a beautiful, rather wistful aria, with a delightful interplay between the voice and orchestra. 'Agitato da fiere tempeste' (Riccardo) – 'for Senesino . . . in a grand style of bravura, and must have had a great effect when accompanied by a good orchestra, and thundered by such a voice'. Act II: 'Di notte il pellegrino' (Costanza) – 'nothing can be more elegant and pleasing'. 'Caro, vieni a me!' (Costanza) – 'truly captivating, and only needs to be sung by a singer of taste and feeling, to be modern now, or at any more distant period from the time of its first performance'. 'Nube che il sole adombra' (Riccardo) – 'a very agreeable air'. 'L'aquila altera conosce i figli' (Pulcheria) – 'a very masterly style of composition'. 'T'amo, sì' (Riccardo and Costanza) – another of Handel's utterly beguiling love duets. Act III: 'All'orror delle procelle' (Riccardo) – 'a song of great execution, not only for that time, but for any time, and any singer. Handel's fire blazes in the orchestra, and the whole composition glows with genius.' 'Morte vieni!' (Costanza) – 'in a very sublime style of pathetic', and with the unusual colour of an obbligato bass flute. 'Quell'innocente, afflitto core' (Pulcheria) – 'in the highest degree graceful and pleasing. I have never met with three successive airs by the same composer, at once so beautiful and so various.' 'Bacia per me la mano del caro idolo mio' (Costanza) – 'one of the finest pathetic airs in all Handel's works . . . uniformly clear and plaintive, from the beginning to the end'. 'Il volo così fido' (Costanza) – a delicate and delightful high-wire aria with piccolo recorder obbligato. 'Volgete ogni desir' (Riccardo) – 'a very sweet and graceful air. . . . Upon the whole, the last act of *Riccardo* is replete with beauties of every kind of composition, and seems not only the best of this particular opera, but of any that I have yet examined.'

Ω Mingardo/Piqu/Lallouette/Scaltriti/Brua/Bertin
Les Talens Lyriques/Rousset
L'Oiseau Lyre 452 201-2 (3 CDs). Recorded 1995.

Siroe, HWV 24

Composition Completed 5 February 1728.
Libretto Nicola Haym, after Pietro Metastasio.
Premiere 17 February 1728, King's Theatre, Haymarket.
Synopsis The story has parallels with Shakespeare's *King Lear*. Cosroe, King of Persia, wants to abdicate and choose a successor from his two sons. The evil Medarse swears allegiance, but the good Siroe is offended and will not swear. Cosroe chooses Medarse and sets in motion a chain of events including attempted assassination by the disguised Princess Emira who loves Siroe but hates Cosroe, jealous tantrums from Princess Laodice who also loves Siroe, and cruel deception by Medarse which almost results in Siroe's death.

Eventually the denouement brings reconciliation for all, and the crown passes to Siroe.

Notes This opera marks the point when everything began to unravel for Handel and the Royal Academy of Music. His finances, always precarious, had dried up almost completely as nobody had renewed their subscriptions. Then on 29 January, just before the premiere, *The Beggar's Opera* by Gay and Pepusch opened at Lincoln's Inn Fields and caused a sensation. Gone were the kings and heroes and all the artifice of Italian opera: this was popular operetta in English. Audiences loved it and promptly deserted the Royal Academy. *Siroe* was therefore not a success, although it did receive eighteen performances, and Burney considered that it 'contains many proofs of the superior abilities of this great composer'. The bass, Boschi, sang King Cosroe, with Senesino, Faustina, and Cuzzoni as Siroe, Emira, and Laodice.

Highlights Act I: 'D'ogni amator' (Emira) – 'may perhaps have been since set to a more graceful melody, but has never been accompanied with so much meaning and ingenuity'. 'Vedeste mai' (Emira) – 'for Faustina . . . extremely pleasing, and must have exhibited the brilliant execution of that singer to great advantage'. Act II: 'Mi lagnerò' (Laodice) – 'sung by Cuzzoni, is a beautiful *Siciliana* of a peculiar cast. The complaint expressed in the words and melody is admirably enforced from time to time by a single note in the violin accompaniment.' 'Fra l'orror' (Medarse) – a thrilling and orchestrally busy aria: 'Handel has set it to an admirable instrumental movement in five parts, strictly fugato . . . rendering the composition interesting by assigning the chief part of the business to the instruments, which so employed, were better worth hearing than the voice.' Burney dismissed the castrato Antonio Baldi as 'a singer of no great abilities'! 'Non vi piacque' (Emira) – 'one of the most elegant, beautiful, and pathetic [arias], in all Handel's works'. Act III: 'Gelido in ogni vena' (Cosroe) – 'so fine a composition of the grand pathetic kind, that it is difficult which most to admire, the richness of the harmony, learning of the modulation, texture

of the parts, or expression of the words'. 'Son stanco . . .
Deggio morire' (Siroe) – 'for Senesino . . . . justly admired
at the time of its performance, and is still new and replete
with refinements, which have been imagined of much later
times'. 'Torrente cresciuto' (Laodice) – 'perhaps the most
elegant, fanciful, and pleasing, of all Handel's dramatic songs
of the bravura kind'. In addition to the arias, each act includes
a sequence of extended recitative, displaying Handel's imaginative skill at moving the action on in tightly organised
dramatic confrontations between the characters.

♩ Fortunato/Baird/Ostendorf/Matthews/Rickards/Urrey
Brewer Chamber Orchestra/Palmer
Newport Classics NCD 60125/1/2/3 (3 CDs). Recorded
1989.

Tolomeo, HWV 25
Composition Completed 19 April 1728.
Libretto Nicola Haym, after Carlo Capece.
Premiere 30 April 1728, King's Theatre, Haymarket.
Synopsis A complicated tale of political ambition and amorous
intrigue set in Cyprus in the first century BC. Tolomeo,
the rightful King of Egypt, is disguised as the shepherd
Osmin and seeking his wife, Seleuce, believed drowned, but
actually also disguised, as the shepherdess Delia. Araspe, the
scheming King of Cyprus, falls in love with 'Delia', and his
volatile sister, Elisa, with 'Osmin'. Then Alessandro,
Tolomeo's supposedly usurping brother, arrives and promptly
falls in love with Elisa. Blackmail, imprisonment, attempted
poisoning, and foiled execution follow, but evil is finally
overcome and Tolomeo, reunited with both Seleuce and
Alessandro, forgives all wrongs and returns to Egypt to claim
the throne.
Notes This was the last new Handel opera mounted by the
Royal Academy of Music before it was disbanded on 1 June
1728. Haym's dedication of the libretto to the Earl of
Albemarle refers to opera in London as 'being on the decline',
and indeed *Tolomeo* had little success, with only seven per-

formances, although it was later revived by Handel in 1730 and 1733. Despite the complex plot, the action is closer to the naturalism and unity of classical drama, and the music is also correspondingly tighter, with generally shorter arias that keep the action moving onwards. Senesino led the cast as Tolomeo, with Cuzzoni as Seleuce, Faustina as Elisa, Boschi as Araspe, and the alto castrato Antonio Baldi as Alessandro.

Highlights Overture: 'the fugue . . . is written on a subject so lively, and is treated with such freedom and spirit . . . the French horns in this fugue were unusual, and have an admirable effect.' Act I: 'Non lo dirò col labbro' (Alessandro) – 'an elegant ballad', and it became one of Handel's most well-known tunes as 'Silent Worship', the version adapted by the Victorian composer Arthur Somervell to his own unrelated English text which begins: 'Did you not hear my Lady / Go down the garden singing? / Blackbird and thrush were silent / To hear the alleys ringing'. 'Quell'onda che si frange' (Elisa) – 'the most elegantly gay and fanciful [aria] imaginable . . . it would please now as much as ever'. 'Fonti amiche, aure leggere' (Seleuce) – 'an elaborate and pathetic composition . . . for Cuzzoni, which did the composer and performer equal credit'. 'Torna sol per un momento' (Tolomeo) – 'a pathetic air . . . for Senesino, of the most soothing and tender kind'. Act II: 'Dite, che fa' (Seleuce and Tolomeo) – 'called the echo song . . . chiefly sung by Cuzzoni; several of the passages, however, were repeated by Senesino, behind the scenes . . . the melody of this air is extremely graceful and pleasing, and the accompaniments are rich and beautiful.' 'Se il cor ti perde' (Tolomeo and Seleuce) – 'one of the most pleasing of all Handel's duets, in the favourite style of the times'. Act III: 'Ti pentirai, crudel' (Elisa) – 'an air of passion and spirit . . . which her [Faustina's] neat execution must have rendered captivating'. 'Torni omai la pace all'alma' (Seleuce) – this is a charming and memorable aria, but Burney was not so impressed: 'pleasing; but not of the first class in the *graziosa* style'. 'Inumano fratel' . . . Stille amare, già vi sento' (Tolomeo) – 'an accompanied recitative . . . and an air . . . so pathetic and masterly in a truly grand dramatic style, that it ought to save the worst opera'. (Burney did not actually think, however, that this was 'the worst opera' – far from it. He recognised that it had never been popular, but considered that many of Handel's arias in it were 'beautiful, and some in his best style of writing'. He was right!) 'Tutta contenta or gode' (Seleuce and Tolomeo) – 'a lively duet', with Handel's characteristic intertwining of the two vocal lines.

🎧 Hallenberg/Gauvin/Spagnoli/Bonitatibus/Basso
Il Complesso Barocco/Curtis
Archiv 477 7106 (3 CDs). Recorded 2006.

The Second Royal Academy Operas 1729–34

Lotario, HWV 26

Composition Completed 16 November 1729.
Libretto Giacomo Rossi, after Antonio Salvi.
Premiere 2 December 1729, King's Theatre, Haymarket.
Synopsis In tenth-century Italy, Berengario, Duke of Spoleto, has usurped the throne and is determined to make the widowed queen, Adelaida, marry his son Idelberto. Berengario is urged on by his scheming wife, Matilda, and assisted by his general Clodomiro. Idelberto does actually love Adelaida, but she spurns him and allies herself instead to Lotario, King of Germany. Berengario and Lotario clash several times in battle, hostages are taken and freed, murder and suicide are attempted, but in the end Lotario is victorious and claims Adelaida. He pardons Berengario and Matilda and gives the throne of Italy to Idelberto.
Notes The first opera produced by Handel's partnership with John Heidegger, *Lotario* made use of the new company of singers he had imported from Italy. It was a gamble to continue the name of the previous company, Royal Academy of Music, and its house style of epic, heroic Italian operas. Born of Handel's obstinacy, and possible misjudgement of his audiences, the venture would ultimately be unsuccessful, even though Handel still enjoyed the patronage and loyal support of

King George II. *Lotario* itself was a flop and disappeared after nine performances. Luckily, however, Handel didn't give up – or we might never have had the great later operas like *Orlando*, *Ariodante*, *Alcina* and *Serse*. Burney described Handel's new venture with an amusing horticultural metaphor: 'Handel had prepared the soil for cultivation by a new *compost*, and had transplanted new exotics from Italy, in order to try the influence of our climate upon them.' The new singers were led by the soprano Anna Maria Strada del Pò (Adelaida), with alto-castrato Antonio Maria Bernacchi (Lotario), tenor Annibale Pio Fabri (Berengario), contraltos Antonia Maria Merighi (Matilda), and Francesca Bertolli (Ildeberto) who specialised in playing men's roles in *travesti*, and bass Johann Gottfried Riemschneider (Clodomiro).

Highlights Act I: 'Per salvarti, idolo mio' (Idelberto) – a gracious air, and Burney pointed out 'the most striking passage': an elegant piece of figuration which reappeared in the finale of the Organ Concerto, Op. 4 No. 2, premiered during a performance of the oratorio *Esther* on 5 March 1735. 'Rammentati, cor mio' (Lotario) – 'an air of great dignity, and susceptible of much taste and expression'. 'Se il mar promette calma' (Clodomiro) – 'admirable for the contrivance of the parts, as well as vocal melody; it . . . may be ranked among his most ingenious and spirited compositions of that kind.' 'Scherza in mar la navicella' (Adelaida) – 'an *aria di bravura*, for Strada, in which Handel has given her many of his favourite divisions . . . it is a spirited song, in which not only the singer, but orchestra, has much to do.' Act II: 'Mente eterne' (Adelaida) – 'truly pathetic, and fit only for a singer possessed of science and feeling'. 'D'una torbida sorgente' (Adelaida) – 'new and ingenious in the accompaniment'. 'Quanto più forte' (Lotario) – 'a cavatina . . . of great beauty, of which the symphony is grand and original'. 'Non disperi peregrino' (Lotario) – 'a charming air, richly accompanied. Several passages in this song occurred to Handel in subsequent compositions, particularly in "Return, O God of Hosts" [*Samson*], where there is a modulation to the minor third of the key.' 'Non sempre invendicata' (Adelaida) – 'has infinite spirit, and affords opportunities for good action as well as singing; while the orchestra supports the situation of the performer with great force and effect'. 'Vi sento, sì, vi sento' (Berengario) – 'an impassioned air . . . in which there is a passage of accompaniment of peculiar energy'. 'Impara, codardo' (Matilda) – 'an air of character . . . which has considerable spirit and originality'. 'Sì, bel sembiante' (Adelaida and Lotario) – 'a very pleasing duet . . . with which, after a cheerful chorus, the opera is terminated'. Burney concluded: 'Upon the whole, though this has many agreeable songs, it abounds with fewer airs on great and masterly subjects than many of his preceding operas; and whether oppressed by opposition and less supported by his singers than formely, his invention seems to have been less fertile than usual.'

♫ Mingardo/Kermes/Davislim/Prina/Summers/Priante
Il Complesso Barocco/Curtis
Deutsche Harmonia Mundi 82876 58797 2 (2 CDs). Recorded 2004.

Partenope, HWV 27
Composition Completed 12 February 1730.
Libretto After Silvio Stampiglia.
Premiere 24 February 1730, King's Theatre, Haymarket.
Synopsis Partenope, queen of the new city of Naples, has three suitors: Emilio, the dominating Prince of Cuma; Arsace, the double-dealing Prince of Corinth, whom she favours, unaware that he has abandoned his fiancée Rosmira, Princess of Cyprus; and the faithful Armindo, Prince of Rhodes. Rosmira appears at court, disguised as a man, 'Eurimene', but is recognised by Arsace, and the scene is set for complicated amorous intrigue, played out against the backdrop of a military struggle between Partenope and Emilio. Eventually peace and true love triumph: Emilio graciously concedes defeat, Arsace is united with Rosmira, and Partenope with Armindo.
Notes A return to top form for Handel: Burney judged *Partenope* 'among the best of Handel's dramatic productions'.

Apart from *Rodelinda*, it was the only one of Handel's London operas so far to have the heroine's name as the title. It also stands apart from the serious, heroic works that surround it, by being one of Handel's lighter operas, with elements of comedy in its investigation of the battle of the sexes. It had only seven initial performances, but was successfully revived the following season. Strada led the cast as Partenope, with the contralto Francesca Bertolli in the trouser-role of Armindo, and the tenor Annibale Pio Fabri as Emilio.

Highlights Overture – Burney did not approve of the fugue – 'on a convulsive and unpleasant theme' – but it now sounds a very decisive way to begin the opera with a flourish. Act I: 'L'Amor ed il destin' (Partenope) – 'abounds with passages of execution of a very agreeable and uncommon kind, that required a flexibility and agility of voice'. 'Dimmi pietoso ciel' (Arsace) – 'has the stamp of a great master upon it'. 'Io ti levo l'Impero dell'Armi' (Partenope) – 'in the style which Hasse and [Leonardo] Vinci were now successfully cultivating, and in which the melody of the voice part was more polished, and the accompaniment more simple and quiet, than any that could be found in the songs of their predecessors'. 'Io seguo sol fiero' (Rosmira) – 'an elaborate hunting song . . . in which the French horns have solo parts'. Act II: 'Care mura in si bel giorno' (Partenope) – 'a short slow air of great dignity and beauty'. 'Voglio amare' (Partenope) – 'extremely graceful and pleasing . . . this air is so smooth and free from wrinkles that it is difficult to imagine it to be near sixty years of age'. 'E vuoi con dure tempre' (Rosmira) – 'an agreeable duet, or rather dialogue, of a peculiar kind . . . in which one of the two lovers, who have quarelled, only upbraids the other from time to time with epithets, *infido*, *ingrato*, without ever singing together'. 'Qual farfalletta' (Partenope) – 'in as modern a style as if it had been composed but last week, and with delightful fluttering effects in the orchestra'. Act III: 'Ch'io parta? sì crudele' (Arsace) – a slow affecting aria, 'has no fault but brevity'. 'Nobil core, che ben ama' (Armindo) – 'a spirited song . . . enlivened and rendered very pleasing by an ingenious accompaniment'. 'Ma quai note di mesti lamenti' (Arsace) – 'this air, at the close of which the hero of the drama falls asleep, is finely written, and will be always elegant and pleasing'.

⋒ Joshua/Streit/Wallace/Foster-Williams/Summers/Zazzo
Early Opera Company/Curnyn
Chandos CHAN 0719-3 (3 CDs). Recorded 2004.

Poro, HWV 28

Composition Completed 16 January 1731.
Libretto After Pietro Metastasio.
Premiere 2 February 1731, King's Theatre, Haymarket.
Synopsis Alessandro (King Alexander the Great) and his treacherous general, Timagene, have invaded India, part of which is ruled by King Poro and part by Queen Cleofide. Poro is captured but swaps indentities with his general, Gandarte, who loves Erissena, Poro's sister. Queen Cleofide decides to make advances to Alessandro as a way of saving her beloved Poro, and Alessandro duly falls in love with her. The resulting love triangle between Poro (disguised), Cleofide, and Alessandro is soured by jealousy and threatened by death. At the last moment the ever-benevolent Alessandro makes everything come right, uniting Poro with Cleofide, and Gandarte with Erissena.
Notes Third time lucky for Handel's Second Academy: *Poro* had fourteen initial performances and a revival later the same year. It marked the return of the alto castrato Senesino to Handel's company, and the production was carefully advertised in the *Daily Journal* as having scenery and costumes 'all entirely new'. There was some tension between Handel and his fashionable librettist, Metastasio, whose approach was somewhat too cool and classical for the red-blooded, passionately baroque composer. So Handel kept making alterations to the text to suit himself. Burney regretted that *Poro* contained 'but few airs in a great and elaborate style', but nevertheless found it 'dramatic and pleasing'. Senesino sang the title role, opposite Strada as Cleofide.

Highlights Act I: 'Se mai più sarò geloso' (Poro) – 'there is a happy and impassioned boldness and expression in the appoggiaturas, which I do not recollect to have seen hazarded by any composer of that period. This cavatina in other respects is admirable.' 'Se mai turbo il tuo riposo' (Cleofide) – Burney did not particularly remark on this aria, but it is a yearning sarabande, with the voice and orchestra in gentle dialogue. 'Se possono tanto' (Poro) – 'which has always been justly admired for its elegance . . . the clear and quiet accompaniment in iterated notes was that which Hasse and Vinci rendered fashionable.' 'Se mai turbo' (Poro and Cleofide) – 'an admirable duet . . . in which the lovers . . . are ironically repeating the former promises which they had made to each other of fidelity and confidence. The composition of this duet is excellent, and in a style truly dramatic.' Act II: 'Caro amico amplesso!' (Poro and Cleofide) – 'another duet in a very different style . . . masterly; and the four instrumental parts of the accompaniment being totally different from the vocal, render the harmony very rich and grateful'. 'D'un barbaro scortese' (Alessandro) – 'in a very spirited and original style'. 'Senza procelle' (Poro) – 'a very pleasing air . . . of which the accompaniments by French horns, flutes, violins, tenor and bass obbligati, must have had an admirable effect when performed by a well-disciplined opera band'. 'Se viver non poss'io' (Gandarte) – 'an exquisite air, *alla Siciliana* . . . which is the best of Handel's innumerable songs in that style'. Act III: 'Serbati a grandi imprese' (Alessandro) – 'has considerable merit as a bravura of the time . . . the voice singing an octave above the bass, while the accompaniment is busy, has a new and good effect'. 'Dov'è? s'affretti' (Poro) – 'is in a grand style of theatrical pathetic. It is not only the best air in this opera, but equal, at least, to any of Handel's best dramatic productions. The plan of accompaniment is majestic, and [the] melody impassioned and expressive.' 'Son confusa pastorella' (Erissena) – 'a very pleasing and characteristic pastoral . . . which was long in high favour, not only with singers, but performers on the German flute'. 'Spirto amato' (Cleofide) – 'written on a short ground-bass, of one bar only, repeated fourteen or fifteen times; while the melody is as free and pathetic as if the composer had been under no such restraint'. 'Caro vieni . . . Dopo tanto penare' (Poro, Cleofide, Erissena, Gandarte, Alessandro, and Timagene) – 'first sung in dialogue . . . afterwards in duo, and finally in chorus, was so simple and pleasing that it soon became a national favourite'.

♫ Banditelli/Bertini/Fink/Lesne/Naglia/Abbondonaz
Europa Galante/Biondi
Opus 111 OPS 30-113/115 (3 CDs). Recorded 1994.

Ezio, HWV 29

Composition 1731– completion date not known.
Libretto After Pietro Metastasio.
Premiere 15 January 1732, King's Theatre, Haymarket.
Synopsis In Imperial Rome in the fifth century AD, the Roman general, Ezio, has defeated Attila the Hun. He returns to claim Fulvia as his bride, from her father, Massimo, a confidant of the Emperor Valentiniano. But Massimo is playing a double game, promising Fulvia to Valentiniano, while actually plotting his death. Onoria, Valentiniano's sister also loves Ezio, but Valentiniano becomes jealous of all the adulation Ezio is receiving and soon believes him guilty of an assassination plot and condemns him to be executed. Eventually Ezio is saved by Varo, Prefect of the Praetorian Guard, and Fulvia unmasks her father's villainy. Valentiniano unites Ezio and Fulvia, and pardons Massimo.
Notes The premiere of *Ezio* marked the first appearance of the Italian bass Antonio Montagnana in Handel's opera company – he sang the part of Varo. Senesino was Ezio, and Strada was Fulvia. *Ezio* was another uncomfortable collaboration with Metastasio, and it was a failure, with only five performances. It is unique in Handel's operas in having no duets or ensemble movements, and maybe there were just too many *secco* recitatives – even though there are also some admirable arias, and indeed some effective moments of

accompanied recitative. In any case, for whatever reason, Handel never revived it. Interestingly, he was revising the oratorio *Esther* at the same time as he composed *Ezio*, and a new musical direction was therefore opening up for him.

Highlights Act I: 'Caro padre' (Fulvia) – 'plaintive', said Burney, 'but not likely to please unless it is performed by a great and favourite singer'. But note the imaginative dialogue of the voice and solo flute. 'Quanto mai felice siete' (Onoria) – 'marked by Handel's originality and contrivance, but seems to be less simple than the poetry requires'. Faint praise for this utterly delightful aria! 'Finchè un zeffiro soave' (Fulvia) – 'an elegant *mezza bravura*, richly and ingeniously accompanied, which the voice, spirit, and abilities of the Strada, must have rendered charming'. Act II: 'Che fò? Dove mi volgo?' (Fulvia) – 'an accompanied recitative, in which the harmony and modulation are extremely masterly, and the words expressed in a manner truly pathetic'. 'Nasce al bosco' (Varo) – 'manifestly intended to exhibit the peculiar power of the singer': it is grandly swaggering, and Handel's first great aria for Antonio Montagnana. 'La mia costanza' (Fulvia) – 'though spirited and pleasing, is not one of Handel's happiest effusions'. Once again Burney damned with faint praise – and he was wrong. 'Ecco alle mie catene' (Ezio) – 'a very beautiful Siciliana for Senesino . . . the melody of which is elegant and impassioned, and the accompaniment delicate, clear, and amical to the voice part'. Act III: 'Guarda pria' (Ezio) – 'full of spirit and dignity, with a busy and masterly accompaniment'. 'Se la mia vita' (Ezio) – 'a magnificent *aria concertata* in ten parts . . . in a grand style of cantabile, and with Senesino's voice and action must have had a great effect'. 'Misera, dove son? . . . Ah, non son io' (Fulvia) – 'all the twelfth scene of this act, for the Strada, consisting of an accompanied recitative . . . and terminated by the air . . . is admirably composed in a grand style of theatrical pathetic.' 'Già risonar d'intorno' (Varo) – 'a military song for Montagnana, accompanied by a trumpet, and composed in Handel's fullest and best style of martial music'.

♫ Fortunato/Baird/Lane/Watson/Urrey/Pellerin/Somary
Manhattan Chamber Orchestra/Auldon Clark
Vox Classics VOX2 7503 (2 CDs). Recorded 1994.

Sosarme, HWV 30 (*Fernando*)

Composition Completed 4 February 1732.

Libretto After Antonio Salvi.

Premiere 15 February 1732, King's Theatre, Haymarket.

Synopsis Prince Argone leads a rebellion against his father, Haliate, King of Lydia, whom he suspects (wrongly) of favouring his bastard brother, Melo. Argone holds his mother, Erenice, and sister, Elmira, captive in the palace, while Haliate lays siege to the city, helped by Sosarme, King of Media, who is in love with Elmira. Meanwhile, Altomaro, trusted counsellor to Haliate, plots to gain the throne for Melo, who is his grandson. Altomaro deceives both Haliate and Argone, but Melo will have no part in the plan and eventually unmasks Altomaro, who commits suicide. Haliate and Argone are reconciled, and Sosarme claims Elmira.

Notes This opera was originally planned as *Fernando, re di Castiglia* and set in Portugal. After composing Act II, Handel changed the character's names (apart from Altomaro) and the location of the action, possibly for reasons of contemporary political sensitivity, but the basic plot and the music remained substantially the same. The cast was led by Senesino (Sosarme), with Strada (Elmira), Montagnana (Altomaro), and the tenor Giovanni Battista Pinacci as Haliate. It was a reasonable success, with eleven performances, and was revived in 1734. Burney judged it to have 'fewer great airs in an elaborate style of composition than several of Handel's more early operas, yet it may be ranked amongst his most pleasing theatrical productions'. It has the distinction of including the only aria Handel ever composed in the remote key of B major ('Rend'il sereno' for Elmira in Act I).

Highlights Act I: 'Fra l'ombre' (Altomaro) – 'for Montagnana, in which the bass voice of this new singer, its depth, power, mellowness, and peculiar accuracy of intonation in hitting distant intervals, were displayed'. 'La turba adulatrice' (Haliate) – 'is excellent in the present theatrical style; in which the agitation and passion of the singer is painted by the instruments in iterated notes'. 'Dite "pace", e fulminate' (Elmira) – 'a capital *bravura* air . . . for the Strada . . . in which her powers of expression and execution are displayed with great abilities in turbulent accompaniments and difficult divisions'. Act II: 'So ch'il ciel' (Melo) – 'original and masterly'. 'Per le porte del tormento' (Sosamre and Elmira) – 'an extremely graceful and pleasing duet'. 'In mille dolci modi' (Sosarme) – 'a very graceful and pleasing air in minuet time'. 'Vola l'augello dal caro nido' (Elmira) – 'a rapid and pleasing air'. Act III: 'S'io cadrò per tuo consiglio' (Haliate) – 'of a very original cast both in melody and accompaniment; indeed it seems impossible to name any dramatic composer who so constantly varied his songs in subject, style, and accompaniment, as Handel'. 'Cuor di madre' (Erenice) – 'an admirable aria *parlante* calculated not only to display the powers of an actor and singer, but the abilities of the principal violin'. 'M'opporrò de generoso' (Sosarme) – 'an air of spirit . . . agitation and fury . . . it has great theatrical merit'. 'Tu caro, caro sei' (Elmira and Sosarme) – 'a very gay and pleasing duet'.

☊ *Fernando* Zazzo/Cangemi/Pizzolato/Abete/Cencic/
Adami/Banerjee
Il Complesso Barocco/Curtis
Virgin Classics 0946 3 65483 2 6 (2 CDs). Recorded 2005.

Orlando, HWV 31
Composition Completed 20 November 1732.
Libretto After Carlo Capece, from Ludovico Ariosto.
Premiere 27 January 1733, King's Theatre, Haymarket.
Synopsis The magician Zoroastro urges the knight Orlando to devote himself to deeds of glory and abandon thoughts of love. Orlando is infatuated with Angelica, Queen of Cathay, but she has fallen in love with the wounded African Prince Medoro, who is also hopelessly loved by the shepherdess Dorinda. Orlando is driven literally mad with jealousy

and wreaks havoc, nearly killing Medoro and Angelica. Eventually, Zoroastro restores Orlando's sanity and Orlando proclaims that he has now mastered himself. He blesses the betrothal of Angelica and Medoro and all sing in praise of love and glory.

Notes The first of three operas based on Ariosto's Renaissance epic, *Orlando Furioso*. *Ariodante* and *Alcina* followed, making up another great trilogy of Handel operas, comparable to *Giulio Cesare*, *Tamerlano*, and *Rodelinda* (see above). One of Handel's best mature operas, *Orlando* is a rich study of character and personality, with various unconventional elements – not least the extraordinary mad scene for Orlando. It turned out to be the last opera Handel wrote for Senesino before he, and most of the rest of the company, defected to the new Opera of the Nobility. Senesino took the title role, with Strada as Angelica, Bertolli as Medoro, Celeste Gismondi as Dorinda, and Montagnana as Zoroastro. *Orlando* was reasonably successful, with an initial ten performances, and six more later in the season.

Highlights Act I: 'Non fù già men forte Alcide' (Orlando) – Orlando's moving affirmation that glory can be gained in pursuit of love. Burney just called it 'an agreeable air'. 'Fammi combattere' (Orlando) – 'a very animated air'. 'Consolati, o bella' (Dorinda, Angelica and Medoro) – 'an agreeable terzetto', as Angelica and Medoro try to comfort Dorinda: Act II: 'Verdi allori' (Medoro) – 'a very graceful and pleasing air'. 'Verdi piante' (Angelica) – 'pathetic and richly accompanied'. 'Ah! Stigie larve . . . Vaghe pupille' (Orlando) – 'the whole last scene of this act, which paints the madness of Orlando, in accompanied recitatives and airs, in various measures, is admirable. Handel has endeavoured to describe the hero's perturbation of intellect.' Act III: 'Sorge infausta' (Zoroastro) – 'an admirable bass song, in Handel's grandest style of writing . . . Montagnana, who sung this air, must have had an uncommon compass and agility of voice to do it justice.' 'Finchè prendi' (Angelica and Orlando) – 'chiefly in dialogue, upon a constantly moving bass . . . the most masterly composition in the opera'. 'Già l'ebro mio ciglio' (Orlando) – 'a beautiful invocation to sleep . . . accompanied by *violetta marina* [a type of viol]'.

🎧 Bardon/Mannion/Summers/Joshua/Van Der Kamp
Les Arts Florissants/Christie
Erato 0630 14636-2 (3 CDs). Recorded 1996.

Arianna in Creta, HWV 32

Composition Completed 5 October 1733.

Libretto After Pietro Pariati.

Premiere 26 January 1734, King's Theatre, Haymarket.

Synopsis An adaptation of the Greek legend of Ariadne, Theseus, and the Minotaur. Teseo (Theseus) arrives on Arianna's (Ariadne's) island of Crete with the annual sacrificial offering of young men and women for the Minotaur. Teseo and Arianna love each other, but Teseo is also loved by Carilda, one of Arianna's friends due to be sacrificed, and Teseo's offer to fight the Minotaur to save Carilda only makes Arianna jealous. Meanwhile both Teseo's friend Alceste and the Cretan general Tauride also love Carilda. All is finally resolved when Teseo kills the Minotaur and claims Arianna, while the faithful Alceste wins Carilda.

Notes This was Handel's first opera following the opening at the Lincoln's Inn Fields Theatre of the new rival company, the Opera of the Nobility, directed by the composer Nicola Porpora under the patronage of the Prince of Wales. Burney commented that 'Porpora was more a man of judgement and experience, than genius', but Handel lost all of his main singers to him, apart from Strada, who took the title role in *Arianna*. Handel recruited a new alto castrato, Giovanni Carestini, as Teseo, and Margherita Durastanti rejoined the company as Tauride. The rival companies immediately went head to head, as the first production of the Opera of the Nobility was Porpora's version of *Ariadne* at the end of December 1733. But Handel still enjoyed the support of the King, and *Arianna*, which opened a few weeks later, was quite popular, with seventeen initial performances. Later in 1734

Handel put on two pasticcios – productions made up of extracts from other works – called *Il Parnasso in festa* and *Oreste*. After that, having come to the end of his contract with Heidegger, he moved his company to the Covent Garden Theatre for the 1735 season. The Opera of the Nobility, who had recruited the famous castrato Farinelli, then took over the King's Theatre, Haymarket. Musical chairs!

Highlights Act I: 'Nel pugnar' (Teseo) – 'which is the first in Carestini's part, is admirable, as a spirited composition intended to display the great and peculiar abilities of that singer'. 'Sdegnata sei con me' (Teseo) – 'a fine cantabile, in which, according to tradition, his [Carestini's] feeling and expression were equally eminent'. 'Sdegno, amore' (Arianna) – 'extremely spirited, and of an original cast'. Act II: 'Oh Patria! . . . Sol ristoro' (Teseo) – 'the beauties of the first scene of the second act [when Teseo dreams that he kills the Minotaur] . . . have not been surpassed in any one of Handel's dramatic works that I can recollect.' 'So che non è più mio' (Arianna) – 'a very beautiful melody, *alla Siciliana*'. 'Son qual stanco pellegrin' (Alceste) – 'a very plaintive and pleasing air . . . with a fine solo part for the violoncello'. 'Se nel bosco' (Arianna) – 'a plaintive, pastoral air'. Act III: 'Ove son? . . . Qui ti sfido' (Teseo) – 'Theseus going to attack the Minotaur, has a fine accompanied recitative and an air . . . of infinite spirit, heightened by a full and rapid accompaniment.' 'Mira adesso' (Arianna and Teseo) – 'admirable, but in a style somewhat ancient'. 'Bella sorge' (Teseo and Chorus) – 'the celebrated air . . . which was long a national favourite . . . the flute players eagerly seized it as their property'.

☊ Katsuli/Nesi/Baka/Paparizou/Karayanni/Magoulas
Orchestra of Patras/Petrou
MDG MDG 609 1375-2 (3 CDs). Recorded 2005.

The Covent Garden operas 1735–7

Ariodante, HWV 33
Composition 12 August to 24 October 1734.

Libretto After Antonio Salvi, from Ludovico Ariosto.
Premiere 8 January 1735, Covent Garden Theatre.
Synopsis Prince Ariodante is happily betrothed to Princess Ginevra, daughter of the King of Scotland. But Polinesso, the unscrupulous Duke of Albany, wants Ginevra for himself and he manipulates her maid, Dalinda, who loves him, to impersonate Ginevra and admit him to her room at night. Ariodante, and his brother Lurcanio, who loves Dalinda, witness this supposed betrayal and Ariodante leaves in despair. Lurcanio accuses Ginevra and the King condemns her. Meanwhile Polinesso hires assassins to silence Dalinda, but they are intercepted by Ariodante who learns the truth and returns to find Lurcanio has killed Polinesso in a duel. All is now revealed and Ariodante and Ginevra are reunited.
Notes Following *Orlando*, *Ariodante* was Handel's second Ariosto-based opera and his first for the Covent Garden Theatre, which he rented from John Rich after the end of his contract with John Heidegger at the King's Theatre. (Ironically, Rich had been the impressario behind the popular *Beggar's Opera*, in 1728, which had first dented the fortunes of Italian opera in London.) Handel took adavantage of the resident troupe of dancers, led by Marie Sallé, and each act ends with a dance sequence. Act II also has a notable final recitative from the stricken Ginevra. Handel particularly exploits the dramatic and virtuoso talents of his new castrato, Carestini – the arias for Ariodante are all demanding and among the best he ever wrote. Strada sang the role of Ginevra; a new young tenor, John Beard, was Lurcanio; a new young soprano, Cecilia Young, played Dalinda; and the contralto Maria Caterina Negri took the part of Polinesso. *Ariodante* was a success, with eleven initial performances, and Burney commented: 'Nothing but the intrinsic and sterling worth of the composition could have enabled Handel at this time to make head, not only against four of the greatest singers that ever trod the opera stage [Senesino, Farinelli, Cuzzoni, and Montagnana, who had defected to the Opera of the Nobility], but against party prejudice, and the resentment,

power, and spleen of the principal patrons of Music among the nobility and gentry of this kingdom.'

Highlights Act I: 'Prendi da questo mano' (Ginevra and Ariodante) – 'a very graceful and pleasing duet'. 'Con l'ali di constanza' (Ariodante) – 'a gay and pleasing *bravura* of a very modern cast'. 'Spero per voi, sì, sì' (Polinesso) – 'has great spirit and originality'. 'Il primo ardor' (Dalinda) – Burney made no comment, but this is a delightful love song. Act II: 'Tu, preparati a morire' (Ariodante) – 'full of rage, distrust, and passion'. 'Scherza infida' (Ariodante) – one of the greatest Handel arias: 'paints his [Ariodante's] growing jealousy, indignation, and despair'. 'Se l'inganno sortisce felice' (Polinesso) – Burney called it 'a light air', but it brilliantly depicts Polinesso gloating over his evil plan. 'Invida sorte avara' (The King) – 'a plaintive and charming *Siciliano*'. 'Il mio crudel martoro' (Ginevra) – 'a very plaintive air . . . by which she [Ginevra] is lulled to sleep'. Act III: 'Numi! Lasciarmi vivere . . . Cieca notte' (Ariodante) – 'a grave and sorrowful cavatina . . . [and] after a long recitative, another air . . . of a bold and original kind'. 'Dopo notte' (Ariodante) – 'a very agreeable *aria di bravura* of considerable agility'. What an understated way to describe this firework of an aria! 'Bramo aver mille vite' (Ariodante and Ginevra) – 'a very pleasing duet . . . upon a plan and subject totally different from any of Handel's opera duets, that I can recollect'.

♭ Baker/Mathis/Burrowes/Bowman/Rendall/Ramey/Oliver
London Voices/ECO/Leppard
Philips 473 955-2 (3 CDs). Recorded 1978.
♭ von Otter/Dawson/Podles/Cangemi/Croft/Sedov/Coadou
Choeur des Musiciens du Louvre/Musiciens du Louvre/
Minkowski
Archiv 457 271-2 (3 CDs). Recorded 1997.
♭ Hunt Lieberson/Gondek/Saffer/Lane/Müller/Cavallier/
Lindemann
Wilhelmshavener Vokalensemble/Freiburger Barockochester/
McGegan

Harmonia Mundi HMU 907146-48 (3 CDs). Recorded 1995.
🎧 Highlights: HMU 907277 (1 CD).
📼 Murray/Rodgers/Howell/Robson/Garrett/Nilon/ Le Brocq
ENO Chorus and Orchestra/Bolton
D. Alden (stage director)
Arthaus Musik 100 064 (1 DVD). Filmed 1996.

Alcina, HWV 34
Composition Completed 8 April 1735.
Libretto After Riccardo Broschi, from Ludovico Ariosto.
Premiere 16 April 1735, Covent Garden Theatre.
Synopsis The heartless sorceress, Alcina, lures men to her
magic island where she changes them into rocks, trees, and
wild beasts. The knight, Ruggiero, is her latest victim, but this
time Alcina has actually fallen in love. Bradamante, Ruggiero's
fiancée, accompanied by her tutor Melisso, disguises herself as
her brother, Ricciardo, to search for Ruggiero. But Morgana,
Alcina's sister, who is loved by Alcina's general, Oronte,
immediately falls in love with 'Ricciardo'. Meanwhile, there is
a young boy, Oberto, on the island searching for his father.
Confusion reigns, until Ruggiero finally rejects Alcina and
breaks her spell. The right couples are reunited and all the
captives are returned to life.
Notes This was Handel's third Ariosto-based opera, following
Orlando and *Ariodante*. It had a lavish production at the Covent
Garden Theatre and was an instant and popular success, providing Strada with her greatest role as the anguished Alcina.
Indeed, nowhere more vividly than in his treatment of all the
characters in *Alcina* does Handel demonstrate compassionate
understanding of human nature. Carestini sang Ruggiero
(although he was initially unimpressed by the wonderful aria,
'Verdi prati'), Young was Morgana, Negri was Bradamante,
Beard was Oronte, and a fourteen-year-old boy, William
Savage, took the role of Oberto (he had recently sung in the oratorio, *Athalia*). *Alcina* had eighteen initial performances, plus
five more the following season, and Burney described it as 'an
opera with which Handel seems to have vanquished his opponents, and to have kept the field near a month longer than his

rival Porpora was able to make head against him . . . few of his [Handel's] productions have been more frequently performed, or more generally and deservedly admired, than this opera.'

Highlights This is difficult – *Alcina* is wonderful from start to finish! Burney began by praising the 'gravity and grandeur' of the Overture and the lovely Act I chorus, 'Questo è il cielo', but then abandoned his usual plan of going through the whole opera. Instead he listed six arias as 'capital airs', four as 'agreeable' (but said there are 'many more' in this category), then declared that 'some may be praised for their uncommon spirit . . . and others for masterly composition'. He concluded by arguing for a revival of the 'entire' opera. Burney's 'capital airs' are 'Di', cor mio' (Alcina) and 'La bocca vaga' (Ruggiero) from Act I; and 'Qual portento' (Ruggiero), 'Mi lusinga' (Ruggiero), 'Ah! mio cor!' (Alcina) and 'Verdi prati' (Ruggiero) from Act II. The 'agreeable airs' are 'O s'apre al riso' (Morgana) from Act I; 'Credete al mio dolore' (Morgana), 'Un momento' (Oronte) and 'Mi restano le lagrime' (Alcina) from Act III. Those 'praised for uncommon spirit' are 'È un folle' (Oronte) from Act II; 'Sta nell'ircana' (Ruggiero) and 'Barbara!' (Oberto) from Act III. And those displaying 'masterly composition' are 'Ombre pallide' (Alcina) from Act II; and the trio 'Non è amore' (Ruggiero, Alcina and Bradamante) from Act III. And as Burney said, many others could be named.

⌒ Fleming/Graham/Dessay/Kuhlmann/Robinson/Naouri/Lascarro
Les Arts Florissants/Christie
Erato 8573-80233-2 (3 CDs). Recorded 1999.
⌒ Auger/Harrhy/Jones/Kuhlmann/Kwella/Davies/Tomlinson
Opera Stage Chorus/City of London Baroque Sinfonia/Hickox
EMI CDS 7497712 (3 CDs). Recorded 1985.
▢ Naglestad/Coote/Schneiderman/Smith/Romei/Ebbecke/Mahnke
Staatsorchester Stuttgart/Hacker
Wieler and Morabito (stage directors)
Arthaus Musik 100 338 (1 DVD). Filmed 2000.

Atalanta, HWV 35

Composition 1 to 22 April 1736.

Libretto After Belisario Valeriani.

Premiere 12 May 1736, Covent Garden Theatre.

Synopsis The shepherd and shepherdess, Aminta and Irene, are in love, but Irene likes to make Aminta jealous by pretending to love Meleagro, who is really the King of Etolia, but disguised as the shepherd Tirsi. Tirsi loves the shepherdess Amarilli, and knows she is really Atalanta, Princess of Arcadia, as does Nicandro, Irene's father and also the confidant of Meleagro. Amarilli is rather bemused to find that she is falling in love with a mere shepherd, Tirsi, but Nicandro eventually reveals Tirsi's true identity, and Mercury, messenger of the gods, arrives to bless the noble couple who will rule wisely and be loved by all.

Notes A pastoral allegory to celebrate the marriage of Prince Frederick of Wales and his bride, Princess Augusta of Saxe-Gotha. Handel gambled on writing a work that might win over the Prince, who was a supporter of the rival Opera of the Nobility. It worked: *Atalanta* was a great success, and a revival later that year was specifically requested by the royal couple. The score was printed immediately after the premiere and sold well by subscription. Strada sang the title role and an impressive new young castrato, Gioacchino Conti, was Meleagro. Burney commented that 'Conti had delicacy and tenderness, with the accumulated refinement of near thirty years, from the time of Handel's first tour to Italy.' Negri and Beard sang Irene and Aminta, and Waltz was Nicandro.

Highlights Act I: 'Care selve' and 'Laschia ch'io parta solo' (Meleagro) – 'Conti's two first songs in the first act, seem to have been written to his new, graceful and pathetic style of singing . . . indeed, Handel was always remarkably judicious in writing to the taste and talents of his performers; in displaying excellence, and covering imperfections.' 'Come all tortorella langue' (Irene) – 'an elegant pastoral'. 'Riportai gloriosa palma' (Atalanta) – 'elegant, gay, and uncommon'. Act II: 'Lassa! Ch'io t'ho perduta' (Atalanta) and 'Amarilli? Oh Dei' (Atalanta and Meleagro) – Burney's only comment was that this aria and duet are both 'more in Handel's own early style than any of the movements in the first act', but both are masterly and dramatic in depicting the inner turmoil of the two characters. The psychological portrayal continues in 'Di'ad Irene, tiranna' (Aminta). 'M'allontano, sdegnose pupille' (Meleagro) – a graceful dialogue between the voice and strings, judged by Burney to be 'more modern'. 'Se nasce un rivoletto' (Atalanta) – 'a pleasing minuet, but not very new', but with various unexpected touches that make it linger in the memory'. Act III: 'Bench'io non sappia ancor' (Atalanta) – 'new and ingenious, and so much the composer's own property, that it cannot be classed with anything else'. 'Caro/Cara, nel tuo bel volto' (Atalanta and Meleagro) – 'an agreeable mixture of *antica e moderna*, or rather Corelli highly polished' – and one of Handel's most mellifluous love duets.

☊ Farkas/Bártfaí-Barta/Lax/Bandi/Gregor/Polgar
Savaria Vocal Ensemble/Capella Savaria/McGegan
Hungaraton HCD 12612-14 (3 CDs). Recorded 1985.

Arminio, HWV 36

Composition 15 September to 14 October 1736.
Libretto After Antonio Salvi, from Jean Galbert de Campistron.
Premiere 12 January 1737, Covent Garden Theatre.
Synopsis Arminio, a German prince, has been betrayed by his father-in-law, Segeste, and captured by the Roman general, Varo, who loves Arminio's wife (Segeste's daughter), Tusnelda. Segeste forms an alliance with Varo and does everything in his power to engineer Arminio's death. But Segeste's plans are complicated by his son Sigismondo (Tusnelda's brother), who loves Arminio's sister, Ramise, and so finds himself torn between love and duty. Thinking Arminio to be dead, Tusnelda tries to kill herself, but she is saved by Sigismondo. Arminio then raises an army, the Romans are defeated, Varo is killed, and the victorious Arminio pardons Segeste.
Notes Composed in haste, *Arminio* was not a success and received only six performances. Audiences were unim-

pressed, and commentators since have tended to dismiss it as unimportant – or worse – but Burney offered a glimmer of light: 'though there are but few captivating airs, and none that I remember to have been revived in modern times [the 1780s], yet fine things frequently occur which catch the eye, and manifest the great master.' Alan Curtis, in his notes to his recent recording, makes an even stronger case for *Arminio*, based on his extensive study of the original manuscript. His approach to the score, and a committed cast of singers, certainly show the opera in the best possible light – it really does have 'fine things' in it. Handel's original cast was led by Annibali and Strada as Arminio and Tusnelda, with Conti and Bertolli as Sigismondo and Ramise, and the bass Henry Theodore Reinhold as Segeste. *Highlights* Act I: 'Il fugir, cara mia vita' (Tusnelda and Arminio) – a rare example of a dramatic duet early in a Handel opera. 'Al par della mia sorte' (Arminio) – a noble aria for the castrato Annibali. 'Posso morir, ma vivere' (Sigismondo) – a striking depiction of Sigismondo's dilemma. Act II: 'Quella fiamma' (Sigismondo) – a brilliant vocal showpiece, with an equally brilliant oboe obbligato. 'Vado a morir' (Arminio) – 'a very fine slow air . . . written in Handel's most solemn and best style'. 'Rendimi il dolce sposo' (Tusnelda) – 'an elegant and original strain, *alla Siciliana*'. Act III: 'Mira il ciel, vedrai d'Alcide' (Varo) – Handel at his grandest, with a rich orchestration of oboes, horns and bassoon, as Varo prepares for war. 'Quando più minaccia il cielo' (Tusnelda and Ramise) – a brief, but affectingly atmospheric duet as hope returns. 'Fatto scorta al sentier della gloria' (Arminio) – an exhilarating, bravura display piece for the defiant hero.

🎧 Genaux/McGreevy/Labelle/Custer/Petroni/Buwalda/Ristori
Il Complesso Barocco/Curtis
Virgin Veritas 7243 5 4561-2 (2 CDs). Recorded 2000.

Giustino, HWV 37
Composition 14 August to 20 October 1736.
Libretto After Niccolò Beregan and Pietro Pariati
Premiere 16 February 1737, Covent Garden Theatre.

Synopsis The widowed Greek Empress Arianna is about to crown the new Emperor Anastasio and marry him, when news comes via General Amanzio of an invasion led by Vitaliano and his general, Polidarte. Meanwhile, Giustino, a country youth, is called to future glory by Fortuna, messenger of the gods. He saves Leocasta, Anastasio's sister, from a bear, and she falls in love with him. The scheming Amanzio betrays Arianna who is captured by Vitaliano and thrown to a sea monster, but rescued by Giustino. Vitaliano is imprisoned, but freed by Amanzio, who makes Anastasio jealous of Giustino so that he banishes him. But Giustino and Vitaliano are revealed to be brothers and they unmask Amanzio. Anastasio declares Giustino his successor and gives him Leocasta as his wife.

Notes Handel began work on *Giustino* and then interrupted it to compose and stage *Arminio*. The title role was taken by Annibali, with Conti and Strada as Anastasio and Arianna. Beard was Vitaliano, and the boy treble, William Savage, played Fortuna. There were six initial performances and three more after Lent, later in the season. *Giustino* was not a success, but Burney commented that it has 'too much merit to be passed over in silence . . . Upon the whole, this opera, so seldom acted, and so little known, seems to me one of the most agreeable of Handel's dramatic productions.'

Highlights Act I: 'Un vostro sguardo' (Anastasio) – 'very pleasing, *alla moderna*. The first close in this air was soon after copied by Arne in his popular song of "Rule Britannia", in *Alfred*.' 'Può ben nascere' (Giustino) – 'a very pleasing cavatina'. 'Allor ch'io forte avrò' (Giustino) – 'a capital air in nine parts, with pleasing solo passages and echoes for the French horn and oboe'. 'Mio dolce amato sposo' (Arianna) – 'in the last air of the first act . . . which is extremely pathetic, Handel has made a very new and curious use of chromatic intervals'. Act II: 'Numi! che'l ciel reggete' (Arianna and Giustino) – 'fragments of a plaintive air are repeated by an echo, after which, while Giustino engages and slays a sea-monster, a most animated and descriptive symphony is played'. 'Mio bel tesoro!' (Arianna and

Anastasio) – Burney was rather hard on this lovely duet, declaring that it 'would have been very graceful and pleasing, if the first bar had not been so often repeated'. 'Sull'altar di questo' (Anastasio) – 'in a very grand and masterly style'. 'Quel torrente che s'innalza' (Arianna) – 'seems written for the display of Strada's powers of execution, with a quiet accompaniment, *alla moderna*'. Act III: 'Il piacer della vendetta' (Vitaliano) – 'though some of the passages have been since in very common use, there are very strong marks of Handel's bold and original genius'. 'Zeffiretto, che scorre nel prato' (Giustino) – 'an admirable *cantabile*, in a very modern style of pathetic; as the next air, "Di re sdegnato" [Anastasio], is of spirit and passion'. 'In braccio a te la calma' (Principals) – 'a charming quintetto, that terminates in a chorus'.

♫ Chance/Röschmann/Kotoski/Gondek/Ely/Lane/Padmore/ Minter
Kammerchor Cantamus Halle/Freiburger Barockorchester/ McGegan
Harmonia Mundi HMU 907130.32 (3 CDs). Recorded 1994.

Berenice, HWV 38
Composition 18 December 1736 to 27 January 1737.
Libretto After Antonio Salvi.
Premiere 18 May 1737, Covent Garden Theatre.
Synopsis The Egyptian Queen Berenice is urged by the Roman Ambassador, Fabio, to marry the young nobleman, Alessandro, to foster good relations between the two countries. Alessandro immediately falls in love with Berenice, but she rejects him because she is betrothed to Prince Demetrio. Demetrio, however, is secretly in love with Berenice's sister, Selene, and plots with an Egyptian enemy to overthrow Berenice in favour of Selene. Meanwhile Berenice tricks Selene into agreeing to marry Prince Arsace. Demetrio's plot and his love for Selene is discovered and he is sentenced to death. Then Berenice has a sudden change of heart, accepting the faithful Alessandro, pardoning Demetrio, and uniting him with Selene.

Notes Handel was unable to attend the premiere of the ill-fated *Berenice*, as he had suffered a stroke a few days before, and it closed after a mere four performances. The title role was sung by Strada, with Conti as Alessandro, Annibali as Demetrio, Bertolli as Selene, and Negri as Arsace. The scoring is restrained, with only strings, oboes and continuo, maybe for reasons of economy, maybe because Handel was battling ill health. Despite the few performances, two extracts from the score became popular favourites: the *Andante larghetto* section of the overture (often referred to as a minuet), and Demetrio's Act II aria, 'Sì, tra i ceppi'. Handel later reused the *sinfonia* that opens Act III in the overture for his *Music for the Royal Fireworks*.

Highlights Overture – 'the slow air, in triple time, is one of the most graceful and pleasing movements that has ever been composed. The two violins are in unison . . . purity itself . . . and the imitation between the treble and bass . . . is happy and pleasing to an uncommon degree.' Act I: 'Nò, che servire altrui' (Berenice) – 'in a very uncommon style, and supported and accompanied with spirit and ingenuity'. 'Nò, soffrir non può' (Demetrio) – 'in a fine style of *cantabile*'. 'Se il mio amor' (Berenice and Demetrio) – 'a very fine duet . . . in which there is an agreeable mixture of ancient and modern styles'. Act II: 'Sempre dolci ed amorose' (Berenice) – 'a mixture of tenderness and spirit that is extremely agreeable'. 'Mio bel sol' (Alessandro) – 'an *aria di cantabile* . . . in an exquisite style of pathetic . . . in which there is not a passage that has suffered by time or fluctuations in taste'. 'Sì, tra i ceppi' (Demetrio) – Burney only looked at the score of the first version of this aria and found it 'dry and laboured in style', but the second version which was substituted in performance has a memorable tune which no doubt explained its subsequent popularity. 'Sì poco et forte' (Selene) – 'has so much originality that I can scarce recollect anything like it, elsewhere'. Act III: 'Chi t'intende?' (Berenice) – 'a very elaborate and fine composition, with a solo part for the oboe . . . this seems the principal *aria d'abilità* of the heroine of the drama'. 'Tortorella che rimira'

(Selene) – 'a very pathetic air . . . in which Handel has an ingenious imitation, in the symphony and accompaniment, of the cooing of the dove'. 'Avvertite, mie pupille' (Berenice) – this wonderfully poignant aria was for some reason cut before performance, and Burney made no mention of it. 'Quella fede, quel volta' (Berenice and Alessandro) – 'a very graceful and pleasing duet'.

𝒪 Baird/Lane/Fortunato/Matthews/Minter/McMaster/
Opalach
Brewer Chamber Orchestra/Palmer
Newport Classics NPD 85620/3 (3 CDs). Recorded 1994.

The final operas: 1737–41

Faramondo, HWV 39
Composition 15 November to 24 December 1737.
Libretto After Apostolo Zeno, from Gautier de Costes de la Calprenède.
Premiere 3 January 1738, King's Theatre, Haymarket.
Synopsis Gustavo, King of Cimbria, swears vengeance on Faramondo, King of the Franks, for the death of his son in battle. But Gustavo's other son, Adolfo, loves Faramondo's sister, Clotilde, and Faramondo himself falls in love with Gustavo's daughter, Rosimonda. King Gernando also wants Rosimonda and allies himself with Gustavo, but Adolfo and Rosimonda save Faramondo from imprisonment and death. Gustavo, betrayed by both his children, then learns that his lieutenant, Tebaldo, and Gernando have abducted Rosimonda and are out to assassinate him. Faramondo foils their plot and Tebaldo reveals on his deathbed that Gustavo's dead son was not his at all – two babies had been switched at birth! The feud is over: Faramondo can marry Rosimonda and Adolfo can marry Clotilde, amid general rejoicing.
Notes After three unsuccessful operas, enormous financial problems (just about managing to pay off his singers), and crippling ill health, the indomitable Handel went for a cure at Aix-la-Chapelle and rose like a phoenix from the ashes. The

Opera of the Nobility had folded at the end of the 1737 season and Handel moved back into the King's Theatre with this new opera. The late start to the season was because all the theatres had been closed for some weeks following the death of Queen Caroline, and Handel had interrupted work on *Faramondo* to compose an anthem for her funeral in December: *The Ways of Zion do Mourn*. Despite competition on the London stage from a new burlesque parodying Italian opera – John Lampe's *The Dragon of Wantley* – and a production mounted on a shoestring, *Faramondo* achieved seven initial performances and one more later in the season. Handel recruited a new company of singers, led by the mezzo-castrato, Gaetano Majorano, known as Caffarelli (Faramondo), Italian mezzo-soprano, Maria Marchesina, known as La Lucchesina (Rosimonda), and French soprano, Elizabeth Duparc, known as La Francesina (Clotilde). The bass Montagnana returned, and several other singers transferred from the defunct Opera of the Nobility.

Highlights Overture – 'one of the most pleasing of all Handel's opera overtures . . . nothing can be more grand than the opening, or more free and spirited than the fugue; and as to the air, it speaks intelligibly to all ears'. Act I: 'Vanne che più ti miro' (Rosimonda) – an agitated and striking aria that Burney dubbed 'curious in its modulation and accompaniment'. 'Sì tornerò' (Faramondo) – 'a slow air, thinly accompanied . . . a fine out-line for a great singer'. 'Se ben mi lusinga' (Faramondo) – 'an air of considerable spirit and execution'. Act II: 'Sì, l'intendesti' (Rosimonda) – 'an air of great spirit and energy . . . in great favour in my own memory . . . the dignity and passion with which the words were expressed, never failed to strike every hearer'. 'Poi che pria' (Faramondo) – 'pathetic, in a style which will never be old'. 'Combattuta da due venti' (Clotilde) – 'Francesina's spirited manner was well displayed . . . the composition is very original'. Act III: 'Voglio che sia' (Faramondo) – 'the fire and spirit . . . make ample amends for preceding trivial movements. This air is is finely planned for the stage, and for a voice of great volume.

The passages are contrasted, and accompaniments pictur-esque and impassioned.' 'Un'aura placida' (Clotilde) – 'an air ... admirably calculated to display her [Francesina's] lark like execution'. 'Virtù, che rende' (Faramondo and Chorus) – 'one of the most agreeable movements in a hunting style that has ever been composed; the score is in nine parts, and those for the French horns remarkably gay and pleasing'.

🎧 Fortunato/Baird/Minter/Lane/Callahan/Castaldi/Gratis/ Singer
Brewer Chamber Orchestra/Palmer
Vox Classics VOX 3 7536 (3 CDs). Recorded 1996.

Serse (Xerxes), HWV 40
Composition 26 December 1737 to 14 February 1738.
Libretto After Silvio Stampiglia, from Niccolò Minato.
Premiere 15 April 1738, King's Theatre, Haymarket.
Synopsis The autocratic Persian King Serse (Xerxes) deter-mines to marry Romilda, daughter of his general, Ariodate. But Serse's brother, Arsamene, already loves Romilda, and she him, and Serse himself is already betrothed to the foreign Princess Amastre, who now arrives at court disguised as a man. Meanwhile, Romilda's sister, Atalanta, loves Arsamene and intercepts a letter from him to Romilda, via his servant, Elviro (disguised as a flower seller), and shows it to Serse. Confusion reigns, jealousy, intrigue and despair ensue, and Arsamene and Romilda nearly lose their lives. Eventually Amastre reveals her true identity, Serse is contrite, and Arsamene and Romilda are united.
Notes A late, great Handel opera, although it only received five performances at its premiere. Burney, and others at the time, were perplexed by 'a mixture of tragic-comedy and buf-foonery', expecting it to be a serious opera. He somewhat grudgingly admitted that 'it gave Handel an opportunity of indulging his native love and genius for humour; and the airs for Elviro, a facetious servant in this opera, are of a very comic cast'. Later commentators have tended to see *Serse* as prefig-uring Mozart's Da Ponte operas, *Così fan tutte* and *Le nozze di*

Figaro, where real emotional depth lies just below the surface of elegant comedy. But Handel was in some ways returning to an earlier tradition of Italian opera, as in *Agrippina* and *Partenope*, where comic characters and scenes were part of an esentially serious work. Many of the arias are also shorter and the whole opera has a momentum that carries it through brilliantly on the stage. Ironically, Handel borrowed (and transformed, rendering the commonplace memorable) various musical elements from his old rival Bononcini, whose *Xerse* was composed on a similar libretto. The cast was led by Cafarelli as Serse, La Lucchesina and La Francesina as Arsamene and Romilda, and Antonia Merighi as Amastre. The opening aria of the opera, 'Ombra mai fu', was later immortalised as 'Handel's Largo'.

Highlights Act I: 'Ombra mai fù' (Serse) – 'a charming slow cavatina . . . in a clear and majestic style, out of the reach of time and fashion'. 'Va godendo vezzoso e bello' (Romilda) – 'a gay air that was sung into fashion by Francesina'. 'Più che penso alle fiamme' (Serse) – 'in a very grand style. The passages are contrasted, and frequent opportunities given for the singer to display his taste and fancy.' 'Un cenno leggiadretto' (Atalanta) – 'gay and pleasing, but in a comic style'. Act II: 'Se bramate d'amar' (Serse) – 'a lively air for Cafarelli . . . with a bass in iterated quavers, very much in the style of Hasse and Vinci; indeed, no music fifty years old can have a younger appearance'. 'Anima infida' (Amastre) – 'a fine mixture of old and new passages and effects, with a Corelli bass, and a modern accompaniment'. 'Sì, la voglio e l'ottero!' (Arsamene) – 'an old melody, with a very modern accompaniment'. 'Voi mi dite che non l'ami' (Atalanta) – 'natural and pleasing'. Act III: 'No, no, se tu mi sprezzi' (Atalanta) – 'admirable, in the *buffo* style'. 'Troppo oltraggi la mia fede' (Romilda and Arsamene) – 'a very pleasing duet . . . of which the bass is remarkably beautiful and masterly'. 'Crude furie degl'orridi abissi' (Serse) – 'curious, spirited, and original'. 'Caro voi siete . . . Ritorno a noi la calma' (Romilda and Chorus) – the final aria and chorus are linked musically and make a

graciously serene conclusion – Handel at his most beguiling.
Burney, however, although he thought the aria was 'beautifully simple', declared that the chorus 'has all the appearance
and effect of common Italian music of the present day'. How
tastes change.

𝄞 von Otter/Norberg-Schulz/Piau/Zazzo/Tro Santafé/
Furlanetto/Abete
Les Art Florissants/Christie
Virgin Veritas 7243 5 45711 2 (3 CDs). Recorded 2003.
▢ Murray/Masterson/Robson/Rigby/Garrett/Booth-Jones/
Macann
ENO Chorus and Orchestra/Mackerras
Hytner (stage director)
Arthaus Musik 100 076 (1 DVD). Filmed 1988.

Imeneo, HWV 41

Composition 9 to 20 September 1738, and October 1740.
Completed 10 October 1740.
Libretto After Silvio Stampiglia.
Premiere 22 Nov 1740, Lincoln's Inn Fields Theatre.
Synopsis Two Athenian maidens, Rosmene and Clomiri, have
been abducted by pirates, but rescued by the young general
Imeneo. He asks their father, Argenio, for Rosmene's hand in
marriage as his reward, but Rosmene is already promised to
another young Athenian, Tirinto, who loves her and is fiercely
jealous. Meanwhile, Rosmene's sister Clomiri has secretly
fallen in love with Imeneo. Argenio tells Rosmene to accept
Imeneo, and so she has to choose between her love for Tirinto
and duty to her rescuer. She feigns madness and claims that a
spirit from the Underworld has decided for her: she will be
Imeneo's. Everyone praises the path of reason and duty in a
final chorus.
Notes '1740. The opera, a tawdry, expensive, and meretricious
lady, who had been accustomed to high keeping, was now
reduced to a very humble state, and unable to support her former extravagance.' Burney's description eloquently summed

up the situation in London, with an audience that had long tired of Italian opera, foreign singers and exotic castrati. Handel, however, persevered for one last season. He moved to the Lincoln's Inn Theatre for what were to be his final two operas. The London Daily Post billed *Imeneo* as an 'operetta', but it was little different really from Handel's previous Italian operas, apart from including the type of comic element he had introduced with *Serse*. The public was not impressed, and *Imeneo* had only two performances – the fewest of any Handel opera. The following year he took it to Ireland, in an English version, renamed *Hymen*, and gave two concert performances of it. They were a great success, alongside his new oratorio *Messiah*. Indeed two of Imeneo's arias – 'De cieca notte' (Act I) and 'Sorge nell'alma mia; (Act II) – evolved along the way into 'The people that walked in darkness' and 'Why do the nations'. Establishing a definitive version of *Imeneo* is more than usually difficult because Handel made so many revisions, additions, and alternatives to cope with voice and cast changes. Burney virtually gave up his usual commentary because the only score available to him was an incomplete draft. The orchestration is once again modest, with just strings, oboes and continuo. The original cast was led by the bass William Savage (his voice had finally broken) as Imeneo, and La Francesina as Rosmene. A new Italian soprano, Maria Monza, never turned up to sing Tirinto, so she was replaced by a castrato, Andreoni. Reinhold sang Argenio, and a 'Miss Edwards' (her first name is uncertain) was Clomiri.

Highlights Act I: 'Se potessero i sospir'miei' (Tirinto) – a beautifully yearning aria as Tirinto despairs of seeing Rosmene again. 'V'è un infelice' (Clomiri) – 'graceful and pleasing', as Clomiri hints to Imeneo that she loves him. 'Esser mia dovrà' (Imeneo) – determination in the face of love and danger. Act II: 'Su l'arena di barbara scena' (Argenio) – a grand aria extolling courage. 'Sorge nell'alma mia' (Imeneo) – 'of great spirit, in a style that was then new', as the hero is caught in the grips of jealousy. 'Consolami, mio bene' (Imeneo, Tirinto and Rosmene) – a heart-rending trio of pleading and indecision. Act III: 'Pieno il core di timore' (Tirinto) – 'grand and original', as Tirinto grapples with his fears. 'D'amor nei primi istanto' (Imeneo) – a brilliant show-piece about love and vanity. It originated in *Deidamia* as an aria for Nerea and was a later addition. 'Miratela: che arriva' (Rosmene) – a masterly and atmospheric accompanied recita-tive for the 'mad scene'. 'Per le porte del tormento' (Rosmene and Tirinto) – the wrong couple united in song, but divided by anguish.

🎧 Ostendorf/Baird/Fortunato/Hoch/Opalach
Brewer Chamber Orchestra and Chorus/Palmer
Vox Cum Laude 1154512 (2 CDs). Recorded 1985.

Deidamia, HWV 42
Composition 27 October to 7 November 1740, and 14 to 20 November 1740.
Libretto Paolo Rolli.
Premiere 10 January 1741, Lincoln's Inn Fields Theatre.
Synopsis A retelling of the Greek myth of the youth of the hero Achilles. Achille (Achilles) is living disguised as a girl, Pyrrha, at the court of King Licomede on the island of Skyros, and has become the lover of Licomede's daughter, Deidamia. Ulisse (Ulysses), also in disguise, and Fenice, the Greek ambassador, arrive to seek out Achille to fight in the Trojan War. Licomede denies that he is on the island, but Ulisse and Fenice court Deidamia and her confidante, Princess Nerea, to discover the truth. Becoming suspicious of 'Pyrrha', they transfer their attentions to her and Achille is soon unmasked. He enthusiastically agrees to go to war, and Ulisse reveals his own true identity. Achille and Deidamia, and Fenice and Nerea, are briefly united before the men leave to face their fate.
Notes The end of an era, and unfortunately not a particularly glorious end: *Deidamia* received only three performances. Burney, however, was impressed by many of the arias (he commented on nearly all of them) and declared that *Deidamia* 'may be numbered among the happiest of Handel's dramatic

productions'. Later commentators have not been as enthusiastic. Once again Handel mixed comic elements into the serious drama, but the tide had turned irrevocably against Italian opera. He composed *Messiah* immediately afterwards, and had a great success with it in Dublin, and from then on his course was set for non-staged music drama in English. La Francesina headed the cast as Deidamia (and received most of the best music), but the soprano, Maria Monza, finally arrived from Italy and Handel expanded the role of Nerea for her. Miss Edwards sang Achille, Andreoni was Ulisse, Reinhold was Licomede, and Savage was Fenice. The orchestration adds occasional horns, trumpets and drums to the usual strings, oboes and continuo.

Highlights Act I: 'Al tardar della vendetta' (Fenice) – 'for a bass voice, is admirable! Rich and ingenious in the accompaniments; and the principal melody pleasing, in a style less robust than is usual in songs for that species of voice'. 'Due bell'alme' (Deidamia) – 'with no violin part; and the violoncello is only accompanied by the harpsichord and lute, in chords, without treble melody; this is a pleasing *cavatina*, in Handel's own early manner.' 'Perdere il bene amato' (Ulisse) – 'an air of two characters [i.e. styles]: in the first part, pathetic, elegant, and worthy of a great singer; in the second, rapid, impassioned, and such as makes a return to the first part welcome'. Act II: 'Se 'l timore' (Deidamia) – 'truly pathetic and touching'. 'Nel riposa e nel contento' (Licomede) – 'admirable in harmony and design'. 'Va', perfido' (Deidamia) – 'extremely animated'. Act III: 'Ai Greci questa spada' (Achille) – 'spirited, military, and characteristic of that hero's intrepidity'. 'M'hai resa infelice' (Deidamia) – 'an air of two characters, well calculated for the stage'. 'Come all'urto aggressor' (Ulisse) – 'an admirable composition, with a fine solo part, originally designed for Caporale's violoncello'. 'Consolami, se brami' (Deidamia) – 'gay and agreeable, but has few new passages'. And that final judgement sums up later criticisms of *Deidamia* as containing many musical elements that Handel had previously used and more creatively.

🎧 Kermes/Bonitatibus/Labelle/Panzarella/Zanasi/Abete
Il Complesso Barocco/Curtis
Virgin Veritas 7243 5 45550 2 (3 CDs). Recorded 2002.

Whatever the verdict on *Deidamia*, however, this survey of Handel's operas should on no account end on a low note. To Burney, and then to Winton Dean, belong the last words, summing up Handel's extraordinary achievements. Burney first:

> When it is recollected that, exclusive of the operas which he had set in Germany and Italy, before his arrival here, this was the thirty-ninth Italian drama which he had composed for the English stage, the fertility and vigour of his invention and music appear astonishing! The arias in this last opera of *Deidamia* are as much contrasted in style, design, and passages, as those he composed thirty years before; and in this particular, Handel's resources seem superior to those of any voluminous opera composer within my knowledge.

Winton Dean has a fascinating epilogue at the end of his second volume about Handel's operas. In it he charts his more than fifty years of studying Handel's dramatic works – operas and oratorios – and how his admiration for the operas has continued to grow. He cites three vital qualities 'that entitle Handel to share the highest rank of the operatic firmament . . . subtlety of characterisation, theatrical flair and an almost inexhaustible flow of lyrical invention':

> Of all the leading opera composers Handel comes nearest to Mozart in his ability to explore the hair-line between comedy and tragedy, and to cross it without curdling the one or debasing the other. Each combines euphony with a finely tempered irony and moves with absolute surefootedness between the sinister and the farcical, the flippant and the tragic. Both possess some of Keats's negative capability, the power to enter other states of being

and interpret them from within; in painting the frailties and foibles of human nature, they reveal the complex truths and turbulent passions beneath, so that while we laugh at the characters' antics we also feel with them.

Selected compilation CDs of opera arias and extracts

∩ Arias for Cuzzoni, Durastanti, Senesino, and Montagnana
Saffer/Hunt/Minter/Thomas/Philharmonia Baroque Orchestra/McGegan
Harmonia Mundi HMX 2907171.74 (4 CDs). Recorded 1990, 1991, 1986, 1989.

∩ *Amor e gelosia*
Ciofi/DiDonato/Il Complesso Barocco/Curtis
Virgin Classics 7243 5 45628 2 (1 CD). Recorded 2003.

∩ Operatic Arias
Daniels/OAE/Norrington
Virgin Veritas 7243 5 45326 2 (1 CD). Recorded 1998.

∩ Opera Seria
Piau/Les Talens Lyriques/Rousset
Naïve E 8894 (1 CD). Recorded 2004.

∩ Opera Arias
Kirkby/Bott/Brandenburg Consort/Goodman
Hyperion CDS 44271/3 (3 CDs). Recorded 1995, 1997 and 1999.

∩ Handel Arias
La Lucrezia, and extracts from *Theodora* and *Serse*
Hunt Lieberson/OAE/Bicket
Avie AV 0030 (1 CD). Recorded 2003 and 2004.

∩ Handel Arias – *As Steals the Morn* . . .
Padmore/Crowe/English Concert/Manze
Hamonia Mundi HMU 907422 (1 CD). Recorded 2006.

∩ Handel – Renée Fleming
Fleming/OAE/Bicket
Decca 475 6186 (1 SACD). Recorded 2003.

♫ Danielle de Niese – Handel Arias
de Niese/Les Arts Florissants/Christie
Decca 475 8746 (1 CD). Recorded 2007.
♫ *Ombra mai fù*
Arias from *Giulio Cesare, Admeto, Radamisto, Rodelinda, Serse, Alcina*
Scholl/Akademie für Alte Musik, Berlin
Harmonia Mundi HMC 901685 (1 CD). Recorded 1998.
♫ Duetti Amorosi – Arias and Duets from *Poro, Serse, Admeto, Muzio Scevola, Rodelinda, Arminio, Teseo*
Rial/Zazzo/Kammerorchester Basel/Cummings
Deutsche Harmonia Mundi 88697214722 (1 CD). Recorded 2007.
♫ *Furore*
Arias from *Serse, Teseo, Giulio Cesare, Admeto, Hercules, Semele, Imeneo, Ariodante, Amadigi*
DiDonato/Les Talens Lyriques/Rousset
Virgin Classics 5 0999 519038 2 4 (1 CD). Recorded 2008.

Oratorios, odes and Passions

Handel didn't invent oratorio, but he certainly made it his own and perfected the style and form in a series of remarkable works. It is quite clear, however, that if the English public had not turned their back on Italian operas, Handel would have continued composing them. So the move from opera to oratorio was not a large one for him. Indeed, the essence of Handelian oratorio is that it brings the drama of the opera house to the concert stage. He even used the term 'sacred drama' for many of these works, and in recent years there have been various attempts to take some of the oratorios back into the opera house – notably *Semele, Theodora, Hercules,* and even *Jephtha.*

In developing his oratorio style, Handel took the elements of recitative and aria from Italian opera, and then developed the special role of the chorus (usually quite limited in opera) from his anthems. For Handel, the chorus had a central, twofold function, acting as a collective 'character' in the drama – part of the action and moving that action onwards (as in *Israel in Egypt*) – and as a *choros* in the classical Greek drama sense of an unnamed group of voices commenting and reflecting on the action (as in *Messiah*). Handel also brought vocal ensembles and orchestral sinfonias to oratorio, and something entirely of his own invention: organ concertos, which he played himself in the interludes between the separate parts of these works.

Charles Burney for once got it wrong when he wrote that Handel 'quitted the stage, and retreated back to a more solemn and solid style for the church'. This was no retreat: it was another way to pursue what he had always cared about. Handel's oratorios are bursting with life and drama. Burney and others, however, put two and two together and made five. Yes, Handel 'was well acquainted with the Holy Scriptures, and was sensible that the sublime sentiments with which they abound would give opportunities of displaying his greatest talents'. Yes, 'he took an ample scope for the exercise of that which was his greatest talent, the sublime in music, and this he displayed to the astonishment of every one in the choruses to these entertainments'. But no, Handel did not give 'another direction to his studies, better suited . . . to the circumstances of a man advancing in years, than that of adapting music to such vain and trivial poetry as the musical drama is generally made to consist of'. Mind you, if Handel did actually say that, as Hawkins claimed he did, he only had himself to blame for the many decades of 'churchiness' to which these works were subjected throughout the nineteenth and much of the twentieth centuries – not to mention the neglect of all but a few of them.

John Mainwaring, Handel's first biographer, identified the problem:

> As the most remarkable characters, events, and occurrences contained in the Holy Scriptures, are intended to be represented in these solemn pieces, it is plainly of their nature to be acted, as well as sung, and accompanied. But

the very sacredness and solemnity of the subjects treated, made even the setting them to music appear to some persons little less than a profanation ... and though music was allowed to lend its assistance in places of worship; yet it seemed to be a dangerous innovation to allow it the further privilege of canvassing in full form religious subjects in places of entertainment. It seemed to be forming a sort of alliance between things usually considered in a state of natural opposition, the church and theatre.

That 'natural opposition' between church and theatre, as Mainwaring calls it, seems much less relevant in our twenty-first-century world, and so with Handel's operas now doing very well on stages everywhere, the new challenge is to reclaim the oratorios for the concert hall, recognising them for the red-blooded works that many of them are. (Perhaps a start could be made by sorting out the pedestrian style of singing recitatives that dulls too many performances and recordings.) The BBC Proms recently gave a rare performance of *Belshazzar*, conducted by the veteran, eternally youthful Handelian, Sir Charles Mackerras. What are the qualities that he hears in Handel's music? 'It's sprightly, it's vivacious, and it's full of passion and rhythmic energy.' As Handel's contemporary, the statesman and writer Horace Walpole quaintly put it: 'Handel has set up an oratorio against the opera, and succeeds.'

St John Passion

The composer of this work is not identified on the manuscript and it is linked to Handel only indirectly through a much later comment by Johann Mattheson, Handel's friend and rival during his Hamburg years: according to Mattheson, who criticised the work at length, it was by 'a world famous composer'. Handel scholars have always been divided, and the *St John Passion* has not been included in the HWV catalogue. It was first performed in Hamburg on 17 February 1704, and is a relatively brief work in the German Lutheran tradition, but unusual in having no chorale settings. Does it sound like the work of a young Handel? Draw your own conclusions . . .

♫ Kleitmann/Moldvay/Brett/Zádori/Verebics/Németh/ Kállay/Gáti
Chamber Choir/Capella Savaria/Németh
Hungaraton HCD 12908 (1 CD). Recorded 1987.

Il trionfo del Tempo et del Disinganno, HWV 46a

Handel's first oratorio, composed in 1707, also became his last, in a second revised version in 1757. It began as *Il trionfo del Tempo et del Disinganno*, was first reworked in 1737 as *Il Trionfo del Tempo e della Verità* with choruses added (see below, HWV 46b), and was further adapted to an English text as *The Triumph of Time and Truth* in 1757 (see below, HWV 71). The original version was composed in Rome to a libretto by one of Handel's patrons, Cardinal Pamphili, churchman, philosopher and poet. A papal decree of 1681 had forbidden the performance of opera, hence the popularity of oratorio, where composers could treat equally dramatic subjects, but without stage action. Apart from that, there was often little difference between them, and Handel's *Il Trionfo* is composed with a succession of recitatives and arias that are similar to his operas. The subject, however, in this particular instance, is more reflective than dramatic: an extended debate between the allegorical figures of Beauty (Bellezza), Pleasure (Piacere), Time (Tempo) and Disillusionment (Disinganno). It was probably first performed at the palace of another of Handel's patrons, Cardinal Ottoboni, with the composer Corelli leading the violins. The score is full of attractive music, including an aria, 'Lascia la spina', that would later reappear as the famous 'Lascia ch'io pianga' in the opera *Rinaldo*. There is also an orchestral Sonata with a prominent part for organ, pre-echoing the organ concertos that Handel would later include in many of his mature English oratorios.

♫ Poulenard/Smith/Stutzmann/Elwes
Les Musiciens du Louvre/Minkowski
Erato ECD 75532 (2 CDs). Recorded 1988.

♫ York/Bertagnolli/Mingardo/Sears
Concerto Italiano/Alessandrini
Naïve OP 30440 (2 CDs). Recorded 2000.
♫ Invernizzi/Aldrich/Oro/Dürmüller
Academia Montis Regalis/De Marchi
Hyperion CDA 67681/2 (2 CDs). Recorded 2007.

La Resurrezione, HWV 47

Handel's first sacred oratorio, on a text by Carlo Capece, was
first performed on Easter Sunday and Monday, 8 and 9 April
1708, at the palace of the Marquis Francesco Ruspoli in Rome.
Aptly, for a piece of musical theatre that was not allowed to be
staged, it takes a view from the wings on the events of Easter
Saturday night and Easter Sunday morning. An Angel disputes
with Lucifer at the gates of Hell, while Mary Magdelene,
Mary Cleopas and St John await – anxiously, and eventually
joyously – the hoped-for resurrection of Christ. Despite a ban
in Rome on female singers, the soprano Margherita Durastanti
(who would later be a member of Handel's London opera
company) took the part of Mary Magdelene at the premiere –
hurriedly replaced by a castrato for the second performance!
Handel's music is fresh and inventive and it provided him with
a rich store of material from which he borrowed in many
subsequent works.

♫ Argenta/Schlick/Laurens/De Mey/Mertens
Amsterdam Baroque Orchestra/Koopman
Erato 0630-17767-2 (2 CDs). Recorded 1990.

Aci, Galatea e Polifemo, HWV 72

A significant work from Handel's Italian period, in the form of
a cantata for three voices and continuo, composed in Naples
in 1708. Mainwaring writes that in Naples, 'as at other places,
he had a palazzo at his command, and was provided with table,
coach, and all other accommodations'. *Aci* was possibly
written to celebrate the wedding of the Duke of Alvito in July
1708, and the music has all the immediacy and bubbling
invention of Handel's early works. The libretto by Nicolo

Giuvo treats the story from Ovid's *Metamorphoses* about the love of the nymph, Galatea, for the shepherd, Acis, thwarted by the jealous rage of the monster Polypheme, who finally crushes Acis to death. But all is not lost, as Acis joins the gods on Mount Olympus and his spilt blood is transformed into a clear running river. Handel returned to the story in 1718 for an English masque, *Acis and Galatea* (see below), but with almost entirely new music. However, he did borrow from *Aci* for various later operas. Then in 1732 Handel brought together the Italian and English versions, *Aci* and *Acis*, calling the result a 'Serenata'. He retained both original languages, added some new music and performed it with singers from his opera company.

🎧 Piau/Mingardo/Naouri
Le Concert d'Astrée/Haïm
Virgin Veritas 7243 5 45557 2 (2 CDs). Recorded 2002.

Ode for the Birthday of Queen Anne, HWV 74 (*Eternal Source of Light Divine*)

Handel held no official position as a composer at the English Court – he was never, for example, Master of the King's (or Queen's) Music – but he was much favoured by successive monarchs and he returned the compliment with music for various special occasions. The forty-eighth birthday of Queen Anne on 6 February 1713 came just as the Peace of Utrecht was being finalised, ending the War of Spanish Succession, and Handel set a text by the poet Ambrose Philips in seven stanzas, each one ending with the words: 'The Day that gave great Anna birth / Who fix'd a lasting peace on Earth'. He set it for three soloists, chorus and orchestra, but nothing is known of the circumstances of any performance. Nowadays the radiant opening counter-tenor movement with trumpet obbligato, *Eternal Source of Light Divine*, is often given on its own. It is one of those transcendent moments in Handel's works where time stands still – the sheer beauty of the music is breathtaking.

🎧 Gritton/Blaze/George
Choir of King's College, Cambridge

Academy of Ancient Music/Cleobury
EMI 5 57140 2 (1 CD). Recorded 2001.

Brockes Passion, HWV 48

Unlike the *St John Passion* (see above), this is definitely
by Handel, although it is unclear exactly when and why
he composed it – a competition has even been suggested.
Handel seems to have sent the score from London to
Hamburg, where it was performed with some success in 1716
or 1717, and for several subsequent years. It is in the form
of a Passion-oratorio, something particularly associated with
Hamburg, where the text is an original piece of writing, rather
than a compilation taken from the Gospels (as was the case
with the two Passions by J. S. Bach). Barthold Heinrich
Brockes was a contemporary of Handel's at the University
of Halle, and his text, written in 1712, was also set by Keiser
and Telemann. Handel made cuts in it to tighten the drama
and dilute the rather sentimental piety. It is a substantial,
but rather short-breathed work, with a succession of 106
brief movements. Handel seems never to have attempted to
perform it in London, but he borrowed extensively from
it, and to good effect, in his first three English oratorios:
Esther, *Deborah* and *Athalia*. Definitely worth a listen, but not
to be compared with Bach's Passions, or Handel's own later
oratorios.

☊ Kleitmann/Gáti/Zádori/Farkas/De Mey/Burzynski/Minter/
Bártfai-Barta
Stadtsingechor Halle/Capella Savaria/McGegan
Hungaraton HCD 12734-36-2 (3 CDs). Recorded 1985.

Acis and Galatea, HWV 49a/b

Classified as a masque, this is in effect an English opera, with
the essential elements of recitative and aria that Handel would
soon take up again in his beloved Italian operas. It was
Handel's second setting of the story from Ovid (see p. 185
Aci, Galatea e Polifemo), composed for the Duke of Chandos
and performed at his mansion, Cannons, probably in 1718.

The English libretto was by John Gay and the whole work is larger in scale than the earlier *Aci*, adding a fourth character – Damon, a countryman who befriends Acis and Galatea – and also a chorus. For the further revision, premiered at the King's Theatre, Haymarket on 10 June 1732 with singers from Handel's opera company, he amalgamated *Aci* and *Acis* and added even more characters. Once again the story inspired Handel to produce some of his most attractive and spontaneous music. His first biographer, John Mainwaring, ventured that this was 'one of the most equal and perfect of all his compositions'.

🎧 Daneman/Petibon/Agnew/Cornwell/Ewing
Les Arts Florissants/Christie
Erato 3984-25505-2 (2 CDs). Recorded 1998.

Esther, HWV 50a/b

Handel's first English oratorio exists in two versions: the first was composed *c.*1718–20 while he was working for the Duke of Chandos, and received only private performances; the second was revised and expanded and premiered on 2 May 1732 at the King's Theatre, Haymarket, with singers from Handel's opera company – although there was no staging, as this was prohibited by a blasphemy law dating back to 1605. The text is based on a translation of Jean Racine's play taken from the Biblical Book of Esther, and recounts how Esther intercedes with her husband, the Persian King Ahasuerus, to spare the persecution of her people, the Israelites. The poets John Arbuthnot and Alexander Pope may have had a hand in the libretto. The first version borrowed music from the *Brockes Passion* for just under half of the numbers, and the second version also borrowed from other earlier pieces, including two Coronation Anthems: *My Heart is Inditing*, and *Zadok the Priest* (to a new text, 'Blessed are all they that fear the Lord'.) *Esther* was well received and often revived, with Handel continuing to make revisions. It is a strongly dramatic work, with particularly powerful and effective choruses.

⊙ Joshua/Bowman/Bickley/Purves/Outram/Kennedy/
Osmond/Smith
London Handel Orchestra and Choir/Cummings
Somm Recordings SOMMCD 238-9 (2 CDs). Recorded
2002.

Deborah, HWV 51

Capitalising on the success of *Esther*, Handel composed his
second English oratorio in February 1733 and gave the first
performance at the King's Theatre, Haymarket, on 17 March.
He used singers from his opera company, led by the soprano
La Strada in the title role, and including the castrato Senesino
and bass Montagnana, which underlined the dramatic nature
of the work. There was also a significant role for eight-part
chorus. *Deborah* was a success and was revived in various later
oratorio seasons up to 1756. Handel composed it quickly,
using music from various earlier works (including the *Brockes
Passion* and the *Coronation Anthems*) which would mainly not
have been previously heard in London. The librettist was
Samuel Humphreys, who took the rather gruesome story
from Chapter 4 of the Old Testament Book of Judges. It tells
of the Israelites in captivity in Canaan, and the prophetess
Deborah who predicts that a woman will cause the downfall of
Sisera the Canaanite commander: he does indeed eventually
die at the hand of the beautiful Jael, who nails his head to the
ground with a tent peg while he sleeps.

⊙ Kenny/Gritton/Denley/Bowman/George/Milhofer/
Campbell/Peacock
Choir of New College, Oxford/Choristers of Salisbury
Cathedral/King's Consort/King
Hyperion CDA 66841/2 (2 CDs). Recorded 1993.

Athalia, HWV 52

Another powerfully dramatic oratorio, close to an opera in
concept. Like *Esther*, it is based on a stage drama by Racine,
this time translated and reworked by Samuel Humphreys.
The story comes from the Old Testament Second Book of

Kings, Chapter 11, and recounts the struggle between Queen Athalia, a worshipper of the pagan god Baal, and the High Priest Joad, over the young boy Joas, who has secretly been raised in the Temple of Solomon and will ultimately be anointed king. Handel composed *Athalia* for a 'Publick Act' (a ceremony to confer degrees) at the University of Oxford, and it was performed at the Sheldonian Theatre on 10 July 1733. Handel himself was offered the degree of Doctor of Music on that occasion, but for some reason he declined. After its success in Oxford, *Athalia* was given in London on 1 April 1735 at the Covent Garden Theatre, and revived the following year, but it never achieved the popularity of some of his other oratorios and Handel put it aside.

⋒ Kermes/Pasichnyk/Lund/Oro/Cooley/Friedrich
Kölner Kammerchor/Collegium Cartusianum/Neumann
MDG 332 1276-2 (2 CDs). Recorded 2003.

Il Parnasso in festa, HWV 73

Between the Oxford and London performances of *Athalia* (see above), Handel plundered the score for a *pasticcio* in the form of an Italian *serenata*, composed to celebrate the marriage of Princess Anne and Prince William of Orange and first performed at the King's Theatre on the eve of the wedding, 13 March 1734. Two thirds of the music came from *Athalia*, the remainder was newly composed and the new libretto was from Greek legend, recounting the festivities for the marriage of Peleus and Thetis, who were to become the parents of Achilles.

⋒ Moore/Sampson/Crowe/Outram/Clegg/Harvey
Choir of the King's Consort/King's Consort/Halls
Hyperion CDA 67701/2 (2 CDs). Recorded 2008.

Alexander's Feast, HWV 75

Handel set two odes by John Dryden in honour of Saint Cecilia, the patron saint of music. The first, written by Dryden in 1687, became the *Ode for St Cecilia's Day* (see below), and the second, written by Dryden in 1697, was

Alexander's Feast – subtitled 'The Power of Music'. The premiere was on 19 February 1736 at the Covent Garden Theatre, with members of Handel's opera company, notably La Strada and John Beard. It was immediately popular, with more performances in 1736 and 1737, and the publication of a subscription score the following year. After that it was frequently revived in successive seasons. Dryden's poem concerns a banquet given by Alexander the Great to celebrate his conquest of Persia, and is also a celebration of the power of music to kindle and inspire the heart of mankind, personified by the secular figure of the lyre player, Timotheus, and the sacred one of Saint Cecilia – credited with the invention of the organ, Handel's own instrument.

Handel's music reflects his enthusiasm for the text and the way it fired his imagination across a wide gamut of moods and styles. It is shorter than most of his other choral works, so he included two concertos at the first performance: one for harp (Op. 4 No. 6), representing Timotheus's lyre, and one for Saint Cecilia's organ (Op. 4 No. 1). He also composed a Concerto Grosso (HWV 318) to be played between Parts I and II. John Hawkins wrote of Handel's success with *Alexander's Feast* that it 'determined him in his resolution to addict himself for the future to this species of composition [i.e. oratorio], and accordingly he persisted in it, with a few occasional deviations, for the remainder of his life'.

🎧 Argenta/Partridge/George
The Sixteen/The Symphony of Harmony and Invention/
Christophers
Coro COR 16028 (1 CD). Recorded 1990.

Il trionfo del Tempo e della Verità, HWV 46b
This revised version of an earlier work, *Il trionfo del Tempo e del Disinganno*, was first performed on 23 March 1737 at the Covent Garden Theatre. It was given two more times the same season, and revived for one performance in 1739. See above (HWV 46a) and below (HWV 71).

☊ McFadden/Scholl/Hariades/Abilgaard
Junge Cantorei/Barockorchester Frankfurt/Martini
Naxos 8.554440-42 (3 CDs). Recorded 1998.

Saul, HWV 53

This was Handel's first collaboration with the librettist Charles Jennens, an Oxford-educated gentleman-scholar from a prosperous landowning family. Jennens and Handel always had an uneasy working relationship, but it was one that bore rich fruit in *Messiah* and other works. Handel composed *Saul* between July and September 1738 and it was first performed at the King's Theatre on 16 January 1739. Further performances followed that year and it was regularly revived. The 'Dead March' from Act III soon became famous. The story comes from the Old Testament Books of Samuel and concerns the tragic figure of King Saul whose murderous jealousy of David, who has slain the giant Goliath, leads to the deaths of both himself and his beloved son, Jonathan, at the hands of the Philistines. Handel took great care over the composition of *Saul* and the manuscript is full of corrections and revisions. The finished work is one of his most powerful and moving oratorios.

☊ Joshua/Bell/Zazzo/Venden/Slattery/Bjarnason/
Waddington/Saks
RIAS-Kammerchor/Concerto Köln/Jacobs
Harmonia Mundi HMC 901877.78 (2 CDs). Recorded 2004.

Israel in Egypt, HWV 54

In December 1737 Handel wrote an anthem for the funeral of Queen Caroline – *The Ways of Zion do Mourn* – and it later became Part I of this three-part oratorio, set to different words ('The sons of Israel do mourn'), and with a new title: 'The Lamentation of the Israelites for the Death of Joseph'. Part II, 'Exodus', is a dramatic narrative of the plagues sent by God upon the Egyptians, and the Israelites' escape from captivity when God parted the waters of the Red Sea. Part III, 'Moses' Song', a celebration of this new-found freedom, was composed first, and so the work was put together in reverse order. The texts were adapted from the Old Testament Books of Exodus and the Psalms, probably by Charles Jennens. The most notable feature of *Israel in Egypt* is the key role of the chorus, who both carry the action and comment on it, more than ever before in a Handel oratorio. The work was first performed at the King's Theatre on 4 April 1739, to little success: audiences actually objected to the extensive use of the chorus and the setting of a Biblical text for an 'entertainment' in a secular context. The sheer range and variety of Handel's writing for the chorus is extraordinary, however, as he captures the character of the whole people of Israel and their struggles.

᠍ Argenta/Van Evera/Wilson/Rolfe Johnson/Thomas/White
Taverner Choir and Players/Parrott
Virgin Veritas 7243 5 62155 2 (2 CDs). Recorded 1989.

Ode for St Cecilia's Day, HWV 76

This was Handel's setting of the first of Dryden's *Odes for Saint Cecilia*, written in 1687 (see above, *Alexander's Feast*, for Handel's setting of the second ode). Unlike in *Alexander's Feast*, there is no narrative here, just an extended poetic tribute to the power of Harmony to bring order – 'What passion cannot music raise and quell!' – and to the individual instruments of music to bring delight – 'the trumpet's loud clamour . . . the soft complaining flute . . . the sacred organ's praise'. Handel responded with characteristically colourful and evocative music for these various instruments, with soprano and tenor soloists, chorus and orchestra. The premiere was on 22 November 1739, alongside a performance of *Alexander's Feast*, at the Lincoln's Inn Fields Theatre.

᠍ Lott/Rolfe Johnson
English Concert and Choir/Pinnock
Archiv 474 549-2 (1 CD). Recorded 1985.

L'Allegro, il Penseroso ed il Moderato, HWV 55

A pastoral ode in three parts on texts by John Milton (Parts I and II) and Charles Jennens (Part III). There are no actual characters, nor a plot as such; instead, the form of the work is a dialogue between two contrasting allegorical moods or 'humours', characterised by the extrovert and actively outgoing (*L'Allegro*) and the introvert and inwardly reflective (*Il Penseroso*), with moderation (*Il Moderato*) urging the virtues of a middle way. All this is played out against the backdrop of nature and the cosmos, and in particular the English countryside and urban landscape, which fired Handel's imagination and led him to indulge in vivid word-setting and explore the full range of his own extrovert and introvert art. Just compare, for example, the glorious clamour of *L'Allegro*'s 'Or let the merry bells ring round' (Part I) with the shimmering beauty of *Il Moderato*'s 'As steals the morn' (Part 3), and the pastoral bliss of *Il Penseroso*'s extended meditation on birdsong, 'Sweet bird, that shunn'st the noise of folly' (Part I). Handel composed the work at speed between 19 January and 4 February 1740 (during a bitterly cold winter, incidentally) and the first performance was 27 February 1740 at the Lincoln's Inn Fields Theatre, where the presence of chorus and orchestra and a team of soloists from Handel's opera company pointed up the theatrical elements of the work.

♩ Brandes/Dawson/Daniels/Bostridge/Miles
Bach Choir/Ensemble Orchestral de Paris/Nelson
Virgin 7243 5 45417 2 (2 CDs). Recorded 1999.

Messiah, HWV 56

This was a major turning point for Handel: the oratorio he composed after what turned out to be his last London opera season and his unsuccessful last opera, *Deidamia*. From *Messiah* onwards he would produce no more theatrical works for the stage. Handel wrote *Messiah* between 22 August and 12 September 1741, and then he was invited to Dublin to present a season of his works, so he took it with him. The first performance was on 13 April 1742, at the end of his Dublin season, and it was an immediate success. The text of *Messiah*

was put together from various books of the Old and New
Testaments by Charles Jennens, who – amazingly – never
really felt that Handel's music did it justice. The scope of the
work is immense, with the Christmas and Easter narratives of
the life, death and resurrection of Christ presented in the
theological context of the mystery of God's plan for the
Redemption of humankind, from Old Testament prophesy to
the New Testament apocalyptic vision of the Last Things in
the Book of Revelation. Jennens avoided using named characters – particularly the figure of Christ, which would have been
seen as blasphemous in the context of secular performance.
Even so, when Handel brought *Messiah* to London after its
triumphant reception in Dublin, there was fierce controversy
in the newspapers about the appropriateness, or not, of such
a subject. The coolly received London premiere was on
23 March 1743 at the Covent Garden Theatre, and *Messiah*
became popular only gradually, helped in part by the later
annual charity performances in the chapel of the Foundling
Hospital. In all, Handel directed *Messiah* thirty-six times
between 1742 and the end of his life, and he continued to
revise the work throughout that time, so that however perfect
Messiah may seem, it does not really exist in any definitive
version. A nice irony!

    See the separate chapter on *Messiah* for further reflections.

♩ Harwood/Baker/Esswood/Tear/Herincx
Ambrosian Singers/ECO/Mackerras
EMI CZS 7 62748 2 (2 CDs). Recorded 1966.
♩ Nelson/Kirkby/Watkinson/Elliott/Thomas
Choir of Christ Church Cathedral, Oxford/Academy of
Ancient Music/Hogwood
Oiseau Lyre 411 858-2 (3 CDs). Recorded 1980.
♩ Schlick/Piau/Scholl/Padmore/Berg
Les Arts Florissants/Christie
Harmonia Mundi HMC 901498.99 (2 CDs). Recorded 1993.
♩ Lott/Palmer/Langridge/Lloyd
Huddersfield Choral Society/RPO/Mackerras

Signum Classics SIGCD 074 (2 CDs). Recorded 1988.
Version arranged by Mozart.

After Handel's return to London from Dublin he abandoned
Italian opera and began to give regular Lenten seasons of oratorios. In the 1743 season he gave *Samson* and *Messiah*; then in
1744, *Semele* and *Joseph and his Brethren*; then he ventured an
extended season from Autumn 1744 to Easter 1745 with
Hercules and *Belshazzar*. It was not a success, so from 1746 he
returned to the Lenten seasons.

Samson, HWV 57

This was Handel's second oratorio to a text by the poet John
Milton (see above: *L'Allegro, il Penseroso ed il Moderato*). The
libretto was adapted by Newburgh Hamilton from *Samson
Agonistes*, based on the Old Testament Book of Judges, along
with extracts from other Milton poems. Handel composed the
first draft of *Samson* in the autumn of 1741, immediately after
finishing *Messiah*, and then put it aside until after his stay in
Dublin, and expanded and completed it in October 1742. The
first performance was at the Covent Garden Theatre on
18 February 1743. It was well received and Handel revived it,
with various revisions, in nine more seasons up to 1759 – the
last performance was only a few weeks before his death. The
action concentrates on the final part of the Biblical story, as
Samson, ensnared by Delilah and now captive and blinded,
recovers his strength enough to pull down the pillars of the
pagan Temple of Dagon, killing the Philistines and himself
along with them. This is another powerful Handel oratorio,
with stirring choruses for the oppressed Israelites. Samson
himself emerges through Handel's music as a heroic and
many-faceted character, and his desolate aria in Act I, 'Total
eclipse! no sun, no moon, all dark', moved audiences all the
more once Handel himself lost his sight towards the end of his
life. Also justly famous is the triumphant soprano aria, 'Let
the bright seraphim', a paean of praise to God, which comes
just before the end.

🎧 Rolfe Johnson/Alexander/Venuti/Prégardien/Blasi/Miles/
Kowalski/Scharinger
Arnold Schoenberg Chor/Concentus Musicus Wien/
Harnoncourt
Teldec 9031-74871-2 (2 CDs). Recorded 1992.

Semele, HWV 58

Disguise is a central element of the story of *Semele*, and the
same might be said of the work itself, for this is Italian opera
masquerading as English oratorio! Gone is the Biblical
subject-matter, and in its place is a decidedly secular and not
at all edifying fable from Ovid's *Metamorphoses*, with a libretto
by the dramatist William Congreve. The beautiful mortal,
Semele, becomes the lover of the god Jupiter, which panders
to her overweening vanity. Jupiter's jealous wife, Juno, seeking
revenge, appears to Semele in disguise and easily persuades
her that she too could be immortal, and so Semele asks Jupiter
to reveal himself to her in his full glory. Unfortunately he does
just that, and Semele is destroyed by his burning brightness.
End of story – and the only moral one can possibly draw from
it is: 'Be very careful what you ask for'! Handel composed
Semele in June and July 1743 and the first performance was
on 10 February 1744 at the Covent Garden Theatre, with a
cast led by one of Handel's operatic divas, La Francesina
(Elisabeth Duparc). Unfortunately the time was not right:
Semele received only four performances, plus a further two
in December 1744, and was never revived. Handel's friend,
Mrs Delany (see separate chapter) noted that '*Semele* has a
strong party against it . . . all the opera people are enraged
at Handel.' Meanwhile the oratorio audience was also unimpressed: in Winton Dean's memorable words, 'where they
expected wholesome Lenten bread, they received a glittering
stone dug from the ruins of Greek mythology'. Glittering
it was indeed, for *Semele* has some of Handel's most glorious
and ebullient music. Jupiter's Act II aria, 'Where'er you walk',
has remained a favourite, and there are many other gems:
among them Semele's arias 'Endless pleasure' (Act I),

'O sleep, why dost thou leave me' (Act II), and 'Myself I shall adore' (Act III).

🎧 Burrowes/Kwella/Jones/Denley/Penrose/Rolfe Johnson/
Davies/Lloyd/Thomas
Monteverdi Choir/English Baroque Soloists/Gardiner
Erato 2292-45982-2 (2 CDs). Recorded 1981.
🎧 Joshua/Summers/Sherratt/Wallace/Croft/Pearson
Early Opera Company/Curnyn
Chandos CHAN 0745 (3 CDs). Recorded 2006.

Joseph and his Brethren, HWV 59

Handel composed *Joseph* immediately after *Semele*, in August and September 1743, but the vital spark that created *Semele* seems not to have ignited here. *Joseph* was, however, quite well received at its first performance at the Covent Garden Theatre on 2 March 1744, so that Handel revived it the following year and in 1747, and then much later for two seasons in the 1750s – each time making his customary changes and revisions. The libretto was by a clergyman, James Miller, based on various earlier sources and recounting part of the Old Testament story from the Book of Genesis. Joseph, sold into slavery in Egypt by his brothers, is an interpreter of dreams and becomes a favourite of Pharaoh, whereupon he is able to engineer the reconciliation of his family. In modern times, *Joseph* has been performed only infrequently and Handel scholars have generally not rated it highly. The one available recording, however, makes a vigorous case for listening again with an open mind, and points out, among other things, the affecting music for Joseph's beloved youngest brother, Benjamin, sung by a boy treble.

🎧 Kenny/Bowman/Denley/George/Burrowes/Ainsley
Choirs of New College, Oxford and the King's Consort/
King's Consort/King
Hyperion CDA 67171/3 (3 CDs). Recorded 1996.

Hercules, HWV 60

Like *Semele*, this was another excursion for Handel into the world of secular 'musical drama' – and indeed this time that was how he described the work. The libretto was by Thomas Broughton, a clergyman and classical scholar, who took the story from Ovid and Sophocles. It concerns the unfounded jealousy of Hercules' wife, Dejanira, for the Princess Iole, and her attempt to rekindle Hercules' love with a supposedly magic garment which she gives him. But it is dipped in the blood of Hercules' dead enemy, Nessus, and it poisons him – at which point, Hercules is raised to the gods on Mount Olympus, and Iole marries his son, Hyllas. Handel composed *Hercules* in July and August 1744 and it was first performed on 5 January 1745 at the King's Theatre, Haymarket, recently vacated by the Earl of Middlesex's Italian opera company, which had run into financial problems. Handel had intended to mount a longer than usual season there for 1744–5, rather than confining it to Lent, but audiences were thin, in large part because oratorios lacked the costumes, scenery, and action of opera – something felt even more keenly when the work performed was actually an opera, as had been the case with *Semele* and was now with *Hercules*. To make matters worse, one of Handel's key singers, Susanna Cibber, was ill on the first night, and the opera faction were conspiring against him, luring people away to other theatres. So *Hercules* never stood much of a chance, and received only two performances. It was revived for just two more performances: one in 1749 and one in 1752. Despite all that, *Hercules* is an impressively heroic work, full of strong music for the principals – Dejanira's *scena*, 'Whither shall I fly?' (Act III), is one of many high points – and with inventive and thrilling choruses commenting on the action: in Act II alone, for example, 'Jealousy! Infernal pest' and 'Wanton god of amorous fires', could not be more different, nor more effective.

🎧 Saks/von Otter/Croft/Dawson/Daniels/Pujol
Les Musiciens du Louvre/Minkowski
Archiv 469 532-2 (3 CDs). Recorded 2000.
💻 Shimell/DiDonato/Spence/Bohlin/Ernman/Kirkbride
Les Arts Florissants/Christie

Bondy (stage director)
Bel Air Classiques BAC 013 (2 DVDs). Filmed 2004.

Belshazzar, HWV 61

> Your most excellent Oratorio has given me great delight in
> setting it to Musick and still engages me warmly. It is
> indeed a Noble Piece, very grand and uncommon, it has
> furnished me with Expressions, and has given me
> Opportunity to some very particular ideas, besides so
> many great Choruses. I entreat you heartily to favour me
> soon with the last Act . . .

Thus Handel wrote to Charles Jennens on 13 September
1744, urging him to complete the libretto of *Belshazzar*. The
delay was due in part to the complexity of combining the
Biblical story of the Fall of Babylon, with various Classical
sources. Jennens took the central narrative from the Book of
Daniel – the writing on the wall that heralds the end of the
dissolute King Belshazzar – and surrounded it with extracts
from the prophesies of Isaiah and Jeremiah, and the historical
writings of Xenophon and Herodotus. Key roles in the drama
are given to Nitocris, Belshazzar's mother, who tries to avert
the tragedy, and particularly to the Chorus – which by turns
represents the oppressed Jews, led by their prophet Daniel;
the arrogant Babylonians, led by Belshazzar; and the besieg-
ing Persians, led by King Cyrus who emerges victorious,
shows mercy to Nitocris and promises Daniel to rebuild the
Temple at Jerusalem. In the end the libretto was far too long
and Handel made cuts, which tightened the dramatic sweep of
the action. He also responded with vivid imagination to the
differing characterisations of the solo voices and especially to
the triple identity of the chorus. But once again, with an excellent cast lined up, he was compromised by the sudden illness
of Susanna Cibber and the indifference of audiences. After
the premiere on 27 March 1745 at the King's Theatre, there
were only two other performances of *Belshazzar* that first
season and only two much later revivals in 1751 and 1758.
Nevertheless, Handel was right: it is a 'Noble Piece'.

♁ Rolfe Johnson/Auger/Robbin/Bowman/Wilson-Johnson/
Robertson/Wistreich
English Concert/Pinnock
Archiv 477 037-2 (2 CDs). Recorded 1990.

Occasional Oratorio, HWV 62

The curious title of this work refers to a dramatic turn of
political events in 1745, when the Young Pretender, the Stuart
Bonnie Prince Charlie, led the Jacobite Rebellion and
marched his army south from Scotland to try to claim the
Crown from the Hanoverian monarchy. King George II's
son, Prince William the Duke of Cumberland, led the oppos-
ing royalist forces, but did not finally gain victory until
16 April 1746 at the Battle of Culloden. In the mean time,
some encouragingly patriotic music was called for and in
January 1746 Handel began work setting a libretto by
Hamilton Newburgh taken from the works of Milton and
Spenser. He worked fast and borrowed music from various of
his earlier works (and also from Telemann's *Musique de table*) –
notably *Zadok the Priest*, which rounds off the oratorio to the
words 'Blessed are all that fear the Lord'. There is neither a
plot nor named characters; instead, the four soloists and chorus expound on the themes of war and liberty, imploring God
to defeat all rebellious enemies and restore peace, and praising Him for his eternal power. Charles Jennens dismissed the
work as 'an oratorio of shreds and patches' – but then he was
sympathetic to the Jacobite cause! The first performance was
given at the Covent Garden Theatre on 14 February 1746,
while the conflict still raged, and was quite well received – the
soprano aria, 'O liberty, thou choicest treasure' (Act II),
became an immediate and lasting hit – but there were only
two further performances (and Handel gave no other oratorios that season), plus a further three at a revival the following
year. After that the *Occasional Oratorio* was put aside.

♁ Gritton/Milne/Bowman/Ainsley/George
Choir of New College, Oxford/Choristers and Choir of the
King's Consort/King's Consort/King

Hyperion CDA 66961/2 (2 CDs). Recorded 1994.

Judas Maccabaeus, HWV 63

In effect this was another *Occasional Oratorio* (see above), composed to celebrate the victorious return of the Duke of Cumberland to London after defeating Bonnie Prince Charlie's army at the Battle of Culloden – hence the famous chorus, 'See the conqu'ring hero comes'. It was Handel's first collaboration with the Reverend Thomas Morell, a Fellow of King's College, Cambridge, who would also supply the texts for *Alexander Balus*, *Theodora*, *Jephtha* and *The Triumph of Time and Truth*. Morell put together the libretto of *Judas* mainly from the First Book of Maccabees, from the Apocrypha. It tells of Judas emerging as the new Jewish leader after the death of Mattathias in 161 BC and pledging to restore his nation's liberty from invading armies from Syria, Samaria and Egypt. At last the desecrated Temple is restored and Judas re-enters Jerusalem in triumph.

Handel composed the music in July and August 1746 and the first performance was on 1 April 1747 at the Covent Garden Theatre. It was an immediate success, with numerous revivals – Handel conducted a total of thirty-three performances in London – and its popularity soon spread to many provincial towns. Unlike many of Handel's other oratorios, it continued to be popular through the nineteenth century and into the twentieth. Less concerned with individual characterisation and personal drama, and more with shared concerns and public display, *Judas* works ideally as a concert oratorio and is rich in colourful, vigorous music – Handel at his extrovert and ceremonial best. Among many famous highlights are the Act I arias, 'Arm, arm, ye brave' and 'Come, ever-smiling liberty'; the aria and chorus 'Sound an alarm! your silver trumpets sound' (Act II); and the aria and duet, 'Oh lovely peace, with plenty crown'd' (Act III).

♁ Harper/Watts/Young/Shirley-Quirk
Amor Artis Chorale/Wandsworth School Boys Choir/Lester/
ECO/Somary

Alto ALC 2002 (2 CDs). Recorded 1971.
☊ Davies/Palmer/Baker/Shirley-Quirk/Keyte/Esswood
Wandsworth School Choir/ECO/Mackerras
Archiv 447 692-2 (3 CDs). Recorded 1976.

Joshua, HWV 64

Joshua was actually composed after the next oratorio,
Alexander Balus, in July and August 1747, but premiered
before it on 9 March 1748 at the Covent Garden Theatre.
There were three further performances that season and
revivals in two later seasons, and it continued to be popular
long after Handel's death. Both *Joshua* and *Alexander Balus*
had libretti by Thomas Morell and both continued the
triumphant militarist style of the *Occasional Oratorio* and *Judas
Maccabaeus*. The Old Testament Book of Joshua supplied
Morell with several stories which he linked together. The
Israelites rejoice at having escaped from captivity in Egypt
and Joshua leads them through various vicissitudes to capture
the cities of Jericho, Ai, and Debir. Interwoven with all this
warmongering is a gentler theme of the love of the young
warrior, Othniel, for the maiden, Achsah, who has one of
Handel's great showpiece arias towards the end of Act III:
'Oh had I Jubal's lyre'. The rest of the score is a satisfyingly
varied mix of heroic, tragic, and pastoral music, with the
Chorus once again very much to the fore.

☊ Ainsley/Kirkby/Bowman/George/Oliver
Choir of New College, Oxford/King's Consort/King
Hyperion CDA 66461/2 (2 CDs). Recorded 1990.

Alexander Balus, HWV 65

Composed in June and July 1747 (just before *Joshua* – see
above), *Alexander Balus* was first performed at the Covent
Garden Theatre on 23 March 1748. There were two more
performances that season, but a revival in 1751 had to be
cancelled because of the death of the Prince of Wales on
20 March, and there was just one further performance in the
1754 oratorio season. Once again Thomas Morell took a story

from the First Book of the Maccabees in the Apocrypha, this time dealing with the era of the new Jewish leader, Jonathan, after the death of Judas Maccabaeus. Jonathan's brother, Alexander Balus, has won a victory against the Syrians, and he agrees a pact with the Egyptian King Ptolomee, sealed by marriage to Ptolomee's daughter, Cleopatra, with whom he has fallen in love. But the duplicitous Ptolomee plots against Alexander and both are eventually killed in battle, leaving the distraught Cleopatra to sing the achingly beautiful aria, 'Convey me to some peaceful shore'. The levels of human interest and intrigue in the story once again brought Handel back closer to the world of his operas, and there is a wealth of engaging music in this neglected work.

☐ Dawson/George/Denley/Daniels/McFadden
Choir of New College, Oxford/Choir of the King's Consort/
King's Consort/King
Hyperion CDA 67241/2 (2 CDs). Recorded 1997.

Susanna, HWV 66

Like *Joshua* and *Alexander Balus*, the next two oratorios are linked by being composed close to each other – *Solomon* in May 1748 and *Susanna* in July and August – and then reaching the stage in reverse order. *Susanna* was performed first, at the Covent Garden Theatre on 10 February 1749. It was quite well received and had a further three performances that season, but for some reason Handel did not revive it until 1759, only a month before he died. The librettist is unknown, but the source was a book of Apocrypha called the Story of Susanna. The title of the final chorus – 'A virtuous wife shall soften Fortune's frown' – encapsulates the action. While Susanna's husband, Joacim, is away, she is lusted after and pursued by two Elders, and when she resists, one of them accuses her of adultery with a young man. She is tried and condemned, but in the nick of time she is proved innocent and reunited with Joacim, who had always believed her faithful. Once again the story could have come from one of Handel's operas: it is highly moral, but played out against a backdrop of 'verdant hills' and 'balmy vales'. So the music, albeit often serious, has a strong flavour of the pastoral to it – something which always brought out the best in Handel. Susanna's lovely aria, 'Crystal streams in murmurs flowing' (Act II), is one of many highlights.

𝆕 Hunt/Minter/Feldman/Parker/Thomas/Thomas
Chamber Chorus of the University of California, Berkeley/
Philharmonia Baroque Orchestra/McGegan
Harmonia Mundi HMU 907030.32 (3 CDs). Recorded 1989.
𝆕 Highlights: HMX 2907358.59 (2 CDs – coupled with highlights from *Theodora*)

Solomon, HWV 67

Composed just before *Susanna* (see above) in May 1748, but first performed after it, on 17 March 1749 at the Covent Garden Theatre, *Solomon* was only given three times and then shelved until Handel's final Lenten oratorio season in 1759, when it reappeared in a revised and expanded version. The unknown librettist drew on a variety of Old Testament sources for the story: the First Book of Kings, the First and Second Books of Chronicles, and the Song of Solomon. After a series of oratorios depicting the various sufferings and struggles of the Israelites, the theme here is the peaceful reign of a great and wise ruler – and audiences would have made the intended connection with King George II, whose coronation had been celebrated by Handel with the famous anthem telling how 'Zadok the priest and Nathan the prophet anointed Solomon king'. Meanwhile, the recent defeat of Bonnie Prince Charlie, and the resolution of war in Europe with the impending treaty of Aix-la-Chapelle, had left people hoping for lasting peace – even if, as many suspected, the political reality was likely to be more complicated. *Solomon*, therefore, has very little dramatic action: it is more a series of tableaux demonstrating the right conduct of enlightened government in a time of peace and prosperity, and it has a wealth of great choruses.

Act I is taken up with praise to God and celebration of Solomon's happy marriage which has forged an alliance with

Egypt. In Act II Solomon sits in judgement over two harlots disputing which of them is the real mother of a young baby. Act III starts with the famous orchestral interlude, the 'Arrival of the Queen of Sheba' – she has come with gifts for Solomon and to admire the Temple he has built to the glory of God. The pastoral element is again marked in both the libretto and the music – Solomon's aria, 'How green our fertile pastures look' (Act III), is just one of the gems of this wonderfully rich score – and the pastoral is clearly linked to the idealised vision of peace and godliness. As Solomon sings in Act I: 'What though I trace each herb and flow'r, / That drink the morning dew, / Did I not own Jehovah's pow'r, / How vain were all I knew'. Finally, music itself has a vital part to play in this Utopian vision: 'Thy harmony's divine, great king, / All, all obey the artist's string', sings the Queen of Sheba in Act III.

☊ Scholl/Dam-Jensen/Hagley/Bickley/Gritton/Agnew/Harvey
Gabrieli Consort and Players/McCreesh
Archiv 459 688-2 (3 CDs). Recorded 1998.
☊ Cameron/Morison/Young/Marshall
Beecham Choral Society/RPO/Beecham
EMI 7243 5 86516 2 (2 CDs). Recorded 1955–6.
The conductor Sir Thomas Beecham was an ardent Handelian: 'mankind has heard no music written for voice which can even feebly rival his for grandeur of build and tone, nobility and tenderness of melody, scholastic skill and ingenuity, and inexhaustible variety of effect'. Beecham made his own performing edition of *Solomon* (either butchering it, or reinventing it for a modern audience, depending on your point of view), and his 1950s recording (recently reissued) offers a fascinating glimpse back to a now-vanished world of Handel performance practice.

Theodora, HWV 68

Theodora is reputed to have been Handel's favourite among his oratorios – and certainly he told Thomas Morell that he valued the chorus at the end of Part II, 'He saw the lovely youth', above even the 'Hallelujah' chorus in *Messiah*. For his libretto, Morell put aside the usual Old Testament and Apocrypha sources in favour of a religious novel by the seventeenth-century writer and scientist, Robert Boyle: *The Martyrdom of Theodora and Didymus*, which was in turn based on the writings of St Ambrose. In fourth-century Antioch, the Roman Governor demands obeisance to Jupiter. When Theodora, virgin leader of a small band of Christians, refuses, she is imprisoned and threatened with rape. The Roman officer Didymus, who loves Theodora and is a secret convert to Christianity, manages to free her, but is himself captured. Finally both are condemned to death and they anticipate the bliss that awaits them in Heaven. Handel composed *Theodora* during June and July 1749 and it was first performed at the Covent Garden Theatre on 16 March 1750. It was not a success with the audience and Handel declared: 'The Jews will not come to it because it is a Christian story; and Ladies will not come because it is a virtuous one.' Handel then made cuts to try to make it more palatable; he revived it in 1755 and was planning a further revival in 1759 shortly before he died. Maybe the main problem for audiences was the tragic nature of the work – Handel usually sent them home happy! But *Theodora*'s seriousness is also its glory. The music is by no means all solemn, but it is deeply affecting throughout, from Theodora's popular aria in Part 1, 'Angels ever bright and fair', to the aria and duet for Didymus and Theodora as they face execution: 'Streams of pleasure ever flowing' and 'Thither let our souls aspire'. And along the way there are gems like the Part 1 aria, 'As with rosy steps the dawn' – surely one of the most hauntingly beautiful things Handel ever wrote.

🎧 Hunt/Lane/Thomas/Minter/Thomas/Rogers
Chamber Chorus of the University of California, Berkeley/ Philharmonia Baroque Orchestra/McGegan
Harmonia Mundi HMU 907020.62 (3 CDs). Recorded 1991.
🎧 Highlights: HMX 2907358.59 (2 CDs – coupled with highlights from *Susanna*)

▪ Daneman/Taylor/Croft/Berg/Galstain/Slaars
Les Arts Florissants/Christie
Erato 0927 43181-2 (3 CDs). Recorded 2000.
▪ Upshaw/Daniels/Olsen/Croft/Hunt
Glyndebourne Festival Opera/OAE/Christie
Sellars (stage director)
NVC Arts 0630-15481-2 (1 DVD). Filmed 1996.

The Choice of Hercules, HWV 69

This is a hybrid work, a brief drama for soloists, chorus and orchestra based on incidental music that Handel had intended for *Alceste*, a play by Tobias Smollett. (There is no musical connection with Handel's earlier full-length music drama, *Hercules*.) Handel composed *Alceste* early in 1750, but then the production of the play was cancelled. Not wanting to waste good music, he turned to Thomas Morell, who came up with a libretto based on a text by the poet and cleric Robert Lowth. Handel set it, adapting and adding to his *Alceste* music, in June and July. The story is simple: the young Hercules is faced with choosing between the rival claims of Pleasure and Virtue, and after a certain amount of soul-searching he embraces his destiny as a true son of Jupiter and elects to follow the path of Virtue. *The Choice of Hercules* was first performed at the Covent Garden Theatre on 1 March 1751 as an additional Part III to *Alexander's Feast*, and then in two later revivals Handel placed it between the existing two parts of the same work, calling it an 'Interlude'. The aria, 'Enjoy the sweet Elysian grove', sung by the Attendant on Pleasure, is one of the highlights of this charming work, and there is a striking trio, 'Where shall I go?', for Hercules, Pleasure, and Virtue – an imaginative representation of the age-old dilemma of the difficulty of choice.

▪ Gritton/Coote/Blaze/Daniels
Choir of the King's Consort/King's Consort/King
Hyperion CDA 67298 (1 CD). Recorded 2001.

Jephtha, HWV 70

Handel's final new oratorio was composed with some difficulty, as he battled with increasingly bad health and loss of sight.

Usually a very quick worker, he took much longer than usual, beginning it in January 1751, then putting it aside at the end of February, taking it up again in June, but not finishing it until the end of August. The first performance was at the Covent Garden Theatre on 26 February 1752. It was well received and Handel gave it twice more that season and then revived it, with revisions, in 1753, 1756 and 1758. *Jephtha* was also Handel's last collaboration with Thomas Morell, who took the story (with significant alterations) from Chapter 11 of the Old Testament Book of Judges. Jephtha leads the Israelites in battle, and secretly vows that if he is victorious he will sacrifice to God the first person he sees on his return. Tragically, that person turns out to be his daughter, Iphis, betrothed to the soldier, Hamor. As the stricken Jephtha prepares to kill his daughter, an Angel appears, explaining that it was the Holy Spirit who inspired Jephtha's vow, and that Iphis can be spared on condition that she lives in perpetual virginity, dedicated to God. At this, everyone rejoices . . .

Handel responded to the moral ambiguities of such a story, illuminating the predicament of his all-too-human characters with music of great compassion and profundity. At the heart of this work – one of Handel's greatest – Jephtha's accompanied recitative, 'Deeper, and deeper still', and the chorus which follows it, 'How dark, O Lord, are Thy decrees', at the end of Act II, display an extraordinary harmonic richness, and are followed by one of Handel's most heartbreaking arias at the beginning of Act III: 'Waft her, angels, through the skies'. Handel's manuscript of *Jephtha* is an eloquent witness to his own personal suffering: his handwriting is notably impaired, and after 'How dark, O Lord' he noted: 'unable to continue owing to a weakening of sight in my left eye'. He also made one significant change to Morell's text in this chorus, replacing 'Whatever God ordains is right', to something bleaker: 'Whatever is, is right' – a line taken from Alexander Pope's *Essay on Man*. For Handel it was blind destiny that inflicted such hardships, not the awesome Jehovah of the Old

Testament, and as a devout New Testament man he struggled with the 'dark impenetrability' of God (to quote Winton Dean), both for *Jepththa* and himself at this darkening point in his life. In the words that open the oratorio: 'It must be so . . .'

🎧 Ainsley/George/Denley/Oelze/Köhler/Gooding
RIAS Kammerchor/Akademie für Alte Musik Berlin/Creed
Brilliant Classics 99956 (3 CDs). Recorded 1994.

The Triumph of Time and Truth, HWV 71

One element of Handel's life's work comes full circle here, and there is an neatness in the final metamorphoses of an Italian oratorio into an English one, by the composer who had so decisively made this genre his own. *The Triumph of Time and Truth* can be traced back via *Il trionfo del Tempo e della Verità* (1737) to *Il trionfo del Tempo e del Disinganno* (1707) – see above, HWV 46a and 46b. Thomas Morell translated the 1737 text into English verse form to fit the music, adding a new character, Deceit, to the existing ones of Beauty, Pleasure, Time, and Truth (or Counsel). Handel advertised *The Triumph of Time and Truth* as 'Altered from the Italian with several new Additions'. That said, there is no new music here: all the additional material comes from borrowings from other works, all of them composed before the previous version in 1737. So in essence this is really a much earlier work than its date of first performance – 11 March 1757 at the Covent Garden Theatre – makes it appear.

After three more performances in 1757, Handel added several more additional movements (none of them original) for two performances in 1758 – his last complete oratorio season. Though hardly one of Handel's greatest works, it has a wealth of attractive music: for example, the lively chorus, 'Oh, how great the glory' (Act I), where Handel elongates the first word, 'Oh' – a masterstroke! There are also several beguiling arias, notably 'Ever-flowing tides of pleasure' (Act I), 'Mortals think that time is sleeping' (Act II), and 'Pleasure! My former ways resigning' (Act III).

☉ Fisher/Kirkby/Brett/Partridge/Varcoe
London Handel Choir/London Handel Orchestra/Darlow
Hyperion CDD 22050 (2 CDs). Recorded 1982.

Selected recordings of oratorio arias and extracts

☉ Handel Arias
La Lucrezia, and extracts from *Theodora* and *Serse*
Hunt Lieberson/OAE/Bicket
Avie AV 0030 (1 CD). Recorded 2003 and 2004.
☉ Handel Arias – *As Steals the Morn* . . .
Padmore/Crowe/English Concert/Manze
Harmonia Mundi HMU 907422 (1 CD). Recorded 2006.
☉ Handel Oratorio Arias
Daniels/Ensemble Orchestral de Paris/Nelson
Virgin Classics 7243 5 45497 2 (1 CD). Recorded 2002.
☉ Great Oratorio Duets
From *Jephtha*, *Joshua*, *Belshazzar*, *Susanna*, *Theodora*, *Solomon*, *Ode for the Birthday of Queen Anne*, *Saul*, *Deborah*, *Alexander Balus*, *Alexander's Feast*, *Esther*.
Sampson/Blaze
Orchestra of the Age of Enlightenment/Kraemer
BIS SACD 1436 (1 SACD). Recorded 2005.

Sacred vocal music

Handel's first surviving music for the church comes from the time he spent in Rome as a young man, although the recently discovered *Gloria* may well date from before that. After he settled in London, Handel wrote sacred music intermittently, and mainly for state occasions, for the rest of his life, beginning with the *Utrecht Te Deum* and *Jubilate* in 1713. He also had a brief period of concentrated composition of sacred anthems while he was employed by the Duke of Chandos between 1717 and 1718.

The survey below covers the main sacred works. In addition there are a few additional anthems, seven German Church Cantatas, and a selection of hymns – notable among these is the tune to *Rejoice, the Lord is King*, composed *c.* 1747 to words by Charles Wesley, and still in popular use today.

Latin church music

Gloria in excelsis Deo

This work only came to light in 2000 in the library of the Royal Academy of Music, London, bound in a volume of vocal arias donated to the Academy in the early nineteenth century. The manuscript is not in Handel's hand, but the work has been verified by the German scholar, Hans Joachim Marx. Handel may have composed it as a young man in Germany before he left for Italy. It is scored for solo soprano, two violins and continuo, and has all the freshness and brio of Handel's early music. Handel later borrowed from it for *Laudate pueri dominum*, and the *Utrecht Jubilate*.

⋔ *Gloria* (and *Dixit Dominus*)
Kirkby/Royal Academy of Music Baroque Orchestra/Cummings
BIS CD-1235 (1 CD) Recorded 1986 and 2001

Dixit Dominus, HWV 232

This setting of Psalm 110 is extraordinarily extrovert and grand. What a supremely confident composer the young Handel was, newly arrived in Rome! He completed *Dixit Dominus* in April 1707 and dated the manuscript (the earliest of his to have survived). In form it is a sacred cantata in nine movements, for two soloists, chorus and orchestra. With hindsight, the opening text is curiously prophetic: 'The Lord said unto my Lord: sit thou on my right hand, until I make thine enemies thy foot-stool'. As yet there were no enemies for Handel, but there would be later when rivalries and resentments set in. For now, with this vigorous and exhilarating calling-card he threw down the gauntlet to the Italians, and it soon paid off as he attracted powerful patrons and his fame began to spread.

🎧 *Dixit Dominus* (and *Gloria*, and Vivaldi's *Gloria*)
Kazimierczuk/Ross/Deam/Fuge/Humphries/Wyn Roberts/O'Connor/Burt/Clarkson
Monteverdi Choir/English Baroque Soloists/Gardiner
Philips 462 597-2 (1 CD). Recorded 1998 and 2001.

***Laudate pueri dominum*, HWV 237 (Psalm 113)**
***Te decus virgineum*, HWV 243 (Antiphon)**
***Nisi Dominus*, HWV 238 (Psalm setting)**
***Haec est regina virginum*, HWV 235 (Antiphon)**
***Saeviat tellus inter rigores*, HWV 240 (Motet)**
***Salve regina*, HWV 241 (Antiphon)**

These six works, plus *Dixit Dominus*, HWV 232 (see above), were grouped together on a recording in 1987 as the 'Second Vespers of the Feast of Our Lady of Mount Carmel', composed by Handel in Rome in 1707. The theory that they were actually performed together in those circumstances has since been challenged, but nevertheless the grouping offers the listener an opportunity to hear a representative cross-section of the sacred vocal music that Handel composed during his Roman period. In their different ways, all of these works demonstrate his suppleness of response to the texts and inexhaustible variety of musical imagination. Not to be missed!

🎧 Carmelite Vespers 1707
Feldman/Kirkby/Van Evera/Cable/Nichols/Cornwell/Thomas
Taverner Choir and Players/Parrott
Virgin Veritas 7243 5 61579 2 (2 CDs). Recorded 1987.

***Silete venti*, HWV 242**

Little is known about the circumstances in which Handel composed this solo motet. Even the text – a meditation on the soul's love for Jesus – is anonymous and has no obvious liturgical function. In style, *Silete venti* follows the model of the many chamber cantatas which Handel had written in Italy as a young man. It probably dates, however, from the 1720s, and

possibly from a visit to Venice in 1729. Whatever its prove-
nance, this is one of Handel's most impressive solo vocal
works – radiant and thrilling – and not surprisingly he borrowed from it several times later. The five short movements
begin with an orchestral Symphonia, which is dramatically
interrupted by the soprano – 'Silete venti!' (Silence, winds!
Cease your rustling, leaves, for my soul reposes in sweetness)
– and a joyful Alleluia concludes the work.

⌒ *Silete Venti* (and *Nisi Dominus*, and *Dixit Dominus*)
Dawson/Sixteen Choir and Orchestra/Christophers
Chandos CHAN 0517 (1 CD). Recorded 1989.

English church music

Chandos Anthems, HWV 246–256a

Handel composed eleven anthems for James Brydges, Duke
of Chandos, between 1717 and 1718 (see the chapter
'Handel's life'). Brydges was rebuilding his sumptuous
mansion, Cannons, at Edgware in North London, and he
eventually built a private chapel. Meanwhile the *Chandos
Anthems* and a *Te Deum* (HWV 281) were performed at the
nearby church of Saint Lawrence, Whitchurch. The Anthems
are for chorus, a range of soloists, and small orchestra. The
texts are from the 1662 *Book of Common Prayer* version of the
Psalms, and the *New Version of the Psalms* (1696) by Nahum
Tate and Nicolas Brady:

1. O be joyful in the Lord, HWV 246
2. In the Lord put I my trust, HWV 247
3. Have mercy upon me, O God, HWV 248
4. O sing unto the Lord a new song!, HWV 249b
5. I will magnify thee, O God my King, HWV 250a
6. As pants the hart for cooling streams, HWV 251b
7. My song shall be alway, HWV 252
8. O come, let us sing unto the Lord, HWV 253
9. O praise the Lord with one consent, HWV 254
10. The Lord is my light and my salvation, HWV 255
11. Let God arise, HWV 256a

Brydges, in a letter to the physician and writer Dr Arbuthnot in 1717, reported that he had received from Handel 'two new anthems, very noble ones, and most think they far exceed the two first', and music historian John Hawkins judged that Handel

> . . . seems to have disdained all imitation, and to have looked with contempt on those pure and elegant models for the church style, the motets of Palestrina, Allegri, and Foggia . . . for these he thought, and would sometimes say, were stiff, and void of that sweetness of melody, which he looked upon to be essential as well to choral as to theatrical music; much less would he vouchsafe an imitation of those milder beauties which shine so conspicuously in the anthems of the English composers for the church, namely Tallis, Byrd, Gibbons, and others . . . in short, such was the sublimity of his genius, and the copiousness of his invention, that he was persuaded of his ability to form a style of his own: he made the experiment, and it succeeded.

'Milder beauties' these anthems certainly are not. Although there are some gently expressive movements, the overall effect is of a virile, multi-coloured response to the carefully chosen Biblical texts. The many choruses, in particular, are a foretaste of the riches to come in the later oratorios: indeed 'Tell it out among the Heathen', in No. 8, which Handel soon reused in an anthem for the Chapel Royal, reappears to thrilling effect in *Belshazzar*. Handel also borrowed from some of his earlier works – the deeply affecting No. 6, 'As pants the hart', for example, was a reworking of an earlier anthem for the Chapel Royal (see below). It is ironic that while Brydges was lavishing large sums of money on Cannons, Handel had to make do with reduced forces for most of these anthems – no violas and no alto voices – but while the glories of Cannons have long disappeared, these endlessly inventive works live on. They deserve to be much more widely performed and recorded.

🎧 *Chandos Anthems* 1–11
Dawson/Kwella/Bowman/Partridge/George
The Sixteen Choir and Orchestra/Christophers
Chandos CHAN 0554-7 (4 CDs). Recorded 1997, 1998 and 1999.

Coronation Anthems, HWV 258–61
Zadok the Priest
Let thy Hand be Strengthened
The King shall Rejoice
My Heart is Inditing

Handel enjoyed a privileged position in relation to royalty. He was not encumbered with an official, salaried position as a composer that would have required him to produce music whenever required, but he did receive royal pensions and was a familiar and valued figure at court. No doubt, given his fiercely independent spirit, this was exactly how he liked it. But when King George I died suddenly in June 1727, George II and Queen Caroline did ask him (rather than John Eccles who was Master of the King's Music) to compose new music for their coronation at Westminster Abbey on 11 October. Handel agreed, but when he was sent suitable texts by the bishops responsible for the coronation, according to Charles Burney, he 'took offence, as he thought it implied his ignorance of the Holy Scriptures: "I have read my Bible very well, and shall chuse for myself," he replied grumpily'. The result was four anthems, each one for a significant moment in the ceremony: *Let thy Hand be Strengthened* came first, at the Recognition, when the King was first presented to congregation; then *Zadok the Priest*, for the Anointing; *The King shall Rejoice*, for the moment the King was crowned; and *My Heart is Inditing*, for the Queen's crowning. Handel perfectly judged the different nuances of each of these key moments, producing marvellously supple music which has lost none of its power to stir and move the listener. It is yet another effortless demonstration of how Handel stood head and shoulders above his contemporaries. King George and

Queen Caroline knew exactly what they were doing when they commissioned him, even if, by all accounts, the performances on the day left something to be desired. Nevertheless, *Zadok* has been performed at every subsequent British coronation, and Handel – never one to let good music languish in obscurity – later recycled most of the anthems in his oratorios *Esther* and *Deborah*.

⋒ *Coronation Anthems* (and *Concerti a due cori* Nos. 2 and 3)
Choir of Westminster Abbey/English Concert/Preston
Archiv 447 280-2 (1 CD). Recorded 1981.
⋒ *Coronation Anthems* (and *Dixit Dominus, Foundling Hospital Anthem*, and *Utrecht Te Deum* and *Jubilate*)
Choir of King's College, Cambridge/Willcocks
Decca 455 041 2 (2 CDs). Recorded 1963.
The classic recording by the Choir of King's College, Cambridge, conducted by Sir David Willcocks, is now over forty-five years old, but still worth considering, and is currently packaged with some other recommendable recordings of Handel's sacred vocal works. Note that *Dixit Dominus* is performed by the Choir of King's College, Cambridge/Cleobury; the *Foundling Hospital Anthem* by the Choir of Winchester Cathedral/Hill; and the *Utrecht Te Deum* and *Jubilate* by the Choir of Christ Church Cathedral, Oxford/Preston.
⋒ The Coronation of King George II, 1727
The Choir of the King's Consort/The King's Consort/King
Hyperion CDA 67286 (2 CDs). Recorded 2001.
This recording, researched and conducted by Robert King, places the *Coronation Anthems* in their original liturgical context, alongside music by Purcell, Blow, Tallis, and Gibbons, and the evocative sounds of tolling cathedral bells, trumpet fanfares and drum processions.

Foundling Hospital Anthem, HWV 268
Handel was an active supporter of the Foundling Hospital charity (or the Society for the Maintenance and Education of

Exposed and Deserted Young Children, to give it its full title)
during the final decade of his life. From 1750 onwards he gave
an annual benefit performance of *Messiah* for the Foundling
Hospital, and eventually bequeathed it a fair copy of the score,
which was made by his assistant John Christopher Smith, the
younger, shortly after Handel's death in 1759. At the outset of
his involvement with the Foundling Hospital, Handel composed a new anthem, which was the final item of his first benefit concert to raise money for a new Hospital chapel on 27
May 1749. Handel chose the various biblical texts himself,
opening with the words, 'Blessed are they that considereth the
poor', from Psalm 41, which set the style and mood of the
work. For the final movement, however, he used the
'Hallelujah' chorus from *Messiah*, and it heralded that work's
connection to the Foundling Hospital. Indeed, the first version of the Foundling Hospital Anthem most likely only comprised the choral movements with orchestra, and Handel
added the movements which involve the four soloists later –
maybe for the official opening of the chapel in April 1753.

♫ *Foundling Hospital Anthem* (and *Coronation Anthems*)
Fisher/Crabtree/Brett/Elwes
Choir of Winchester Cathedral/Brandenburg Consort/Hill
Argo 440 946-2 (1 CD), Recorded 1993.

Funeral Anthem for Queen Caroline, HWV 264
(*The Ways of Zion do Mourn*)
This is one of Handel's most deeply affecting works, imbued
with rich, dark colours. Queen Caroline was a great lover of
music and supporter of Handel, so he would have felt her loss
personally. She died on 20 November 1737 and was buried
in Westminster Abbey on 17 December. Handel's anthem,
which lasts over forty minutes, was composed within a week
in early December and performed at the end of the service.
'The composition was exceedingly fine, and adapted very
properly to the melancholy occasion', commented Handel's
former patron, the Duke of Chandos. What the Duke may or
may not have noticed were the subtle musical references

throughout to Caroline's German ancestry, including quotations of Lutheran chorale melodies, which give the work at times a rather archaic quality. The biblical texts of the eleven movements were chosen by Edward Willes, Sub-dean of the Abbey, beginning with 'The ways of Zion do mourn', from Lamentations. Nine of the movements are for chorus and orchestra, and Handel introduces four soloists for 'The righteous shall be had in everlasting remembrance' and 'They shall receive a glorious kingdom'. He later added an introductory orchestral *sinfonia*, and reused the entire work as Part I of his oratorio *Israel in Egypt*: 'The Lamentation of the Israelites for the Death of Joseph'.

♫ *Funeral Anthem for Queen Caroline*
(and *Te Deum for Queen Caroline*, HWV 280)
Van Der Sluis/Pushee/Van Berne/Van Der Kamp
Alsfelder Vokalensemble/Brockorchester Bremen/Helbich
CPO 999 244-2 (1 CD). Recorded 1993.

Utrecht Te Deum, HWV 278
Utrecht Jubilate, HWV 279
The Treaty of Utrecht brought to a favourable conclusion Britain's involvement in the War of Spanish Succession (among other things, Britain gained sovereignty over Gibraltar). Peace was finally proclaimed on 5 May 1713 and celebrations were held in St Paul's Cathedral on 7 July. Handel was ready with a festive *Te Deum* and *Jubilate*, both of which were performed during the service. In fact, shrewd operator that he was, Handel had been ready for some time, having completed the *Te Deum* back in January. He had followed that in February with the *Ode for the Birthday of Queen Anne*, and he completed the *Jubilate* the same month. It was all part of his plan to make a career for himself in England, which would of course be easier if he was also accepted at court – and indeed the Queen awarded him a pension of two hundred pounds per year in December 1713. Handel cleverly referred to existing models for his *Te Deum* and *Jubilate*, particularly those by Purcell, still regularly sung

on special occasions, but the resulting works are flamboyantly his own. The scoring is for five soloists, five-part chorus, and an orchestra that includes timpani and trumpets, for grand effect. These two Latin hymns had been incorporated into the English Prayer Book by the Anglican Church after the split from Rome at the Reformation, and Handel set them in translation: 'We praise thee, O God', and 'O be joyful In the Lord'. He divided them into eight movements and six movements respectively, alternating soloists and chorus, and sensitively balancing the mood and effect of each movement to the words of the text. Charles Burney later commented:

> The grand *Te Deum* and *Jubilate*, which he set on this occasion, were composed with such force, regularity, and instrumental effects, as the English had never heard before. Purcell's *Te Deum*, in design, and expression of the words, is perhaps, superior to all others; but in grandeur and richness of accompaniment, nothing but national partiality can deny Handel the preference.

♫ *Utrecht Te Deum* and *Jubilate* (and *Ode for the Birthday of Queen Anne*, *Foundling Hospital Anthem*, and *Alceste* incidental music)
Kirkby/Nelson/Brett/Covey-Crump/Elliott/Thomas
Choir of Christ Church Cathedral, Oxford/Academy of Ancient Music/Preston
Decca 458 072-2 (2 CDs). Recorded 1979 (*Utrecht Te Deum* and *Jubilate*).

Dettingen Anthem, HWV 265
Dettingen Te Deum, HWV 283

On 27 June 1743 King George II led his army to victory against the French at Dettingen, in south-west Germany. In the event, this was only one of a whole series of battles to be fought in the War of Austrian Succession, which was not resolved for another five years until the treaty of Aix-la-Chapelle in October 1748. But Handel seized the chance to compose a grand, celebratory *Te Deum* and an accompanying *anthem* for the King's return. Given the size of the work, and large forces employed, he may well have been expecting a great public ceremony of thanksgiving, but these were politically uneasy times and the King did not return to England until November. It was therefore exactly five months after the Battle of Dettingen, on 27 November, that the two works received their first performance in the more modest surroundings of the Chapel Royal – no doubt the *Te Deum* raised the roof! The gentler *Dettingen Anthem* includes new settings of texts already used in the *Coronation Anthems* ('The King shall rejoice', and 'Exceeding glad shall he be'), and would have fared rather better in the Chapel's intimate acoustic. What is so striking about the *Te Deum* is that although it begins in bright, primary colours with all the bombast and noise of victory, as it goes on, while retaining the grandeur, more muted shades also appear, the music becomes more detailed, and it ends simply and prayerfully: 'O Lord, in Thee have I trusted'. A lesser composer would never have looked for such subtlety in a public piece – although even kings need to learn humility!

♫ *Dettingen Te Deum* and *Dettingen Anthem*
Varcoe/Tipping/Christophers/Pearce/Choir of Westminster Abbey/English Concert/Pinnock/Preston
Archiv 410 647-2 (1 CD). Recorded 1982 and 1983.
♫ *Dettingen Te Deum* (and *Zadok the Priest*, Organ Concerto No. 14)
Davies/Marlow/Choir of Trinity College, Cambridge/Academy of Ancient Music/Layton
Hyperion CDA 67678 (1 CD). Recorded 2007.

Among a number of other shorter, occasional anthems which Handel composed for various occasions, are four for the choir and musicians of the Chapel Royal at St. James's Palace: *I Will Magnify Thee*, HWV 250b, *As Pants the Hart*, HWV 251a and 251d, *O Sing Unto the Lord a New Song*, HWV 249a, and *Let God Arise*, HWV 256b. Handel was appointed 'Composer of

Musick' to the Chapel Royal in February 1723 and granted a further royal pension. Perhaps the best of these anthems, imaginative and beautifully responsive to the text of Psalm 42, is *As Pants the Hart*, HWV 251d, which dates from *c.*1722 (there are also three other versions of this anthem, HWV 251a, b and c).

♫ Music for the Chapel Royal
Choir of the Chapel Royal/Musicians Extra-ordinary/Gant
Naxos 8.557935 (1 CD). Recorded 2005.

A more recent reminder of the splendour of these sacred vocal works and their contribution to special occasions is preserved on a recording of the Handel Tercentenary Concert given at Westminster Abbey on 23 February 1985. There are extracts from the *Coronation Anthems*, the *Ode for the Birthday of Queen Anne*, the *Funeral Anthem for Queen Caroline*, and the *Utrecht Jubilate*, along with 'Waft her, angels, to the skies' from *Jephtha*, the 'Hallelujah' chorus from *Messiah*, the first *Concerto a due cori*, and the Organ Concerto, Op. 7 No. 5.

♫ Handel Tercentenary Concert
Tinsley/Rolfe-Johnson/Bowman/Wilson-Johnson/Preston/
Steele-Perkins
London Philharmonic Choir/Westminster Abbey Choir
English Chamber Orchestra/Leppard
BBC Radio Classics 15656 91522 / IMP LC 3007 (1 CD).
Recorded 1985.

Secular vocal music

There is an enormous amount of secular vocal music by Handel for all sorts of combinations of voices and instruments, and using at least five languages: Italian, English, French, Spanish, and German. Of prime importance, and abounding in glorious music, are the Italian cantatas.

Italian cantatas

Italy was Handel's finishing school and the Italian cantatas mark an important stage in the perfecting of his career as a dramatic composer. Winton Dean claims that 'almost all the cantatas might be viewed as scenes from unwritten stage works', and certainly in composing so many of them he amassed a huge stockpile of music from which he could and did borrow freely for his later operas. It is arguable whether Italy really gave Handel more practical skill as a composer – so much of that was innate and already developed in Halle and Hamburg – but Italy did give him style, and the understanding of how best to use his talents. And in return he also had something to offer the Italians. As John Mainwaring, Handel's first biographer, put it:

> I think it is highly probable, that whatever delicacies appear in Handel's music, are owing to his journey into Italy; and likewise that the Italians are much indebted to him for their management of the instrumental parts that accompany the voice.

The solo voice cantata had long been a popular genre in Italy, and its undisputed master was Alessandro Scarlatti. In Rome, where successive popes had closed the opera houses, cantatas were composed for performance at private, evening gatherings of the aristocracy. In effect this was a clever ploy to get round the ban on public opera, because the cantatas are certainly dramatic, though usually written for only one voice. Handel's patrons, the Cardinals Pamphili and Ottobone, and the Marquis Ruspoli, were members of these 'Arcadian Academies', as they were called, and while Handel was 'composer in residence' in Ruspoli's two mansions, the Bonelli Palace in Rome and a country estate at Vignanello, north of the capital, he was 'desired to furnish his quota' of cantatas, as John Mainwaring put it. Handel seized the task with relish and probably contributed at least eighty canatas during his time in Italy, between 1706 and 1710. Most of them are for solo voice and continuo, often also with obbligato instruments (e.g. violin, flute, or oboe) dueting with the voice. Each is generally around ten minutes in length – although there are some notable longer ones, like *Clori, Tirsi e Fileno* – and alternates recitatives and *da capo* arias. They are mainly on classical subjects drawn from Greek antiquity, chiefly about the joys and sorrows of love, and Handel usually plays up the dramatic aspects of each story – his cantatas are definitely headed for the theatre! And of course during the same period Handel did write an opera for Florence (*Rodrigo*, 1707) and one for Venice (*Agrippina*, 1709) – two Italian cities that were outside the Pope's immediate jurisdiction.

A complete survey of these cantatas is beyond the scope of this book, but there are many lovely works to explore. Here are brief notes on ten representative cantatas that have been recorded (coupled with others) by singers who excel in this intimate and dramatic art, beginning with Janet Baker and including Ann Murray, Lorraine Hunt Lieberson, Natalie Dessay, Véronique Gens, Gérard Lesne, Magdalena Kožená, and Emma Kirkby.

Ah! crudel, nel pianto mio, HWV 78

This cantata was probably composed in August 1708 and performed the following month at the Palazzo Bonelli in Rome, home of the Marquis Ruspoli. The text is about unrequited love, with the singer moving from despair, to accusation, and finally to hope that constancy may yet be rewarded.

ᴖ Bach and Handel Solo Cantatas
(*Ah! crudel nel pianto mio* and *Armida abbandonata*, arr. Leppard)
Baker/ECO/Leppard
EMI 7243 5 74284 2 (2 CDs). Recorded 1967.

Clori, Tirsi e Fileno (*Cor fedele*), HWV 96

Composed in Rome in September or October 1707, for the Marquis Ruspoli, just before Handel left to go to Florence for the premiere of his opera *Rodrigo*, this is the most extended and grandest of the cantatas of this period. The story tells of the pretty shepherdess, Clori, who continually puts off choosing between two shepherds, Tirsi and Fileno – both love her, but are also exasperated by her!

🎧 *Clori, Tirsi e Fileno*
Hunt/Feldman/Minter
Philharmonia Baroque Orchestra/McGegan
Harmonia Mundi HMU 907045 (1 CD). Recorded 1990.

Il delirio amoroso (Da quel giorno fatale), HWV 99

This was possibly the first cantata that Handel composed in Rome, in January 1707, to a text by Cardinal Pamphili, and performed at his *palazzo* in May that year. It describes the anguish of the young maiden, Clori, at the death of her lover, Tirsi.

🎧 Handel: *Delirio* (*Il Delirio amoroso*, extract from *Aci, Galatea e Polifemo* and *Mi palpita il cor*)
Dessay/Le Concert d'Astrée/Haïm
Virgin Classics 0946 332624 2 (1 CD). Recorded 2005.

Armida abbandonata (Dietro l'orme fugaci), HWV 105

The story comes from the poet Tasso, about the sorceress Armida, abandoned by the crusader, Rinaldo, and torn between her desire for vengeance and her continuing love for him. Handel probably composed and performed it during the same month, June 1707, at the Palazzo Bonelli.

🎧 *Delirio Amoroso* – Italian Secular Cantatas (*Clori, mia bella Clori, Armida abbandonata*, and *Il Delirio Amoroso*)
Murray/The Symphony of Harmony and Invention/Christophers
Coro COR 16030 (1 CD). Recorded 1997.

Agrippina condotta a morire (Dunque sarà pur vero), HWV 110

The precise date of composition is unclear, and the text is anonymous, but this cantata was probably performed in Rome in 1708 by the soprano castrato, Pasqualino Tiepoli. The subject is the anger and despair of the famous Roman empress Agrippina. Her machinations helped to put her son, Nero, on the throne, but now he has turned on her and condemned her to death.

ဘ Three Cantatas (*La Lucrezia*, *Armida abbandonata*, and *Agrippina condotta a morire*)
Gens/Les Basses Réunies
Virgin Veritas (1 CD). Recorded 1998.

Apollo e Dafne (La terra è liberata), HWV 122

This dramatic cantata, composed towards the end of Handel's time in Italy, was probably not completed until he returned to Hamburg in 1710. The anonymous text is based on Ovid's *Metamorphoses* and tells of the unrequited love of the god, Apollo, for the nymph, Daphne, who is eventually transformed into a laurel tree as a means of escaping his advances. Handel set it for soprano and bass, with wind, strings and continuo. This is absolutely an opera in miniature (it lasts just over half an hour), full of confident and varied music – the young Handel in absolute control of his art.

ဘ *Apollo e Dafne* (and *Silete venti*)
Gauvin/Braun
Les Violons du Roy/Labadie
Dorian xCD-90288 (1 CD). Recorded 2000.

Mi palpita il cor, HWV 132c

There are three versions of this cantata, each with different solo instruments: oboe, HWV 132b; flute, HWV 132c; and flute and oboe, HWV 132d. HWV 132c seems to be the earliest of the three, composed soon after Handel moved to London in 1710. The anonymous text tells of a young man who anguishes over whether his beloved Cloris will return his love or not.

ဘ Cantatas for Alto Solo (*Splenda l'alba in oriente*, *La Lucrezia*, *Mi palpita il cor*, and *Carco sempre di Gloria*)
Lesne/Il Seminario Musicale
Virgin Classics 0777 7590592 2 (1 CD). Recorded 1990.

La Lucrezia (O numi eterni), HWV 145

One of Handel's most striking cantatas, composed in 1708, probably for the soprano, Margherita Durastanti, who would later become one of the star singers in his London operas. Set in Ancient Rome, the text by Cardinal Pamphili recounts the aftermath of the legend of the Rape of Lucrezia. In a passionate monologue, Lucrezia rails against her attacker, Tarquinius, and calls for vengeance.

⋒ Handel Arias
La Lucrezia, and extracts from *Theodora* and *Serse*
Hunt Lieberson/OAE/Bicket
Avie AV 0030 (1 CD). Recorded 2003 and 2004.

Tra le fiamme, HWV 170

Cardinal Pamphili again provided the text for this cantata, composed in Rome in 1707 or 1708. A lover is likened to a moth fatally drawn towards the light of a flame, or to Icarus who flew too near to the sun.

⋒ Handel: Italian Cantatas (*Il Delirio amoroso*, *La Lucrezia*, and *Tra le fiamme*)
Kožená/Les Musiciens du Louvre/Minkowski
Archiv 469 065-2 (1 CD). Recorded 1999.

Tu fedel? tu constante?, HWV 171

One of his earliest cantatas, Handel probably began composing it in Florence and completed it in Rome in 1707. The subject is a woman's rejection of her inconstant lover, and the original singer was probably once again the fiery Margherita Durastanti.

⋒ Italian Cantatas (*Tu fedel? tu costante?*, *Mi palpita il cor*, *Alpestre monte*, and *Tra le fiamme*)
Kirkby/Academy of Ancient Music/Hogwood
L'Oiseau-Lyre 414 473-2 (1 CD). Recorded 1985.

Italian duets

Alongside his Italian cantatas, Handel composed a series of vocal duets – there are twenty of these listed in the HWV

Catalogue. Lightly accompanied by continuo instruments, they were intended for performance at intimate musical gatherings, and they owe something to the duets of Handel's older Italian contemporary, Agostino Steffani. Handel seems to have composed them at various times between 1706 and 1745: some in Italy, some in Hanover, and the remainder in London. Like the solo cantatas, the texts deal mainly with the joys and sorrows of love – made more direct by the involvement of two voices. They are beguiling miniatures, ranging widely in mood and style. As John Mainwaring observed:

> They were composed in the vigour of his faculties, not for the theatre, but for the closet. Nothing was to be sacrificed to the rude, undiscerning ear of the multitude; nor were invention and harmony to be given up for the poor purchase of an encore.

A good way to sample these duets is on a recent CD which brings together a representative selection of nine of them, including the two that were recycled for inclusion in *Messiah: Nò, di voi non vo' fidarmi* and *Quel fior che all'alba ride*.

Ahi, nelle sorti umane, HWV 179
Nò, di voi non vo' fidarmi, HWV 189
Caro autor di mia doglia, HWV 182a
Quel fior che all'alba ride, HWV 192
Conservate, raddoppiate, HWV 185
Tanti strali al sen mi scocchi, HWV 197
Va', speme infida, HWV 199
A mirarvi io son intento, HWV 178
Sono liete, fortunate, HWV 194

♫ Arcadian Duets
Claycomb/Dessay/Gens/Lascarro/Panzarella/Petibon/
Mijanovic/Mingardo/Asawa/Agnew
Le Concert d'Astrée/Haïm
Virgin Veritas 7243 5 45524 2 (1 CD). Recorded 2001 and 2002.

Two other duets are included on a vintage recital from Janet Baker and Dietrich Fisher-Dieskau: *Giù nei Tartarei regni*, HWV 187 and *Quando in calma ride il mare*, HVV 191.

🎧 Janet Baker with Dietrich Fischer-Dieskau (*Giù nei Tarterei, Quando in calma ride il mare*, and music by A. Scarlatti, D. Scarlatti, Monteverdi, and Lawes)
Baker/Fischer-Dieskau/ECO/Leppard
Testament SBT 1321 (1 CD). Recorded 1970.

German arias, HWV 202–10

These arias are both a Handel rarity and a Handel mystery. He set very few texts in his native German and it is not known for sure why he chose these particular poems by Barthold Heinrich Brockes, who was a contemporary of Handel's at the University of Halle. It seems likely that Handel had further contact with Brockes in Hamburg after setting his German Passion in 1716, and would therefore have received a copy of a collection of Brockes's poems published in 1721 and reprinted in 1724. Scholars examining the music paper that Handel used have deduced that he wrote the arias in three batches (two plus five plus two) in London between 1724 and 1726. Brockes' poetry delights in the God of creation: 'Singe, Seele, Gott zum Preise', begins the fifth aria – 'Sing, my soul, in praise of God, / Who in so wise a manner / Makes all the world so beautiful'. Handel responds sympathetically to all these texts, with music of great delicacy. 'Süsser Stille, sanfte Quelle' is perhaps the most beautiful, but each of the arias is worth exploring. They are reflective, chamber works, scored for a solo soprano, with a violin dueting gracefully with the voice, and continuo.

🎧 Nine German Arias (and Three Oboe Sonatas)
Sampson/Degand/King's Consort
Hyperion CDA 67627 (1 CD). Recorded 2006.

A CD with soprano Emma Kirkby and tenor Charles Daniels offers an ideal way to explore some of Handel's shorter and lighter vocal pieces, composed in a variety of languages. It includes the charming sequence of French airs, *Sans y penser*, HWV 155, like a miniature French cantata from the court of Louis XIV, composed for the Marquis Ruspoli in Rome in 1707, and a selection of mainly English songs, plus one each in German and Spanish.

⌒ The Occasional Songs
Kirkby/Daniels/Miller/Sharman/Nicholson
Somm SOMMCD 226 (1 CD). Recorded 2000.

Finally, a curiosity: a collection of three 'English Cantatas' (classed as 'doubtful and spurious' by *The New Grove Dictionary of Music and Musicians*) and seven English songs (probably by Handel), recorded by The Brook Street Band. Nothing definite is known about the history of the cantatas – *So Pleasing the Pain is*, *With Roving and with Ranging*, and *To Lonely Shades* (none of them is in the HWV catalogue) – but each consists of music from existing Italian arias (there are no recitatives) taken from the operas *Flavio*, *Ottone* and *Giulio Cesare* and put to new (anonymous) English texts on the subject of love, with reduced instrumentation for two violins and continuo. Intriguing!

⌒ Handel's English Cantatas
Kennedy/Bruce-Payne/The Brook Street Band
Avie AV 2153 (2 CDs). Recorded 2008.

Orchestral music

Handel learned his mastery of the orchestra in the opera house and most of his orchestral music is bound up in some way or another with the theatre. No surprise then to find that it is flamboyant and exciting – and often frustrating, because its origins and definitive forms are frequently elusive. Stanley Sadie began his *BBC Music Guide* on Handel's concertos with one of the most perceptive judgements you will ever read about the composer. Commenting on Handel's 'dependence on circumstances, his readiness to rely on his freedom of invention and his gift for happy caprice', Sadie makes the point that it is often hard to identify a 'definitive' version of a work. He goes on: 'We have to solve this problem as best we can in each case, and learn to put up with Handel's large-scale carelessness, recognising that it is all an integral part of a genius which operated exclusively on a large scale, and which disdained to concern itself with minutiae.'

Handel's first biographer, John Mainwaring, made a similar point:

> In his music for instruments there are the same marks of a great genius [as in his vocal music], and likewise some instances of great negligence. He often attended more to the effect of the whole, than to the artificial contexture of the parts, for which Geminiani is so justly admired. In his fugues and overtures he is quite original. The style of them is peculiar to himself, and no way like that of any master before him. In the formation of these pieces, knowledge and invention seem to have contended for the mastery.

The survey below covers the main orchestral works, but as always with Handel there are other things to be discovered – an overture here, a sinfonia there, an isolated allegro, or gigue, or hornpipe etc. – rich pickings from Handel's 'large-scale carelessness', and they turn up from time to time as fillers on CDs.

Orchestral concertos

Concerti Grossi, Op. 3
No. 1 in B flat major, HWV 312
No. 2 in B flat major, HWV 313
No. 3 in G major, HWV 314
No. 4 in F major, HWV 315
No. 5 in D minor, HWV 316
No. 6 in D major, HWV 317

The music publisher John Walsh seems to have been mainly responsible for assembling these works as Handel's Op. 3 – just as he had been for the Op. 1 Solo Sonatas and the Op. 2 Trio Sonatas. Handel never composed any purely free-standing orchestral works (unlike Corelli, for example), so these concertos originally functioned as interludes to his operas and oratorios, and also borrowed music from them and from other works. They were popularly called 'Oboe Concertos' during Handel's lifetime, which was rather misleading, but the *concerto grosso*, made popular particularly by Corelli, was essentially a form which contrasted a *concertino* small group of instruments, with a larger *ripieno* group – and Handel often liked to have oboes in his *concertino*.

In an age of publishing piracy and scant control of copyright, it is likely that Handel had nothing to do with the first edition of Op. 3 in 1734. The opportunist publisher, John Walsh, decided that there was money to be made out of a collection of concertos by Handel – the genre was very popular, with Corelli leading the field – and he set about assembling a set from instrumental movements in various works. No matter that the expectation would be for works for strings only (as Corelli's were), because Handel had not actually written any. Once Handel became aware of the publication of Op. 3, however, he did immediately negotiate with Walsh to replace a spurious, anonymous work (given as Concerto No. 4) with an authentic one for the reprinted edition a few months later. (Both No. 4 Concertos can be heard on the Goodman recording.) So these concertos are something of a ragbag, but the music in them is great – and it is now all by Handel!

No. 1 is scored for two recorders, two oboes, two bassoons, strings and continuo, and is probably the earliest of the set, dating from Handel's first years in London *c*.1710, or possibly even before that in Hanover. No. 2 is scored for two oboes, one bassoon, strings and continuo, and shares some material with the *Brockes Passion*, composed *c*.1716. No. 3 is scored for either flute or oboe, strings and continuo, and was most likely compiled and transcribed – badly! – by Walsh, using movements from the *Chandos Anthems* and *Te Deum* and a

keyboard fugue composed around the same time, *c.*1717–18.
Modern editions and recordings have corrected Walsh's
errors. No. 4 is scored for two oboes, one bassoon, strings and
continuo, and was probably composed for a benefit performance of the opera *Amadigi*, on 20 June 1716, and played in one
of the breaks between the acts. No. 5 is scored for one oboe,
one bassoon, strings and continuo, and as with No. 3, some of
the material comes from the *Chandos Anthems* – but this concerto was assembled by Handel, not Walsh, some time before
1727, when there is a dated manuscript version of it. No. 6 is
scored for one flute, two oboes, one bassoon, strings and continuo, and has a chequered history. Walsh's original two-
movement version is now rarely played; instead, the complete
three-movement work, from which the first movement originally came, is substituted. This was composed *c.*1720–1, and
two movements were subsequently used in Handel's opera
Ottone (1722). Walsh's second movement turns out to have
been an organ concerto movement (and is recorded as an
appendix in the Goodman recording of the complete Organ
Concertos).

☊ Six Concerti Grossi, Op. 3
Brandenburg Consort/Goodman
Hyperion CDH 55075 (1 CD). Recorded 1992.
☊ Concerti Grossi, Op. 3
Handel and Haydn Society/Hogwood
L'Oiseau-Lyre 421 729-2 (1 CD). Recorded 1988.
☊ Concerti Grossi, Op. 3
English Baroque Soloists/Gardiner
Erato 2292-45981-2 (1 CD). Recorded 1980.

**Concerto Grosso in C major, 'Alexander's Feast',
HWV 318**
This work stands literally and metaphorically between the
Op. 3 and Op. 6 sets of *concerti grossi*. Handel completed it on
25 January 1736 and it was first performed the following
month on 19 February, between the two parts of the oratorio,
Alexander's Feast. Unlike the Op. 3 concerti, somewhat

randomly put together, this concerto follows the traditional form of the Italian *concerto grosso*, with a solo *concertino* group of two violins and cello, in dialogue with a larger *ripieno* group of strings – to which Handel adds two oboes for extra colour. He also reverses the traditional slow-fast-slow-fast progression of movements, ending with a delightful dance with a catchy rhythmic snap.

♩ HWV 318 with Concerti Grossi, Op. 6, Vol. 3
Collegium Musicum 90/Standage
CHAN 0622 (1 CD – Concerti 10–12 and HWV 318, 'Alexander's Feast'). Recorded 1997.
♩ *Ombra mai fù*
Arias from *Giulio Cesare*, *Admeto*, *Radamisto*, *Rodelinda*, *Serse*, *Alcina*, and Concerto Grosso, HWV 318, 'Alexander's Feast'
Scholl/Akademie für Alte Musik, Berlin
Harmonia Mundi HMC 901685 (1 CD). Recorded 1998.

Concerti Grossi, Op. 6
No. 1 in G major, HWV 319
No. 2 in F major, HWV 320
No. 3 in E minor, HWV 321
No. 4 in A minor, HWV 322
No. 5 in D major, HWV 323
No. 6 in G minor, HWV 324
No. 7 in B flat major, HWV 325
No. 8 in C minor, HWV 326
No. 9 in F major, HWV 327
No. 10 in D minor, HWV 328
No. 11 in A major, HWV 329
No. 12 in B minor, HWV 330

For this second set of concertos Handel himself took the initiative: having decided to compose completely original works, he worked at enormous speed. He began immediately after completing the *Ode for St Cecilia's Day* on 24 September 1739, finishing the twelve concerti just over a month later and dating the manuscripts of all but one of them as he completed them. The sequence of composition differs slightly from the published edition: No. 1 (completed 29 September), No. 2 (4 October), No. 3 (6 October), No. 4 (8 October), No. 5 (10 October), No. 7 (12 October), No. 6 (15 October), No. 8 (18 October), No. 12 (20 October), No. 10 (22 October), No. 9 (score undated – completed some time between 22 and 30 October), and No. 11 (30 October). Maybe because he was in a hurry to finish the set, Handel relied more heavily on borrowings from other works for the last two concerti (Nos. 9 and 11). In the months after composition, Handel premiered most of these concertos between the acts of his oratorios, although they were not individually identified. They were finally published by John Walsh in April 1740 as *Twelve Grand Concertos* – a literal English translation of the Italian *concerti grossi* – and as they were Handel's Op. 6 (although this only appeared on the title page for the second printing), the direct parallel with Corelli's famous Op. 6 set (published in 1714) would not have been lost on English audiences who had long delighted in those works. And indeed this time the scoring was for traditional, Corellian string forces, with a *concertino* group of two violins and a cello contrasted with the larger string ensemble (although Handel did also provide optional oboe parts for Nos. 1, 2, 5 and 6, doubling string lines in the *ripieno*). What is so extraordinary about these concerti is the inexhaustible variety of Handel's imagination. In just over two-and-a-half hours of music they offer a microcosm of his world. Everything is here – from noble overtures and heart-rending adagios, to buoyant allegros and vigorous fugues, while along the way a pleasantly rustic musette, a soothing air, or a witty hornpipe catches your ear with that easy gift for melody that makes Handel's music so memorable. Op. 6 is truly a Handelian treasure trove to explore at length and at leisure! Not surprisingly the comparison has often been made with Bach's set of 'Brandenburg' Concertos – another 'high-water mark' of the Baroque.

The music historian John Hawkins is worth quoting at this point, just because he is so spectacularly wrong:

As to these twelve Concertos, they appear to have been made in a hurry, and in the issue fell very short of answering the expectations that were formed of them, and inclined men to think that the composition of music merely instrumental, and of many parts, was not Handel's greatest excellence.

Would Hawkins stand by that view if he could now hear Andrew Manze's revelatory recording with the Academy of Ancient Music?

♩ Concerti Grossi, Op. 6
Academy of Ancient Music/Manze
Harmonia Mundi HMU 907228.29 (2 CDs). Recorded 1997.
Also HMX 2907228 (1 CD) a selection of 6 Concerti from the same recording: Nos. 1, 2, 3, 5, 10, 11
♩ Concerti Grossi, Op. 6 (Vols. 1–3)
Collegium Musicum 90/Standage
Chandos CHAN 0600 (1 CD – Concerti 1–5). Recorded 1996.
CHAN 0616 (1 CD – Concerti 6–9) Recorded 1997.
CHAN 0622 (1 CD – Concerti 10–12 and HWV 318, 'Alexander's Feast'). Recorded 1997.
♩ Concerti Grossi, Op. 6, *Fireworks Music* and *Water Music*
Orpheus Chamber Orchestra
DG 471 758-2 (3 CDs). Recorded 1990, 1993 and 1994.

Concerti a due cori
No. 1 in B flat major, HWV 332
No. 2 in F major, HWV 333
No. 3 in F major, HWV 334

The title refers to two 'choirs' of wind instruments that dialogue with each other and with the accompanying strings who form the the nucleus of the orchestra, binding everything together. No. 1 just has oboes and bassoon, while Nos. 2 and 3 add horns. As with the Organ Concertos and the Op. 6

Concerti Grossi, Handel seems to have composed these
concertos for performance between the various parts of his
oratorios. There is evidence that No. 3 was intended for *Judas
Maccabaeus* on 1 April 1747, and it is likely that No. 1 was for
Joshua on 9 March 1748 and No. 2 for *Alexander Balus*, later
the same month on 28 March. No. 3 also has the most original music of the set, while the first two are full of borrowed
music from Handel's earlier oratorios and operas – including
two choruses from *Messiah*: 'And the glory of the Lord' in
No. 1, and 'Lift up your heads' in No. 2. As always, what
Handel borrows, he also transforms, and these are exuberant
works, with the musical material tossed back and forth
between the two wind choirs. The *Allegro ma non troppo* of
No. 2 (which comes from *Esther*), with its leaping ground-
bass, is particularly memorable.

 Concerti a due cori (1–3)
Academy of Ancient Music/Hogwood
L'Oiseau-Lyre 411 721-2 (1 CD). Recorded 1983.
 Concerti a due cori (with *Music for the Royal Fireworks*)
English Concert/Pinnock
Archiv 415 129-2 (1 CD). Recorded 1984.

Instrumental concertos

Organ Concertos, Op. 4
No. 1 in G minor, HWV 289
No. 2 in B flat major, HWV 290
No. 3 in G minor, HWV 291
No. 4 in F major, HWV 292
No. 5 in F major, HWV 293
No. 6 in B flat major, HWV 294 (for organ or harp)

These works and the Op. 7 set bring us particularly close to
Handel because he composed them for himself to play (see the
chapter on 'Handel the performer'). In effect, he invented
the genre: before Handel, organ concertos did not exist. In the
1730s, when he began to promote oratorios in addition to his

opera productions, he created these works to play himself in the interludes between the various acts – thus keeping the audience entertained and maybe, in the absence of stage action, providing an extra enticement to buy tickets. Handel had always directed his works from the keyboard – a harpsichord for operas, and now an organ (to support the choir) for oratorios – and he would improvise on either instrument in his own inimitable style. So the concertos grew largely out of this art of improvisation, refined and formalised and provided with orchestral accompaniment. As John Hawkins put it:

> Finding that his own performance on the organ never failed to command the attention of his hearers, he set himself to compose, or rather, make up, concertos for that instrument, and uniformly interposed one in the course of the evening's performances.

Not, however, that the organ concertos all followed a particular pattern – far from it. One of the delights of both sets is just how dissimilar most of these concertos are. They manage to retain that elusive freedom of improvisation – no wonder that even if audiences did not appreciate a particular new oratorio, they would still be won over by the concerto, or concertos, played alongside it. And in an age of casual plagiarism, Handel was evidently concerned that when the Op. 4 set was published in 1738 – with the title *Six Concertos for the Harpsichord or the Organ* – they should have his own absolute authentication: 'These Six Concertos were publish'd by Mr. Walsh from my own Copy Corrected by my Self, and to him only have I given my Right therein'. Incidentally, the title page reference to 'Harpsichord or Organ' was a shrewd piece of salesmanship: many music lovers at the time would possess a harpsichord, but only a few would have access to an organ!

Concertos Nos. 2 and 3 were most likely composed first and performed with the oratorio *Esther* on 5 March 1735. Both of them make use of earlier material from the Op. 2 Trio Sonatas. No. 5, a reworking of the Recorder Sonata, Op. 1 No. 11, was probably then performed with a revival of

Deborah on 26 March the same year. The manuscript of No. 4 is dated 25 March and was given with *Athalia* on 1 April. No. 6, the most popular concerto of the set, was originally composed for harp and first performed with *Alexander's Feast* on 19 February 1736, along with No. 1, the last concerto to be composed, and in many ways the one that comes closest to reflecting the art of improvisation that lay behind it.

Richard Egarr calls the Op. 4 Concertos 'amazing, personal works' and his recent research into their possible ornamentation (preserved on an eighteenth-century barrel organ!) has resulted in a recording which completely re-evaluates these works. 'I tried to create cadential "noodling" afresh each time in concert and during the recording process', he writes. 'Handel's "amazing fullness, force, and energy" must be allowed to speak.' To quote John Hawkins again:

> Few but his intimate friends were sensible that on this instrument he had scarce his equal in the world; and he could not but be conscious that he possessed a style of performing on it that at least had the charm of novelty to recommend it.

🎧 Organ Concertos, Op. 4
Egarr/Academy of Ancient Music
Harmonia Mundi HMU 807446 (1 CD). Recorded 2006.
🎧 Organ Concertos, Op. 4
Van Asperen/OAE
Virgin Veritas 7243 5 45174 2 (1 CD). Recorded 1994.

Organ Concerto in F major (No. 13), 'The Cuckoo and the Nightingale', HWV 295
Organ Concerto in A major (No. 14), HWV 296a
Beware the confusion over Handel's organ concertos! Three sets were published by John Walsh for harpsichord or organ: Six Concertos, Op. 4 (1738); A Second Set of Six Concertos (1740); A Third Set of Six Concertos, Op. 7 (1761). That should make eighteen concertos, but in fact only the first two of the Second Set were original; the other four were

transcriptions of the Concerti Grossi, Op. 6 Nos. 1, 5, 6, and 10. So there are generally reckoned to be fourteen concertos, plus a number of incomplete or spurious ones. No. 13 was completed on 2 April 1739 and first performed at the premiere of *Israel in Egypt* two days later on 4 April. The nick-name, 'The Cuckoo and the Nightingale', comes from the sprightly birdsong calls in the second movement. No. 14 seems also to have been composed early in 1739 (the manu-script is undated) and first performed on 20 March that year, with *Alexander's Feast*, at a charity concert organised 'for the Benefit and Increase of a Fund established for the Support of Decay'd Musicians and their Families'.

♩ Five Organ Concertos: Op. 4 No. 2; Op. 7 Nos 3, 4, 5; and HWV 295
Preston/English Concert/Trevor Pinnock
Archiv 447 300-2 (1 CD). Recorded 1982 and 1983.
♩ Organ Concerto No. 14 (with *Dettingen Te Deum* and *Zadok the Priest*)
Marlow/Choir of Trinity College, Cambridge/Academy of Ancient Music/Layton
Hyperion CDA 67678 (1 CD). Recorded 2007.

Organ Concertos, Op. 7
No. 1 in B flat major, HWV 306
No. 2 in A major, HWV 307
No. 3 in B flat major, HWV 308
No. 4 in D minor, HWV 309
No. 5 in G minor, HWV 310
No. 6 in B flat major, HWV 311

Handel, late in life . . . was afflicted with blindness; which, however it might dispirit and embarrass him at other times, had no effect on his nerves or intellects, in public: as he continued to play concertos and voluntaries between the parts of his Oratorios to the last, with the same vigour of thought and touch, for which he was ever so justly renowned.

Charles Burney goes on to say that at first Handel relied on his memory to play some of his old concertos, but as the urge to compose never left him, he began to rely more and more on his powers of improvisation, which must have made for a distinctly seat-of-the-pants experience for his orchestral musicians:

> For, giving the band only the skeleton, or ritornels of each movement, he played all the solo parts extempore, while the other instruments left him, *ad libitum*; waiting for the signal of a shake, before they played such fragments of symphony as they found in their books.

In other words, spot the cadence – the right cadence – and then play hopefully!

The final set of Organ Concertos shares this improvisatory quality in the way it was put together. John Christopher Smith, the younger, Handel's assistant, probably helped John Walsh, the younger to assemble the set from various disparate sources after Handel's death, and it was published in 1761. The manuscript of No. 1 is dated 17 February 1740 and it was first performed with the premiere of *L'Allegro, il Penseroso ed il Moderato* ten days later on 27 February. No. 2 was dated 5 February 1743 and performed with *Samson* on 18 February. It includes a movement marked simply 'Organo ad libitum: Larghetto' – in other words, it would have been improvised by Handel as the mood took him. No. 3 was composed in January 1751 and performed after *Alexander's Feast* on 1 March, in a concert that also included the premiere of *The Choice of Hercules*. This was Handel's last orchestral composition and includes an 'Organo ad libitum' Adagio and fugue. No. 4 is not an original complete work, but was presumably assembled by John Christopher Smith from various single movements, including the Adagio, HWV 303, for two organs and orchestra, and there is an 'Organo ad libitum' third movement. The score of No. 5 is dated 31 January 1750 and it was first performed at the premiere of *Theodora* on 16 March that year, including two 'Organo ad libitum' movements. No. 6, like

No. 4, was another work of disparate movements put together to make a concerto (presumably to keep the uniformity of sets of six works), although there is some evidence that the two outer movements, derived from an earlier *sinfonia*, may have been played at the premieres of *Joshua* and *Susanna* on 9 March 1748 and 10 February 1749. The Concerto is completed with an 'Organo ad libitum' middle movement. A final word, however, for the final movement: marked rather prosaically 'a tempo ordinario'; it is one of those Handel pieces that lodges in the memory – energetic but somewhat wistful, straightforward but quirky in rhythm and form. It can only come to life (and in some recordings it doesn't!) under the hands of a skilled improviser. Try the Ton Koopman recording and recapture something of Handel's own rich imagination at play.

Given the high level of improvisation inherent in these works, it is obvious that no two recordings of them will even be similar. Some organists do improvise, others have chosen movements from other works by Handel to make up the movements. As you get to know these intriguing works you will probably want to sample a range of approaches. Two complete sets, however, stand out: those by Ton Koopman (mentioned above) and by Paul Nicholson. Nicholson's has the added interest of being performed on the organ of St Lawrence, Whitchurch, near to where Cannons, the mansion of the Duke of Chandos, once stood. It's an organ (albeit rebuilt) that Handel himself knew well.

♩ Organ Concertos, Op. 4 and Op. 7
Koopman/Amsterdam Baroque Orchestra
Apex 2564 62760-2 (2 CDs). Recorded 1986.
♩ Organ Concertos, Op. 4 and Op. 7
Nicholson/Kelly/Brandenburg Consort/Goodman
Hyperion CDD 22052 (2 CDs). Recorded 1996.

Oboe concertos
No. 1 in B flat major, HWV 301
No. 2 in B flat major, HWV 302a
No. 3 in G minor, HWV 287 (for flute or oboe)

Nothing is very certain about these concertos! Only the first two were published during Handel's lifetime, by John Walsh in 1740. There are no original manuscripts and their dates of composition are not known. No. 2, however, borrows music from two of the *Chandos Anthems*, so that would place it no earlier than *c.*1718, although it is possible that Walsh put the work together himself at a much later date. Nos. 1 and 3, if indeed they are by Handel, are probably from much earlier in his life, possibly from 1705 when he was still in Hamburg. The G minor Concerto did not appear in print until the mid-nineteenth century, although an early manuscript copy has recently come to light in Rostock, which attributes it to either flute or oboe. Many eighteenth-century wind players would have been proficient on both instruments, and indeed this work sounds equally idiomatic on the flute. All three concertos are charming – whether they are by Handel or not!

๏ Oboe Concertos, HWV 310, 302a and 287; Concerto Grosso, 'Alexander's Feast', HWV 318; Sonata à 5, HWV 288
Reichenberg/English Concert/Pinnock
Archiv 415 291-2 (1 CD). Recorded 1984.
๏ Oboe Concertos (and Sonatas)
Goodwin/St James Baroque Players/Bolton
Meridian CDE 84303 (1 CD). Recorded 1985.
๏ Handel at Home (Flute Concerto, HWV 287, and chamber arrangements of movements from *Alcina*, *Solomon*, and *Semele*)
Brown/London Handel Players
Somm SOMMCD 055 (1 CD). Recorded 2005.

Recorder concertos
Are there any? French recorder player, Hugo Reyne, argues that there are, and presents the results of his research into some original and alternative versions of various concertos from Handel's Opp. 3 and 4 (including the popular Op. 4 No. 6 which is already known in versions for organ and harp), plus two other concertos possibly by Handel in manuscript collections in Weisentheid and Rostock. The musical results

are convincing and enjoyable – after all, Handel used the recorder extensively in his stage works – and demonstrate just how complicated it can be to establish definitive versions of many of Handel's works. And maybe the conclusion is that, for the practical and pragmatic Handel, it might not really have mattered very much.

𝕲 Six Concertos for Recorder
Reyne/La Simphonie du Marais
Musiques de la Chabotterie, Vendée 605004 (1 CD). Recorded 2006.

Occasional orchestral works

Water Music
Suite No. 1 in F major, HWV 348
Suite No. 2 in D major, HWV 349
Suite No. 3 in G major, HWV 350

Handel's first biographer, John Mainwaring, provided a much-quoted story associated with the *Water Music*, concerning the accession to the throne of King George I in 1714. The new king, previously Elector of Hanover and Handel's employer, was said to be displeased at Handel's long absence from Germany and therefore when the King arrived in London

> Handel, conscious how ill he had deserved at the hand of his gracious patron . . . did not dare to show himself at court. To account for his delay in returning to his office, was no easy matter. To make an excuse for the non-performance of his promise was impossible.

According to Mainwaring, the situation was resolved in a most ingenious manner by a courtier and friend of Handel's, Baron Kilmanseck:

> The King was persuaded to form a party on the water.
> Handel was apprised of the design, and advised to prepare

some Music for that occasion. It was performed and
conducted by himself, unknown to his Majesty, whose
pleasure on hearing it was equal to his surprise . . . Handel
was restored to favour, and his Music was honoured with
the highest expressions of the royal approbation.

Unfortunately, the story just doesn't add up. Not only is
there no evidence that Handel fell into disfavour with King
George I, it is now generally agreed that the *Water Music* was
first performed during the King's river trip on Wednesday
17 July 1717 – an occasion designed specifically to bolster the
King's magnificence and prestige in the eyes of his somewhat
sceptical people. It was also designed to distance him from
the politically meddlesome Prince of Wales, who was not
invited. So, although Handel's music seems not to have been
composed to placate the King, it was certainly a gesture of
allegiance to him – which was a shrewd move, because in
Hanover Handel had always been a favourite of the Prince
and Princess of Wales. So maybe Mainwaring's story has a
grain of truth in it after all.

According to a report sent to Berlin by Friedrich Bonet, the
Prussian Ambassador to London:

About eight in the evening the King repaired to His barge,
into which were admitted the Duchess of Bolton,
Countess Godolphin, Mad. de Kilmanseck, Mrs Were and
the Earl of Orkney, the Gentleman of the Bedchamber in
Waiting. Next to the King's barge was that of the
musicians, about 50 in number, who played on all kinds of
instruments, to wit trumpets, horns, hautboys, bassoons,
German flutes, French flutes, violins, and basses; but there
were no singers. The music had been composed especially
by the famous Handel, a native of Halle, and His Majesty's
Principal Court Composer. His Majesty approved of it so
greatly that he caused it to be repeated three times in all,
although each performance lasted an hour – namely twice
before and once after supper. The evening was all that
could be desired for the festivity, the number of barges and

above all of boats filled with people desirous of hearing
was beyond counting. In order to make this entertainment
the more exquisite, Mad. de Kilmanseck had arranged a
choice supper in the late Lord Ranelagh's villa at Chelsea
on the river, where the King went at one in the morning.
He left at three o-clock and returned to St. James's about
half past four. The concert cost Baron Kilmanseck £150
for the musicians alone. Neither the Prince nor the
Princess took any part in this festivity.

The *Daily Courant* of 19 July 1717 published a very similar
story, adding that on the King's return journey, 'the Music
continuing to play till he landed'. Quite a night for the
musicians!

The 'Celebrated Water Musick', as it was soon called,
became very popular during Handel's lifetime, in all sorts
of groupings of extracts, and some of these were published
by John Walsh during Handel's lifetime. But the complete
collection of pieces was not published until 1788, long after
his death, and as there is no original manuscript we cannot
know the exact sequence of movements. Some modern
recordings still mix and match, but the complete *Water Music*
is now usually organised into three suites, grouped together
by key: F major, D major, and G major. Suite No. 1 in F major
is scored for strings with horns, bassoons, and oboes – a festive sound given an extra ceremonial edge in Suite No. 2 in
D major by the addition of trumpets. Meanwhile Suite No. 3
in G major uses flutes and recorders with the strings for a
more intimate sound – ideal perhaps for the music played at
supper. All in all the *Water Music* is a rich and cosmopolitan
mix of musical styles – French, Italian and English – and on
the best modern recordings with authentic instruments
(valveless horns are an absolute necessity), the sheer exuber-
ance of the big extrovert movements is infectious. And then
Handel will suddenly produce a movement of quietly seduc-
tive beauty to twist your emotions in quite another direction.
What a showman!

🎧 *Water Music* and *Fireworks Music*
English Baroque Soloists/Gardiner
Philips 464 706-2 (1 CD). Recorded 1983 and 1991.
🎧 *Water Music* and *Fireworks Music*
Le Concert Spirituel/Niquet
Glossa GCD 921606 (1 CD). Recorded 2002.
🎧 *Water Music* and *Fireworks Music*
Le Concert des Nations/Savall
Auvidis ES 8512 (1 CD). Recorded 1993.

Music for the Royal Fireworks in D major, HWV 351

The grand display of Royal Fireworks in Green Park
was designed to celebrate the signing of the Peace of
Aix-la-Chapelle (7 October 1748), ending the War of
Austrian Succession, although it did not actually take place
until six months later on 27 April 1749. A huge amount of
planning was necessary, and the responsibility was shouldered
by the Duke of Montague, who found himself caught up in a
disagreement between the King and Handel about the music:

> I think Hendel [sic] now proposes to have but 12 trumpets
> and 12 French horns; at first there was to have been
> sixteen of each, and I remember I told the King so, who, at
> that time, objected to their being any musick; but, when I
> told him the quantity and nomber of martial musick there
> was to be, he was better satisfied, and said he hoped there
> would be no fidles. Now Hendel proposes to lessen the
> nomber of trumpets &c. and to have violeens. I don't at all
> doubt but when the King hears it he will be very much
> displeased.

Did Handel get his own way in the end? We can't be sure,
because although the score specifies strings doubling some of
the wind parts, that may have been only for subsequent performances, when it is known that Handel did include strings.
So it may well be that the first performance was for a formidable line-up of wind and brass: twenty-four oboes, twelve
bassoons and a contra-bassoon, nine horns, nine trumpets,

and three pairs of kettledrums plus side-drums. Anticipation of the event reached fever pitch and when the music was publicly rehearsed in Vauxhall Gardens, much against Handel's better judgement, twelve thousand people turned up and caused a traffic jam that blocked London Bridge for three hours! Then on the great day itself it rained and part of the pavilion housing the display caught fire – nevertheless the music was judged a great success.

The *Fireworks Music*, which turned out to be Handel's last purely orchestral work, comprises a grandiose overture in the French style, alternating slow and fast sections, followed by a suite of five celebratory dances: 'Bourrée', 'La paix', 'La Réjouissance', Menuet I and Menuet II. Recordings of the *Fireworks Music* vary in the forces employed: Charles Mackerras led the way in 1959 with his massed all-wind version – famously recorded in the middle of the night (the only time he could get all the players together!) at St Gabriel's Church, Cricklewood, North London. The recording session began at 11 p.m. on 13 April and finished at 2.30 a.m. on 14 April – the day of the two-hundredth anniversary of the death of Handel! Trevor Pinnock also offers a more recent wind-only version, on period instruments, while Gardiner and Niquet include strings. And there are many more alternatives available of this justifiably popular work – Handel was unsurpassed at music for great occasions.

♪ *Music for the Royal Fireworks* / *Concerto a due cori* in F/ *Water Music* suite and other works ed. Mackerras
Wind Ensemble/Pro Arte Orchestra/LSO/Mackerras
Testament SBT 1253 (1 CD). Recorded 1956, 1959 and 1977.
♪ *Music for the Royal Fireworks*, and Concerto in F major, HWV 331/336, Concerto in D major, HWV 335a, Passacaille, Gigue and Menuet, and Occasional Suite in D major
English Concert/Pinnock
Archiv 453 451-2 (1 CD). Recorded 1996.

☊ *Water Music* and *Fireworks Music*
English Baroque Soloists/Gardiner
Philips 464 706-2 (1 CD). Recorded 1983 and 1991.
☊ *Water Music* and *Fireworks Music*
Le Concert Spirituel/Niquet
Glossa GCD 921606 (1 CD). Recorded 2002.

Finally, for a quirky taste of Handel's orchestral music opulently played in the grand tradition of the 1950s, look no further than Sir Thomas Beecham's suite, *Love in Bath*. In 1945 Beecham made orchestral arrangements of twenty-two short movements, mainly from the operas, for a ballet called *The Great Elopement*. Absolutely not for the purists, but Beecham conducts it all with such disarming flair!

☊ *Love in Bath* suite, arr. Beecham (and *Solomon*, arr. Beecham)
RPO/Beecham
EMI 7243 5 86516 2 (2 CDs). Recorded 1956, 1957 and 1959.

Chamber music

Handel's chamber music is a minefield! It is littered with uncertainties about authenticity, dates, and attributions to particular instruments. Violin, flute, recorder, and oboe each claim a number of solo and trio sonatas, but precisely which ones, and how we can be sure, are not always easy questions to answer. What can be said with certainty is that Handel, essentially a man of the theatre, seems to have been casual about his chamber music – though not uninterested in it. He happily provided notable players of the day, in particular favourite players from his opera orchestra, with solo sonatas for performance in public concerts, without intending to create any definable repertoire, or even keep a particular track of what he wrote.

The story is similar for Handel's trio sonatas. He started composing them from a young age for colleagues and patrons, following in the steps of Corelli, whose first set of popular trios had been published in 1683, two years before Handel was born. Eleven further sets followed from Corelli, but Handel did not publish any of his own trios until many years later, and then only after a certain amount of persuasion.

It is worth noting that solo sonatas at that time were actually for three players and trio sonatas for four. The solo, melodic line of a sonata, and the two solo lines of a trio were supported by a bass line, usually played on the cello, which provided not only harmonic support but also further melodic interplay. The bass line was also played on a keyboard, usually a harpsichord, with an improvised accompaniment above it.

Solo and trio sonatas both followed two basic forms: the *sonata da chiesa* (church sonata) which generally had four abstract movements – slow-fast-slow-fast – and the *sonata da camera* (chamber sonata) which was mostly made up of dance movements. Handel generally favoured the *sonata da chiesa* – its abstract movements allowed him more freedom for his imagination – but he would occasionally also include dance movements, making a hybrid of the two kinds of sonata.

Handel would often have taken part in performances of his chamber music, playing the harpsichord and no doubt using all his famed improvisatory skills to exploit the elements of dialogue and conversation that underline the inherent theatricality of these works. The delicate restraint of private music-making often associated with chamber works is largely absent here; instead it is easy to hear in these sonatas and trios all the pathos, joy, and drama of Handel's operatic arias and duets, something that the best recordings bring out to thrilling effect.

Handel's complete chamber music was recorded in 1991 by the ensemble L'Ecole d'Orphée on original instruments and has recently been reissued in a bargain-priced box of six CDs. The performances are admirable and provide an ideal one-stop survey of this area of Handel's output: details are given alongside other recommendations in each of the categories below.

Solo sonatas

The problems begin immediately with Opus 1! This was a collection of sonatas published first by Jeanne Roger in Amsterdam in 1730 and then by John Walsh in London in 1732. Between them, the two versions contain fourteen sonatas. However, extensive research in the 1970s revealed that both versions were unreliable, and the opportunist Walsh emerged as the villain of the piece. The Roger edition was actually a forgery, printed by Walsh himself to get around the royal monopoly Handel had been granted in 1720 to publish his own works. Walsh had in effect borrowed, transposed and rewritten the sonatas as the whim took him, without any consultation with Handel.

Moreover, at least two of the sonatas (Nos. 10 and 12 for violin) appear not to be by Handel at all. Conveniently, all fourteen sonatas have been brought together on one recording: five for recorder (HWV 360, 362, 365, 367a, 369), four for violin (HWV 359a, 361, 364a, 371), four for flute (HWV 359b, 363b, 367b, 379), and one for oboe (HWV 366), plus six other works allied to Op. 1. Each of the Op. 1 Sonatas then reappears in collections devoted exclusively to each of these particular instruments, and outlined below.

🎧 20 Sonatas, 'Opus 1'
Beckett/Beznosiuk/Goodwin/Wallfisch/Nicholson/Tunnicliffe
Hyperion CDA 66921/3 (3 CDs). Recorded 1994.

Violin sonatas

Sonata in G major, HWV 358 (violin or recorder?)
Sonata in D minor, HWV 359a
Sonata in A major, Op. 1 No. 3, HWV 361
Sonata in G minor, Op. 1 No. 6, HWV 364a
Sonata in F major, Op. 1 No. 12, HWV 370
Sonata in D major, Op. 1 No. 13, HWV 371
Allegro in C minor, HWV 408
Andante in A minor, HWV 412

Sonata in A major, 'Roger', Op. 1 No. 10
Sonata in E major, 'Roger', Op. 1 No. 12

There seem to be five genuine Handel Violin Sonatas: HWV 358, 359a, 361, 364a and 371. Three of these can be dated and they cover almost the full range of Handel's career. HWV 358 comes from 1707, when he was a young man in Italy (although doubts have been raised as to whether this is a violin or recorder sonata); HWV 361 was composed c.1725 (unusually, the manuscript has survived); and HWV 371 in 1750 (although the opening was sketched in Rome in 1707). Andrew Manze plays these five sonatas alongside the two spurious ones, Nos. 10 and 12 from Roger and Walsh's Op. 1 (see above), and two other movements which date from the mid-1720s. In his notes he sets the tone for his many-faceted performances of these works:

> Handel's sonatas are masterpieces in miniature of a composer more famous for his grander structures. Perhaps the sonata was but a toy theatre in Handel's world of architectural splendours. Nevertheless, the characters which wordlessly inhabit its stage are no less lifelike, no more an illusion, than the many heroes and heroines who people the operas and oratorios.

⌒ Complete Violin Sonatas
Manze/Egarr
Harmonia Mundi HMX 2907259 (1 CD) Recorded 1998.
⌒ Chamber Music (complete): CD 2
L'Ecole d'Orphée – Holloway/Sheppard/Carolan
Brilliant Classics 92192-1/6 (6 CDs). Recorded 1991.

Flute sonatas

Sonata in E minor, Op. 1 No. 1a, HWV 379
Sonata in E minor, Op. 1 No. 1b, HWV 359b
Sonata in G major, Op. 1 No. 5, HWV 363b
Sonata in B minor, Op. 1 No. 9b, HWV 367b
Halle Sonata No. 1 in A minor, HWV 374
Halle Sonata No. 2 in E minor, HWV 375

Halle Sonata No. 3 in B minor, HWV 376
Sonata in D major, HWV 378

There are either five or eight authentic Handel flute sonatas, depending on whether you accept as genuine the so-called 'Halle' Sonatas, published by Walsh in 1730. There is no conclusive evidence either way, except that stylistically there is no reason to exclude them, but whether they do date from early in Handel's career when he was still a student in Halle is pure conjecture. The D major Sonata, HWV 378, however, with its beautifully expressive opening Adagio, probably does go back to Handel's Italian period. This sonata was only discovered in a wrongly attributed manuscript in Brussels in the 1980s, whereas the remaining four sonatas formed part of Roger and Walsh's Op. 1 in 1730 and 1732. Of these four, HWV 379, dating from 1727–8, is the only one to exist in a manuscript that denotes it exclusively for the flute; the other three (HWV 359b, 363b and 367b) are reworkings of violin, oboe, and recorder sonatas respectively, with changes of key to make them more idiomatic for the flute. 'These sonatas contain some of the most passionate and exciting music ever composed for the flute,' declares Jed Wentz in his CD notes, and he looks to the world of Baroque opera, and the expressive techniques of the Italian singers whom Handel knew well, for inspiration on how to play them: 'to animate the notes on Handel's page, to make them cajole, enrage and enchant the listeners of today.'

○ Flute Sonatas
Wentz/Musica ad Rhenum
Challenge Classics CC 72046 (1 CD) Recorded 1997
○ Chamber Music (complete): CD 1
L'Ecole d'Orphée – Preston/Sheppard/Toll/Carolan
Brilliant Classics 92192-1/6 (6 CDs). Recorded 1991.

Oboe sonatas

Sonata in C minor, Op. 1 No. 8, HWV 366
Sonata in B flat major, 'Fitzwilliam', HWV 357
Sonata in F major, HWV 363a

The earliest of Handel's three oboe sonatas, HWV 357 (nick-named the 'Fitzwilliam' because the manuscript is now housed in the Fitzwilliam Museum in Cambridge), was prob-ably composed in Italy or Hanover in the early years of the eighteenth century. The other two date from Handel's early years in London. Examination of the manuscript of HWV 366 suggests that it belongs to 1711–12 when Handel was working on the operas *Rinaldo* and *Il pastor fido*. HWV 363a is the original version of the G major Flute Sonata, HWV 363b, published as Op. 1 No. 5. It belongs to a similar period as the previous oboe sonata, and the opening Adagio even borrows music from an aria in *Rinaldo*. According to Charles Burney, Handel claimed that the oboe was his 'favourite instrument' when he was young (see below, Trio Sonatas HWV 380–93), and these three sonatas explore its chameleon nature, ranging in mood from the plaintive and the pastoral to the outright skittish – all of it caught particularly well by David Reichenberg on his recording.

♫ Chamber Music (complete): CD 2
L'Ecole d'Orphée – Reichenberg/Sheppard/Carolan
Brilliant Classics 92192-1/6 (6 CDs). Recorded 1991.
♫ Three Oboe Sonatas (with Nine German Arias)
Bellamy/King's Consort
Hyperion CDA 67627 (1 CD). Recorded 2006.

Recorder sonatas

Sonata in G minor, Op. 1 No. 2, HWV 360
Sonata in A minor, Op. 1 No. 4, HWV 362
Sonata in C major, Op. 1 No. 7, HWV 365
Sonata in D minor, Op. 1 No. 9a, HWV 367a
Sonata in F major, Op. 1 No. 11, HWV 369
Sonata in G major, HWV 358 (recorder or violin?)
Sonata in B flat major, HWV 377

The recorder was a hugely popular solo instrument in England in the early years of the eighteenth century when

Handel arrived in London, so it is not surprising that it got the lion's share of the Op. 1 Sonatas – and indeed some wonderful solo moments in his operas. Soon the recorder would be overtaken by the flute, which ultimately proved to be both more expressive and more powerful, so these sonatas, composed in the mid-1720s, stand at the instrument's zenith. There is also a sixth sonata, HWV 377, composed around the same time, but not included in Op. 1, and a possible earlier sonata, HWV 358, which dates from 1707–10 and has been attributed to either recorder or violin (the manuscript does not specify). It is usually claimed by players of both instruments and it is unlikely that Handel would have minded either way!

What is important is the quality of imagination and invention in all of these works. HWV 367a, for example, is in a most unusual seven movements – a miniature drama of shifting moods and styles – wordless but eloquent, and challenging all the musical resources of the performer. Once again these sonatas are a reminder that even if we are in the concert hall for Handel's chamber music, we have never actually left the theatre.

☊ Recorder Sonatas
Petri/Jarrett
RCA RD 60441 (1 CD). Recorded 1990.
☊ Chamber Music (complete): CD 6
L'Ecole d'Orphée – Pickett/Beckett/Sheppard/Carolan
Brilliant Classics 92192-1/6 (6 CDs). Recorded 1991.

Trio sonatas

Trio Sonatas, Op. 2 (1733)
No. 1 in B minor, HWV 386b
No. 2 in G minor, HWV 387
No. 3 in B flat major, HWV 388
No. 4 in F major, HWV 389
No. 5 in G minor, HWV 390
No. 6 in G minor, HWV 391

The six Trios published by John Walsh *c.*1732 as Op. 2 were composed by Handel over a long period. One at least, No. 2, seems to have been a work from his youth – the copy owned by Charles Jennens marks it 'composed at the age of 14'. As with Op. 1 there seems have been some sharp dealing from Walsh, with a supposedly pirated edition appearing first in Amsterdam. Actually, Walsh himself was responsible for this and it may have been his ploy to get Handel to collaborate on a proper, 'corrected' edition for London. No manuscripts have survived, so there is still much left to conjecture.

The music of Op. 2, however, certainly repays attention and the very first Trio is one of the best. It is one of the later works, probably composed sometime around 1720, and pairs the newly fashionable flute with the violin to expressive effect, particularly in the gracious third movement based on a favourite idea borrowed by Handel from an opera by Reinhard Keiser. No. 4 also varies the instrumentation, although there is some confusion here: should it be again for flute with violin, or the flute's still-popular rival, the recorder? The more limited range seems to suggest the recorder, although the score says flute. Certainly the other four trios are for the more usual pairing of two violins. Nos. 3 and 5 are mature works, and Handel borrowed from them later when composing his Organ Concertos. No. 6 was probably composed much earlier, maybe *c.*1707 when Handel was in Italy. As for Trio No. 2, if Handel really did compose it in 1699 or 1700, then it demonstrates how confidently assured he already was as a composer.

🎧 Chamber Music (complete) CD 3
L'Ecole d'Orphée – Holloway/Comberti/Preston/Pickett/Sheppard/Woolley/Toll
Brilliant Classics 92192-1/6 (6 CDs). Recorded 1991.
🎧 Trio Sonatas, Op. 2 (and HWV 392 and 393)
Academy of St Martin-in-the-Fields Chamber Ensemble
Philips 412 595-2 (2 CDs). Recorded 1980, 1982 and 1983.

Trio sonatas, Op. 5 (1739)

No. 1 in A major, HWV 396
No. 2 in D major, HWV 397
No. 3 in E minor, HWV 398
No. 4 in G major, HWV 399
No. 5 in G minor, HWV 400
No. 6 in F major, HWV 401
No. 7 in B flat major, HWV 402

This second volume of trio sonatas was published by John Walsh's son in 1739. The title specifies *Seven Sonatas or Trios for Two Violins or German Flutes* and the set differs from Op. 2 because these are mainly not original works: rather, they are made up of movements arranged from existing orchestral works, including overtures from some of the *Chandos Anthems* and dance music from some of the operas. The manuscripts indicate, however, that Handel himself was involved in the choice, ordering and revision of movements, and there are also some newly composed movements in Nos. 1, 3, 5 and 6. In fact No. 6 borrows only from an early trio not included in Op. 2, so it is the closest to being a work written expressly for this set.

Op. 5 is very unusual for the time in having seven trios, rather than the usual collection of six, and Handel scholar Anthony Hicks suggests that Walsh added another trio, probably without Handel's knowledge, which he had put together himself. This was very likely No. 4, which borrows from *Athalia*, *Il Parnasso in festa*, *Radamisto*, *Terpsichore* and *Alcina* – all rich sources of music which Walsh was no doubt keen to exploit.

Throughout these works Handel delights in the interplay of the two solo instruments, as they imitate and oppose each other – the whole set feels like a parallel collection, albeit wordless, to the great duets that grace his operas. How eloquent, for example, and how moving, is the opening Largo of No. 6, and then how exciting the scurrying fugue that follows. The pattern of contrast is repeated with the expressive central Adagio, followed by an energetically striding Allegro.

Finally the instruments unite harmoniously for the urbane conversation of the final Andante. Vintage Handel!

♪ Chamber Music (complete): CD 4
L'Ecole d'Orphée – Holloway/Comberti/Sheppard/Carolan
Brilliant Classics 92192-1/6 (6 CDs). Recorded 1991.
♪ Seven Trio Sonatas, Op. 5
London Handel Players – Brown/Butterfield/Webber/Collyer/
Sharman/Cummings
Somm SOMMCD 044 (1 CD). Recorded 2005.

Sinfonia in B flat major, HWV 338
Trio Sonata in C minor, HWV 386a
Trio Sonata in F major, HWV 392
Trio Sonata in G minor, HWV 393
Trio Sonata in E major, HWV 394
Trio Sonata in C major, HWV 403

Not surprisingly, given Handel's prolific activities as a composer, various other trio sonatas have come to light from time to time. Three of them were discovered in manuscript in a collection in Dresden and published in 1879 when Friedrich Chrysander compiled his Handel-Gesellschaft edition. Chrysander also published a C minor version of Op. 2 No. 1 (HWV 386). The first of the Dresden Trios (HWV 392) probably dates from Handel's time in Italy, c.1706–7, and material from it reappears, reworked, in Op. 5 No. 6 (see above). The authenticity of the other two Dresden Trios (HWV 393 and 394) is more doubtful. Two other trios are also included on the recording by L'Ecole d'Orphée: HWV 338 (called a 'Sinfonia') could well be a very early work, composed in Hamburg in c.1704–6; in contrast, HWV 403 was probably written in 1738 and then immediately reused for orchestral movements in the oratorio *Saul*.

♪ Chamber Music (complete): CD 5
L'Ecole d'Orphée – Holloway/Comberti/Bury/Sheppard/
Woolley/Carolan
Brilliant Classics 92192-1/6 (6 CDs). Recorded 1991.

Trio Sonata in B flat major, HWV 380
Trio Sonata in D minor, HWV 381
Trio Sonata in E flat major, HWV 382
Trio Sonata in F major, HWV 383
Trio Sonata in G major, HWV 384
Trio Sonata in D major, HWV 385

The authenticity of this final collection of trio sonatas hangs on an anecdote recounted by Charles Burney in 1784: 'The late Mr Weideman was in possession of a set of Sonatas, in three parts, which Handel composed when he was only ten years old.' Carl Friedrich Weideman was a flautist in Handel's opera orchestra and had been given the Trios by his flute pupil, the Earl of Marchmont, who had 'picked them up as great curiosities' during his travels in Germany. Weideman then showed them to Handel, 'who seemed to look at them with much pleasure, and laughing, said, "I used to write like the Devil in those days, but chiefly for the hautbois, which was my favourite instrument." '

That sounds quite conclusive, but modern scholars are not so sure. The original manuscript is lost, the copyist's paper dates from later, the musical style seems too mature for a ten-year-old, the range and double-stopping for the second part indicates a violin not an oboe, and Handel never borrowed any of the music in these trios for his later compositions – very unlike him. So was he mistaken when he appeared to recognise these trios? The question hangs in the air as you listen to these works – very tantalising! Generally the set is not particularly imaginative – many of the movements sound as though they could be by anyone. Occasionally, however, the emotional weight seems right (for example, the *Affetuoso* of HWV 381), and all of HWV 380 just might be by the precocious young Handel – surely no ordinary ten-year-old!

♙ Trio Sonatas for Oboe and Violin
Convivium – Robson/Wallfisch/Tunnicliffe/Nicholson
Helios CDH 55280 (1 CD). Recorded 1998.

Keyboard music

Handel composed an enormous amount of solo keyboard music, much of it during his early career in Germany and Italy. Some of it was subsequently organised into suites, but many shorter pieces remained uncollected, including preludes and short dances that sometimes seem like hastily written-down improvisations. And indeed improvisation is the key to Handel's keyboard music. Where each movement in a Bach suite seems intensely worked-out, many of Handel's feel more like written-down improvisations and leave you thinking that maybe there would have been more to the music when he himself played it. Given what we know about him as a virtuoso harpsichordist (see the chapter on 'Handel the performer'), he no doubt regarded the instrument as primarily something on which he would make *new* music every time, even if his imagination was set running by ideas or pieces that already existed. The act of carefully capturing something on paper, so that it would be fixed for all time, probably interested him much less. What has been captured, however, time and time again in this music, is Handel's unmistakable and unfailing vitality.

Keyboard Suites Vol. 1 (1720)

No. 1 in A major, HWV 426
No. 2 in F major, HWV 427
No. 3 in D minor, HWV 428
No. 4 in E minor, HWV 429
No. 5 in E major, HWV 430
No. 6 in F sharp minor, HWV 431
No. 7 in G minor, HWV 432
No. 8 in F minor, HWV 433

The publication of this first book of keyboard suites was in no way carefully planned. In 1720 Handel was completely taken up with thoughts of opera and the newly founded Royal Academy of Music, and had to divert his attention to deal with an annoying case of plagiarism, as he explained in the preface:

> I have been obliged to publish some of the following
> Lessons, because surrepticious [sic] and incorrect Copies of
> them had got Abroad. I have added several new ones to
> make the Work more useful, which if it meets with a
> favourable Reception, I will still proceed to publish more,
> reckoning it my duty, with my Small Talent, to serve a
> Nation from which I received so generous a protection.

Note the word 'lessons' here. Teaching and learning form a
large part of the intention of these works. In the early years of
Handel's career, when many of these suites were written, he
was perfecting his own craft as well as providing valuable
study material for others.

The Suites were published with a French title – *Suites de
pièces pour le clavecin composées par G. F. Handel* – and although
Handel allied himself in that way to the French harpsichord
tradition, he did not just confine himself to the usual pattern
of elegant dances. Instead, these works are a cosmopolitan
mix, including Italian and German elements. He actually
ignores some of the usual dances – the Polonaise, Rigaudon,
and Bourrée, for example – but does not hesitate to import
other types of movements as they suit him – notably Allegro,
Adagio, and Air with variations. So, in a way, the suite just
provided a starting point for his forward-looking thought
processes, which at times seem to anticipate sonata form.

These works came to be known as 'The Eight Great
Suites', and there is indeed an impressive grandeur and
gesture to their style. Certainly they provided a challenge
to contemporary players. Handel's first biographer, John
Mainwaring, explained:

> The first set, which were printed by his own order,
> will always be held in the highest esteem, notwithstanding
> those real improvements in the style for lessons which
> some Masters have since hit upon. Handel's have one
> disadvantage, owing entirely to their peculiar excellence.
> The surprising fullness and activity of the inner parts,
> increases the difficulty of playing them to so great a

degree, that few persons are capable of doing them justice. Indeed there seems to be more work in them than one instrument should seem capable of dispatching.

If the organ concertos bring us close to Handel the mature composer on the instrument he loved, these keyboard suites reveal the younger, often impetuous Handel, absolute master of the harpsichord, giving free rein to his imagination. The more you listen to them, the more original touches you find in them. This is an area of Handel's output that is ripe for rediscovery.

Among the highlights of the first set of Suites (to take just one example from each) is a gracious and joyous Courante in No. 1, with a richly embellished melody – a good example of the importance of the inner parts noted by Mainwaring – and in fact all the Courantes in these suites are a delight. Then in No. 2, rather than opening with the usual Prelude – the traditional warm-up for the fingers – Handel writes an Adagio which is almost an operatic aria, with extensive ornamentation. No. 3 is notable for its Air with a set of five variations. The air is already heavily ornamented, so the variations seem a little prosaic – this does feel like a 'lesson' – but there are flashes of brilliance. In No. 4 Handel launches straight in with an exhilarating fugue as the first movement, and No. 5 has as its final movement another set of variations, made popular with the nickname 'The Harmonious Blacksmith'. Again it starts prosaically and whips up quite a head of steam by the end. No. 6 finds Handel at his most emotionally searching in the fragmented line of the opening Prelude, while the extraordinary opening Overture of No. 7 is orchestral in scope and seems to burst out of the confines of the harpsichord. It is matched at the end of the Suite by the heroic grandeur of the Passacaille. In complete contrast, the opening Prelude of No. 8 has an intimate and plaintive melancholy.

♩ The Eight Great Suites (with Six Fugues, HWV 605–10, and Two Fugues HWV 611–12)
Nicholson (harpsichord)
Hyperion CDD 22045 (2 CDs). Recorded 1994.

Keyboard Suites, Vol. 2 (1733)
No. 1 in B flat major, HWV 434
No. 2 in G major, HWV 435
No. 3 in D minor, HWV 436
No. 4 in D minor, HWV 437
No. 5 in E minor, HWV 438
No. 6 in G minor, HWV 439
No. 7 in B flat major, HWV 440
No. 8 in G major, HWV 441
No. 9 in G major, HWV 442

Once again, this was not a carefully planned volume of keyboard pieces, and did not reflect the sort of compositional progression that Handel followed, for example, between the Op. 3 and Op. 6 *concerti grossi*. It is a further miscellany of suites, published by John Walsh in 1733, that mainly date back to Handel's youth, alongside some newer works which he may have composed for the royal Princesses Anne and Caroline after being appointed their music teacher in 1723. Sophie Yates writes in her CD notes that the variation to the opening Allemande of No. 8, for example, 'has the air of a study, designed to bring dexterity and rhythmic control to the fingers of the young Princess Anne', and adds: 'It is interesting to imagine what Handel might have been like as a harpsichord teacher'. Yes indeed!

Brahms took up the theme of the *Aria con variazioni* in Suite No. 1 for his *Variations and Fugue on a Theme of Handel*, but the really amazing movement here is the opening improvisatory Prelude: full of virtuosic swagger, it must have been an absolute *tour de force* when Handel played it. Then No. 2 is not actually a suite at all, but a vast Chaconne with twenty-one variations. Once again it must have made an extraordinary effect on Handel's two-manual Ruckers harpsichord. Handel's gigues are always buoyant, but the one in Suite No. 3 skips along in a particularly breezy and ear-catching fashion. Very life-enhancing. No. 4 is one of the more straightforward suites, no doubt intended for teaching, but it ends with a grand Sarabande – reminiscent of the traditional 'Folia' theme, famous across Europe and used for countless sets of variations – and finally a whirlwind of a Gigue, over almost before it has started! (Incidentally, the Sarabande was made famous in a dramatically orchestrated version in Stanley Kubrick's 1975 film *Barry Lyndon* – you can see a clip on www.youtube.com.) In No. 5 also, it is the Gigue that stands out, with the unusual time signature of 24/16. On a larger scale than the one in the previous suite, it is an even bigger whirlwind. In complete contrast, the gentle opening Allemande of No. 6 is richly discursive with its intertwining parts, and No. 7 has an equally eloquent Sarabande, rather like a soliloquy. The joyous Allegro of No. 8 transcends its simple construction of successions of arpeggios and scales, and the flamboyant opening Prelude of No. 9 is a characteristic Handel flourish.

♩ Harpsichord Works – 1720 and 1733
Sophie Yates (harpsichord)
Chandos CHAN 0644, 0669, 0688 (3 CDs). Recorded 1998 and 2001.
♩ Suite No. 1, HWV 434, and Brahms, *Variations on a Theme of Handel*, Op. 24
Schiff (piano)
Elatus 2564 61762-2 (1 CD). Recorded 1994.

That last recording is of course played on the piano, not the harpsichord. So what about the piano for Handel? Unlike Bach, Handel has so far attracted less attention from pianists. But those that have recorded Handel, in very different ways, and are worth investigating include Andrei Gavrilov and Sviatoslav Richter, Keith Jarrett, Murray Perahia, and Anne Queffelec.

♩ Keyboard Suites, Vol. 1 (Eight Suites, 1720)
Gavrilov and Richter (pianos)
EMI 7243 5 86540 2 (2 CDs). Recorded 1979.
♩ Keyboard Suites, Vol. 2 (Eight Suites, 1733)
Gavrilov and Richter (pianos)
EMI 7243 5 86543 2 (2 CDs). Recorded 1979.
♩ Handel – Suites for Keyboard
Jarrett (piano)
ECM New Series 4452982 (1 CD). Recorded 1993.

⌒ Handel Suites (HWV 427, 428, 430, 435) and Scarlatti
Sonatas (selection)
Perahia (piano)
Sony SK 62785 (1 CD). Recorded 1996.
⌒ *Oeuvres pour piano*: Suites, HWV 430, 431, 433, 435, 436
Queffelec (piano)
Mirare MIR 010 (1 CD). Recorded 2005

Six Fugues (1735)
No. 1 in G minor, HWV 605
No. 2 in G major, HWV 606
No. 3 in B flat major, HWV 607
No. 4 in B minor, HWV 608
No. 5 in A minor, HWV 609
No. 6 in C minor HWV 610

Not published until 1735, but probably composed *c.*1716–17,
these fugues display not only Handel's command of form, but
also, when it suited him, his quiet disregard for it. Each fugue
is in four parts, for example, but quite often the fourth is not
brought in until near the end, for added effect – Bach would
not have approved. But as the nineteenth-century writer and
Handel enthusiast, Samuel Butler, pointed out: 'Bach was
fugue-ridden; Handel wrote fugues. Fugues were Handel's
servants and Bach's masters' (quoted by Christopher Hogwood
in the notes to his recording, *The Secret Handel* – see below).
Nevertheless, Handel is more than capable of using fugue
form to explore big ideas – just try the magnificent No. 5, with
its pre-echo of the chorus 'And with his stripes' from *Messiah*.

⌒ Six Fugues, HWV 605–10, and Two Fugues HWV 611–12
(with The Eight Great Suites)
Paul Nicholson (harpsichord)
Hyperion CDD 22045 (2 CDs). Recorded 1994.

Suite, HWV 428 (arr Muffat)
Fugue No. 6 in C minor, HWV 610
Air and Variations in E major, HWV 430

Suite for two keyboards in C minor, HWV 446
Three Minuets in A major, HWV 545, 546, 547
Air in F major, HWV 464 (from *Water Music*)
Bourrée and Hornpipe in F major, HWV deest (from
Water Music)
Air in B flat major, HWV 469
Concerto in G major, HWV 487
Air Lentement in G minor, HWV 467
Allemande in B minor, HWV 479
Courante in B minor, HWV 489
Chorale, 'Jesu meine Freude', in G minor, HWV 480
Chaconne in G major, HWV 435

These works are grouped together by Christopher Hogwood
on a fascinating recording called *The Secret Handel*, and played
on the clavichord. The strings of the clavichord are struck,
rather than plucked like the harpsichord, and the sounds it
produces are much softer and gentler – ideal for practice, and
indeed for playing in secret, which was exactly what Handel
did as a young child when he hid a clavichord in a room at the
top of the house after his father had forbidden him to have
anything to do with music (see 'Handel's life', 1691). Handel
seems to have remained fond of the clavichord for the rest of
his life. Hogwood describes an instrument now in Maidstone
Museum which has the inscription: 'This clavichord belonged
to Handel, who used it in composition when travelling.'
Hogwood also quotes Bernard Granville, one of Handel's
friends (see the chapter on Mrs Delany), who claimed that
Handel said that 'the Clavichord must be made use of by a
beginner, instead of Organ or Harpsichord'.

When the young Handel was finally allowed a teacher,
Friedrich Zachow, he compiled a manuscript copybook with
extracts from many contemporary composers. Hogwood
includes an Air and Variations by one of these composers in
the copybook, Johann Philipp Kreiger, and a couple of pieces
by Zachow, as well as a wide variety of works by Handel himself, including a performing version of Suite No. 3 in D minor,
HWV 428 (see above), embellished by Gottlieb Muffatt.

♠ The Secret Handel
Hogwood (clavichord)
Metronome MET CD 1060 (2 CDs). Recorded 2002.

Finally, a Handel curiosity: a CD of works played on the chamber organ built by Goetze and Gwynn for the Handel House Museum in London – a copy of the type of eighteenth-century instrument by Richard Bridge and Thomas Parker which Handel would have known well. The organ is housed in Handel's parish church, St George's, Hanover Square, and on it Paul Ayres plays a varied programme of pieces by Handel and inspired by him. Some of the Handel pieces are originally for organ, others are transcriptions; and some of the 'inspired' works are the result of a competition designed to encourage new repertoire for one-manual chamber organ.

♠ Handel-Inspired
Ayres
Priory PRCD 894 (1 CD). Recorded 2007.

Messiah

Whole books have been written about *Messiah*. It is Handel's supremely iconic work and never loses its power to move and inspire. There is a story that after writing out the 'Hallelujah' chorus, Handel is reported to have exclaimed to his servant with tears in his eyes: 'I did think I did see all Heaven before me, and the great God Himself seated on His throne, with his Company of Angels.' Such is the power of myth which has grown up around this work.

It is extraordinary then to discover (as mentioned in the section on the oratorios) that the librettist Charles Jennens was never really satisfied with what Handel had done with his arrangement of carefully chosen texts from the Bible. The story unfolds in a series of Jennens's letters to his close friend, the classical scholar, Edward Holdsworth:

> Handel says he will do nothing next Winter, but I hope I shall persuade him to set another Scripture Collection I have made for him, and perform it for his own Benefit in Passion Week. I hope he will lay out his whole Genius and Skill upon it, that the Composition may excell all his former Compositions, as the Subject excells every other Subject. The Subject is *Messiah*.
>
> (10 JULY 1741)

> I heard with great pleasure at my arrival in Town, that Handel had set the Oratorio of *Messiah*; but it was some mortification for me to hear that instead of performing it here he was gone into Ireland with it. However I hope we shall hear it when he comes back.
>
> (2 DECEMBER 1741)

> His *Messiah* has disappointed me, being set in great haste, tho' he said he would be a year about it, and make it the

best of all his Compositions. I shall put no more Sacred
Works into his hands, to be thus abus'd.

(17 JANUARY 1743)

As to the *Messiah*, 'tis still in his power by retouching the
weak parts to make it fit for a publick performance; and I
have said a great deal to him on the Subject; but he is so
lazy and so obstinate, that I much doubt the Effect.

(21 FEBRUARY 1743)

Messiah was perform'd last night, and will be again
tomorrow, notwithstanding the clamour rais'd against it,
which has only occasion'd it's being advertis'd without its
Name . . . 'Tis after all, in the main, a fine Composition,
notwithstanding some weak parts, which he was too idel
[sic] and too obstinate to retouch, tho' I us'd great
importunity to perswade him to it. He and his Tode-eater
Smith [Handel's assistant John Christopher Smith] did all
they could to murder the Words in print; but I hope I
have restor'd them to Life, not without much difficulty.

(24 MARCH 1743, THE DAY AFTER THE FIRST
LONDON PERFORMANCE)

I don't yet despair of making him retouch the *Messiah*, at
least he shall suffer for his negligence; nay I am inform'd
that he has suffer'd, for he told Lord Guernsey, that a
letter I wrote him about it contributed to the bringing of
his last illness upon him; and it is reported that being a
little delirious with a Fever, he said he should be damn'd
for preferring Dagon (a Gentlemen he was very
complaisant to in the Oratorio of *Samson*) before the
Messiah. This shews that I gall'd him: but I have not done
with him yet.

(15 SEPTEMBER 1743)

Handel has promis'd to revise the Oratorio of *Messiah*, and
He and I are very good Friends again. The reason is he

has lately lost his Poet Miller [James Miller, librettist of *Joseph and his Brethren*], and wants to set me at work for him again.

(7 MAY 1744)

In July 1744 Jennens sent Handel the text for Act I of *Belshazzar*, and Handel responded in placatory mood: 'Be pleased to point out these passages in the *Messiah* which You think require altering.' Finally, the following year, Jennens wrote again to Holdsworth, summing up the whole *Messiah* affair:

> I shall show you a collection I gave Handel, call'd *Messiah*, which I value highly, and he has made a fine Entertainment of it, tho' not near so good as he might and ought to have done. I have with great difficulty made him correct some of the grossest faults in the composition, but he retain'd his Overture obstinately, in which there are some passages far unworthy of Handel, but much more unworthy of the Messiah.
>
> (30 AUGUST 1745)

The irony of all this is that Handel's crowning genius in *Messiah* was actually to have transfigured the texts, making the music indispensable to them. For anyone brought up knowing the texts of the Authorised Version of the Bible and also listening to *Messiah*, it eventually becomes almost impossible to hear the words without the music. So try this *Messiah* test: can you read the following fragments of text in a musical vacuum, without hearing any fragments of *Messiah*?

> *Comfort ye . . . Behold a virgin shall conceive . . . And the glory of the Lord shall be revealed . . . O thou that tellest good tidings to Zion . . . For unto us a child is born . . . He shall feed his flock . . . Behold the Lamb of God . . . He was despised . . . How beautiful are the feet . . . I know that my Redeemer liveth . . . Behold, I tell you a mystery . . . The trumpet shall sound . . . Worthy is the Lamb that was slain.*

If your answer is 'No', then the point is made. If it is 'Yes', then the full richness of *Messiah* still awaits you!

And there is another *Messiah* test, guaranteed to sort out the good from the bad recordings. You might call this the Yoke Test, and it refers to perhaps Handel's most challenging chorus: 'His yoke is easy', at the end of Part I. If a choir can negotiate the long athletic lines, and if a conductor can keep the voices airborne, balancing them and then building to the two sweeping cadence points, then this is one the most wonderful moments in all Handel's works. If not, then you probably won't like the rest of the performance either, so try another one!

'His yoke is easy' is actually one of Handel's borrowings, and it demonstrates his keenness of ear in combining words and music. On 1 July 1741 he composed an Italian duet, *Quel fior che all'alba ride*, for two sopranos and continuo. The text of the opening movements runs: 'Quel fior che all'alba ride / il sole poi l'uccide, / e tomba ha nella sera'. It means 'A flower that smiles at daybreak / is then slain by the sun, / and entombed by evening'. By 28 August, when Handel completed the first draft of Part I of *Messiah*, he had transformed this duet into a four-part chorus with orchestra, to the text: 'His yoke is easy / his burthen is light / his burthen, / his burthen is light'. In the process of rewriting, the Italian word 'ride' had become the English 'easy', both words carrying the soaring and twisting musical line on the long-held 'ee' vowel. Effectively, the smile of the flower had been translated into the lightness of the burden carried by the follower of Christ. Masterly!

Mrs Delany

Handel's circle included many famous and fascinating people, but perhaps none as sympathetic and appealing as Mary Delany – someone with whom he enjoyed an easy friendship during the many years they knew each other.

When Mary died in 1788 she was as old as the century. Almost eighty years earlier, she (aged ten) and Handel (aged twenty-five) had had a decisive first meeting:

> In the year '10 I first saw Mr Handel who was introduced to my uncle by Mr Heidegger, the . . . most ugly man that was ever formed. We had no better instrument in the house than a little spinet of mine, on which the great musician performed wonders. I was much struck with his playing, but struck as a child, not a judge, for the moment he was gone, I seated myself at my instrument and played the best lessons I had then learned. My uncle archly asked me if I thought I should ever play as well as Mr Handel. 'If I did not think I should,' cried I, 'I would burn my instrument!' Such was the innocent presumption of childish ignorance.

Mary Granville, as she was in 1710, was niece to Sir John Stanley, a commissioner of customs, and the rest of her family was solidly military, with a long history of loyal service to the Crown. But the Granvilles fell on hard times just a few years later in 1714, when Queen Anne died and the Jacobites (who had hoped to restore the Stuarts to the throne) had to yield to the Whigs, who forced through the Hanoverian succession.

In 1718 Mary was persuaded by her family to marry the elderly and odious Alexander Pendarves, in the hope of reversing their fortunes. Mary was disgusted by the whole business, but obedient and faithful. However, it was to no avail: Pendarves died in 1724 without changing his will, in which he left everything to his niece. But widowhood was the making of Mary, freeing her to live a relatively independent life in London in a way that would have been impossible as a spinster. An anonymous portrait, painted some time in the 1720s, shows her as an open-faced, clearly intelligent and spirited young woman. (This is reproduced in the National Portrait Gallery exhibition catalogue, edited by Jacob Simon – see 'Further reading'). Little wonder that she had many suitors, including John Wesley, but she did not remarry until 1743, when she became the second wife of a clergyman, Dr Patrick Delany.

Throughout her long life Mary was a great letter writer and she corresponded regularly with her sister, Anne. She also had a brother, Bernard, and all three of them were great admirers of Handel and his music. Mary was a brilliantly cultured woman – she also corresponded with the writer Jonathan Swift – and a keen musician herself, so she took a lively interest in Handel's operatic ventures. On 11 November 1727 she wrote to Anne: 'I was yesterday at the rehearsal of Mr Handel's new opera called *King Richard the First* – 'tis delightful.' But all was not well generally with Italian opera in London and later that month Mary wrote again:

> I doubt operas will not survive longer than this winter, they are now at their last gasp; the subscription is expired and nobody will renew it. The directors are always squabbling, and they have so many divisions among themselves that I wonder they have not broke up before; Senesino goes away next winter, and I believe Faustina, so you see harmony is almost out of fashion.

In January of the following year there was a further threat to Italian opera when *The Beggar's Opera*, a popular ballad-opera, was premiered:

> Yesterday I was at the rehearsal of the new opera composed by Handel [*Siroe*]; I like it extremely, but the taste of the town is so depraved, that nothing will be approved of but the burlesque. *The Beggar's Opera* entirely triumphs over the Italian one.

And in May 1728, Mary reported to Anne the imminent collapse of the Royal Academy of Music:

> There is to be but four opera nights more, and then adieu to harmony of that kind for ever and ever. Senesino and Faustina have hired themselves to Turin and to Venice for the next winter and the carnival following.

Fortunately it was not adieu, and less than a year later the situation had improved: 'The subscription for the Opera next winter goes on very well, to the great satisfaction of all musical folks.' That satisfaction was not, however, always uncritical on Mary's part. She certainly knew what she liked and what she didn't as far as individual singers were concerned – and also in the music itself. At a rehearsal for *Lotario* in November 1729 she mainly approved of the castrato Bernachi and the tenor Fabri, but as for the females:

> La Strada is the first woman; her voice is without exception fine, her manner perfection, but her person very *bad*, and she makes *frightful mouths* . . . The last is Bertoli, she has neither voice, ear, nor manner to recommend her; but she is a perfect beauty, quite a Cleopatra.

And Mary was not uncritical of Handel's music at times, although in the most tactful way. On arriving at the premiere of *Lotario* on 2 December she was given some bad news about a friend: 'whether it was owing to that, or that the opera really is not so meritorious as Mr Handel's generally are, but I never was so little pleased with one in my life.' But that was a rare example of discontent: generally Mary defended Handel against all-comers. In March 1734 she wrote:

> I went [to the opera] with Lady Chesterfield in her box . . . 'Twas *Arbaces*, an opera of Vinci's, pretty enough, but not to compare with Handel's compositions. . . . I went to the oratorio at Lincoln's Inn, composed by Porpora . . . some of the choruses and recitatives are extremely fine and

touching, but they say it is not equal to Mr Handel's oratorio of *Esther* or *Deborah*.

By this time, Mary was living quite close to Handel in Brook Street, and the following month she staged 'a very pretty party'. She borrowed a harpsichord and invited a glittering line-up of aristocratic and musical friends. Once again, her sister Anne heard all about it:

> I must tell you of a little entertainment of music I had last week . . . I never was *so* well entertained at *an opera*!
> Mr Handel was in the best humour in the world, and played lessons and accompanied Strada, and all the ladies that sang from seven o'the clock till eleven. I gave them tea and coffee, and about half an hour after nine had a salver brought in of chocolate, mulled white wine and biscuits. Everybody was easy and seemed pleased.

Presumably Handel either dined before, or went home to a substantial late supper afterwards. Given his prodigious appetite, he would certainly not have been satisfied with just a few biscuits! Neither in fact was Mary: 'Bunny staid with me after the company was gone, eat a cold chick with me, and we chatted until one o' the clock.' 'Bunny' was Mary's nickname for her brother, Bernard, who had recently moved into a house in nearby Park Street. Mary's mother (also called Mary) was another recipient of her letters and from time to time they included news of Handel. In March 1735 Mary and her sister, Anne, were much taken with Handel's skill as an organist, which they were lucky to observe both in public and in private:

> We were together at Mr Handel's oratorio *Esther*. My sister gave you an account of Mr Handel's playing here for three hours together: I did wish for you, for no entertainment in music could exceed it, except his playing on the organ in *Esther*, where he performs a part in two concertos, that are the finest things I ever heard in my life.

The following month Mary was with her sister at the first rehearsal of the opera *Alcina* at Handel's house and reported back to her mother:

> I think it is the best he ever made, but *I have thought so of so many*, that I will not say positively *'tis the finest*, but 'tis *so fine* I have not words to describe it. Strada has a whole scene of charming recitative – there are a thousand beauties. Whilst Mr Handel was playing his part, I could not help thinking him a necromancer in the midst of his own enchantments.

What a vivid description of Handel: 'a necromancer in the midst of his own enchantments'! On occasions Mary was even treated to a sneak preview of Handel's operas on her own. On 27 November 1736 she wrote gleefully to her sister, 'Mr Handel has two new operas ready – *Erminius* and *Justino* [*Arminio* and *Giustino*]. He was here two or three mornings ago and *played to me both the overtures*, which are charming.' A later rehearsal of *Arminio*, the following January at Covent Garden, confirmed her first impression: 'I think it is as fine a one as any he has made, as I hope you will, 'tis to be acted next Wednesday. From the rehearsal I came home with my *neighbour Granville!*'

The next few years must have been particularly pleasant, with both her brother and Handel living close by. But Mary Pendarves was not destined to remain an attractive young widow in Brook Street. On 9 June 1743 she married Patrick Delany from Dublin. She had known him for years and they had become close after his first wife died in 1740. Delany was also a music-lover and an admirer of Handel – indeed at the Dublin premiere of *Messiah* he had been so moved by the aria, 'He was despised', sung by Susanna Cibber, who had a somewhat scandalous private life, that he cried out: 'Woman, for this, be all thy sins forgiven!'

Mary's affectionate nickname for her husband was 'D.D.' – short for both Doctor of Divinity and Dr Delany. They continued to live for a while in London, but in May 1744 he was

appointed Dean of Downpatrick in Ireland – adding another
D.D. to his name – and then the opportunites to hear
Handel's music became more rare. In the mean time the
letters to Anne (now also married) continued as Mary
made the most of the time still left to her in London. On
10 November 1743 she wrote:

> Mrs Percival came to invite us to dine with her yesterday,
> and to go in the morning to Whitehall Chapel to hear
> Mr Handel's new *Te Deum* [the *Dettingen Te Deum*]
> rehearsed, and an anthem. It is excessively fine, I was all
> rapture and so was your friend D.D. as you may imagine;
> everybody says it is the finest of his compositions; I am not
> well enough acquainted with it to pronounce that of it, but
> it is heavenly.

And on 24 January 1744:

> I was yesterday morning at Mr Handel's to hear the
> rehearsal of *Semele*. It is a delightful piece of music, quite
> new and different from anything he has done: but I am
> afraid I shall hear no more music this year, and that will be
> a loss to me – but the *harmony of friendship* must make up
> that loss . . . Francescina [the soprano, Elisabeth Duparc]
> is improved, and sings the principal part in it.

Mary's final weeks in London allowed her to sample the
oratorio season, which had by now replaced Handel's operas:
'*Semele* is to be performed next Friday; D.D. subscribes for
me, and I hope not to miss one of the charming oratorios,
except when I give up my ticket to him.' She was an acute
observer of the first night on 10 February:

> I was yesterday to hear *Semele* . . . There is a four-part song
> that is delightfully pretty; Francesina is extremely improved,
> her notes are more distinct, and there is something in her
> running-divisions that is quite surprizing. She was much
> applauded, and the house full, though not crowded; I
> believe I wrote my brother word that Mr Handel and the

Prince had quarelled, which I am sorry for. Handel says the *Prince* is quite out of *his* good graces!

And Mary was there again a week or so later:

Semele is charming; the more I hear it the better I like it, and as I am a subscriber I shall not fail one night. But it being a profane story D.D. does not think it proper for him to go; but when *Joseph* or *Samson* is performed I shall persuade him to go – you know *how much* he delights in music. They say *Samson* is to be next Friday, for *Semele* has a strong party against it, viz. the fine ladies, *petits maîtres*, and ignoramus's. All the opera people are enraged at Handel . . .

All this oratorio-going in the Lenten season began to give the new Mrs Delany creative ideas of her own:

The oratorios fill very well, not withstanding the spite of the opera party: nine of the twelve are over. *Joseph* is to be performed (I hope) once more, then *Saul*, and the *Messiah* finishes; as they have taken very well, I fancy Handel will have a second subscription; and how do you think *I have lately been employed*? Why, I have made a drama for an oratorio, out of Milton's *Paradise Lost*, to give Mr Handel to compose to; it has cost me a great deal of thought and contrivance; D.D. approves of my performance, and that gives me some reason to think it not bad, though all I have had to do has been collecting and making the connection between the fine parts. I begin with Satan's threatenings to seduce the woman, her being seduced follows, and it ends with the man's yielding to temptation; I would not have a word or a thought of Milton's altered; and I hope to prevail with Handel to set it without having any of the lines put into verse, for that will take from its dignity. This, and painting three pictures, have been my chief morning employment since I came to town.

For whatever reason, however, Handel didn't set Mary's text and nothing more was said about it. But what if he had?

What would poor D.D. have done? Would he have considered it a sufficiently 'sacred' story to attend a performance of it during Lent? We shall never know! Meanwhile, the Delanys' stay in London was drawing to a close. On 22 March 1744 she wrote, 'Last night, alas! was the last night of the oratorio: it concluded with *Saul*: I was in hopes of the *Messiah*. I have been at ten oratorios . . .' But there was a parting gift before she moved to Ireland: 'Today I shall have a treat that I shall most ardently wish you and my mother your share of. Handel, my brother, and Donnellan *dine here*, and we are to be entertained with *Handel's playing over* Joseph *to us*.'

Mary took her advocacy of Handel to Ireland with her – but there were limits. On a cold day just before Christmas 1745 she wrote to Anne:

Last Monday the Dean and I went to the rehearsal of the *Messiah*, for the relief of poor debtors; it was very well performed, and I much delighted. You know how much I delight in music, and that piece is very charming; but I had not the courage to go to the performance at night, the weather was so excessively bad and I thought it would be hazardous to come out of so great crowd so far, that is my kind guardian thought so for me . . .

But she did make it to a charity performance of *Deborah* in Dublin on 25 January 1746 – and with her critical faculties intact:

On Tuesday last I went to hear *Deborah* performed, for the support of one of the infirmaries. It is a charming piece of music, and was extremely well performed; we have a woman here, a Mrs Storer, who has a very sweet and clear voice, and though she has no *judgement* in music, Dubourg [violinist and conductor] manages her so well in his manner of accompanying her, as to make her singing very agreable.

Back in London on a visit in January 1747, and staying in Pall Mall, Mary was delighted to receive a call from Handel:

'Just as I came to this place [in writing this letter], in came Mr Handel, and he has prevented my adding any more . . .' Handel might equally well have found her occupied with drawing or painting – she was a talented amateur artist. At that point she was taking one of his works, *L'Allegro, il Penseroso ed il Moderato*, as her inspiration: ' "The Allegro" is a drawing, I have imagined in imitation of Mr Handel's "Let me wander", etc., and I have brought in all the images as well I could. "Pensero" is in embryo.'

Mary's visits to London often coincided with the Lenten season of oratorios – not by chance, presumably. She was back on 1 March 1750: 'To-morrow oratorios begin – *Saul*, one of my beloved pieces – I shall go.' Incidentally, Mary's sister, Anne, who received all these letters, would have considered herself every bit as much a devotee of Handel. Writing to her brother in December 1750, she observed:

I hope you find Handel well. I beg my compliments to him: he has not a more real admirer of his great work than myself; his wonderful *Messiah* will never be out of my head; and I may say *my heart* was raised almost to heaven by it.

Mary would have agreed about the power of *Messiah*: 'That sublime and awful piece of music . . . 'tis heavenly.' *Messiah* was a work to subdue and impress even a wild young violinist and conductor, Giovanni Marella, who was all the rage in Ireland in December 1750, as Mary explained to her brother:

Morella [sic] conducted it and I expected would have *spoiled it*, but was agreeably surprized to find the contrary; he came off with great applause. I thought it would be impossible for his wild fancy and fingers to have kept within bounds; but Handel's music inspired and *awed him* . . . Pray make my compliments to Handel. Is *Theodora* to appear next Lent?

Meanwhile the inclement Irish weather once again got the better of her:

We went to the rehearsal of *Joshua* last Tuesday; were charmed with it – never heard it before, but it was so cold on Thursday I had not the courage to go to the night performance of it.

On the other hand, there were times when Mary did go to a performance and must have wished she had stayed away – on 12 March 1751, for example:

Tuesday . . . in the afternoon, went to hear *Samson*, *murdered most barbarously*; I never heard such a performance called music in my life! what should be grave we turned to merriment.

From a distance in Ireland Mary was able to receive copies of Handel's oratorios as they were published, but also the increasingly sad news of his declining health. In 1751, the year when Handel had such problems completing *Jephtha*, she wrote:

I have got *Theodora*, and have great pleasure in thrumming over the sweet songs . . . Did you hear that poor Handel has lost the sight of one of his eyes? I am sure you (who so truly taste his merit) will lament it: so much for England!

And in November the following year, after Handel had undergone an eye operation: 'Poor Handel! How feelingly must he recollect the "total eclipse". I hear he has now been couched, and found some benefit from it.'

'Total eclipse! No sun, no moon!' was the moving aria in which Samson bemoaned his own blindness. That thought stayed with Mary as she went to a rehearsal of *Messiah* in the week before Christmas:

It was very tolerably performed. I was a little afraid of it, as I think the music is very affecting, and I found it so – but am glad I went, as I felt comfort from it . . . I could not help thinking with great concern of poor Handel, and lamenting his dark and melancholy circumstances; but his

mind I hope will still be enlightened for the benefit of all
true lovers of harmony.

And once again back in London on a visit, Mary attended
what turned out to be the final performance of *Messiah* that
Handel ever conducted, at the Foundling Hospital Chapel on
15 May 1754:

D.D. gave Miss Mulso [a family friend] a ticket for the
Messiah, and I took her with me – my brother called for us
both; the music was too fine, I never heard it so well
performed. The chapel is fine, and the sight of so many
poor children brought up (I hope to good purpose), was a
pleasant sight.

The following year, she spiritedly deplored the current taste
of London audiences: 'The oratorio was miserably thin; the
Italian opera is in high vogue, and always full, though one song
of the least worthy of Mr Handel's music is worth all their
frothy compositions.' In March 1756, while opera thrived at
the Haymarket Theatre, under the management of Francesco
Vanneschi, Mary continued to chart the fluctuating fortunes of
the oratorio at Covent Garden: 'I was last night at *Judas
Maccabaeus*, it was charming and full. *Israel in Egypt* did not
take, it is too solemn for common ears.' And later that Lent
season: 'The oratorio last night was *Jephtha*; I never heard it
before; I think it is a very fine one, but very different from any
of his others.' And Mary was pleased that a performance of
Messiah in May, conducted by John Christopher Smith, the
younger, to benefit the Foundling Hospital charity, was so
popular that it had to be repeated a fortnight later: 'I am sure
it pleased our friend Handel, and I love to have him pleased.'
But there could still be disappointments. Returning to
London in February 1758, she reported to Anne:

D.D. treated Sally [Mary's god-daughter] with the *Triumph
of Time and Truth* last night, and we went together, but it
did not please me as usual; I believe the fault was in my

own foolish spirits, that have been of late a good deal
harrassed . . .

Mary was in Ireland when Handel died on 14 April 1759 and
did not write to her sister until 5 May:

> I could not help feel a damp on my spirits, when I heard
> that great master of music was no more, and I shall now be
> *less able* to bear any other music than I used to be. I hear he
> *has* showed his *gratitude* and *his regard* to my brother by
> leaving him some of his pictures; he had *very good* ones. I
> believe when my brother last wrote to me, which was from
> Calwich, he had not had an account of his legacy; it was
> from Mrs Donnellan I had it, to whom Handel was left
> 50 pounds. I want to know what the pictures are? I am
> sure you were pleased with the honours done him by the
> Chapter at Westminster.

The pictures Handel left to Bernard Granville were two
Rembrandts, one of which had originally been a present from
Granville. Mrs Donnellan, an old friend of Mary's, had been
left her legacy in the fourth codicil to Handel's will, signed on
11 April, only three days before he died. For Mary herself
there was nothing – except the music, and that legacy never
left her.

The last touching glimpse of Mary Delany is as an old lady
at a party she gave at her home on 15 March 1784, shortly
before the Handel Commemoration celebrations. By then she
was again widowed and had moved back to London. Her
happy second marriage had ended with Patrick Delany's death
in 1761 – and that same year her sister Anne also died. So
Mary became a close friend and mentor to Anne's daughter
(also called Mary), and whereas in her first widowhood she
had been a vivacious socialite, in her second she became
everyone's favourite aunt. As a hobby, in her seventies she
developed a delicate new technique of flower illustration with
paper collage work. She called it 'paper mosaick', and over a
thousand of these collages are now preserved in the British

Museum (see Ruth Hayden's book in 'Further reading'). Mary also continued to move in the best circles, enjoying close friendships with the Duchess of Portland, King George III and Queen Charlotte, and taking Charles Burney's brilliant, but socially inexperienced daughter, Fanny, under her wing.

Mary Hamilton was another young friend of Mrs Delany's old age (she had a position at the court with Queen Charlotte), and in her diary after the party in 1784 she wrote:

> The music consisted of some of Handel's finest songs . . . I was so enchanted with the song of 'I know that my redeemer liveth', that I was going to desire Sir William [her uncle] to play it again, but looking towards dear Mrs Delany I forbore . . . the tears were trickling down her venerable cheeks.

Mrs Delany, indefatigable at eighty-four, then went to four of the five Handel Commemoration concerts, writing to a friend, 'The effect was wonderful.'

After Handel

> Handel is not a mere composer in England: he is an
> institution. What is more, he is a sacred institution.

Strong words from the critic and dramatist, George Bernard
Shaw, writing at the end of the nineteenth century, but he was
accurately reflecting how Handel's reputation had evolved
since his death. From the vantage point of the 2009 anniversary the picture once again looks quite different, so here is a
selection of key dates and events that charts the continuing
story of Handel.

1759

3 May John Christopher Smith, the younger, directs a benefit
performance of *Messiah* for the Foundling Hospital charity.
24 May A memorial concert of Handel's sacred music, including the *Foundling Hospital Anthem* and the *Coronation Anthems*,
is conducted by John Christopher Smith, the younger.
27 August Handel's executors direct that the contents of his
house in Brook Street should be sold to his servant, John
Duburk.
10 October The residue of Handel's estate is paid to his niece
in Germany, Johanna Flörcke.

1760

25 October Death of King George II.
Anonymous publication of the first Handel biography:
Memoirs of the Life of the Late George Frederic Handel by John
Mainwaring.

1761

John Walsh, the younger, publishes Handel's Organ Concertos,
Op. 7.

Publication of *Georg Friederich Händels Lebensbeschreibung* by Johann Mattheson – an edited and expanded translation of Mainwaring's biography.

1762

15 July Louis-François Roubiliac's monument to Handel is unveiled in Westminster Abbey.

1776

Publication of *A General History of the Science and Practice of Music* by John Hawkins.

1784

26 May–5 June The supposed centenary of Handel's birth is celebrated with five Commemoration Concerts at Westminster Abbey and the Pantheon. William Coxe comments:

> The British Monarch [King George III] presided at the Commemoration of Handel; the most splendid tribute ever paid to posthumous fame. In the same Abbey where his body lies interred, those anthems which he had composed for the funeral service of Queen Caroline, together with the most celebrated pieces of his compositions, were judiciously selected for the celebration of his own memory; and performed in the highest style of instrumental perfection and vocal excellence. It was an honour to the profession, to the nation, and to the Sovereign . . . and those who attended the Commemoration in Westminster Abbey, that spring-tide of harmony, have heard him in all his glory.

This establishes a tradition of annual Handel Commemorations which continues until 1791 and inspires similar celebrations in Birmingham, York, Manchester, and Sheffield. These encourage the performances of Handel's oratorios, particularly *Messiah*, in towns and cities throughout the UK and the tradition gains momentum through the nineteenth century.

1785

23 February Centenary of Handel's birth.

Publication of *An Account of the Musical Performances in Westminster Abbey . . . in Commemoration of Handel* by Charles Burney.

William Cowper recalls the Commemoration in Book 6 of his epic poem *The Task*, simultaneously praising Handel and deploring the use of the Bible as the text for *Messiah*:

> Remember Handel? Who, that was not born
> Deaf as the dead to harmony, forgets,
> Or can, the more than Homer of his age?
> Yes – we remember him; and while we praise
> A talent so divine, remember too
> That His most holy book, from whom it came,
> Was never meant, was never used before,
> To buckram out the memory of a man.

Samuel Arnold, organist and composer to the Chapel Royal, advertises a proposed complete edition of Handel's work. This was the first attempt to publish a complete edition of the music of any composer. Many volumes were issued up to 1797, but the edition was never completed.

1789

6 March Premiere in Vienna of Mozart's arrangement of *Messiah* for Baron van Swieten's 'Society of Associated Cavaliers'. Mozart also made arrangements of *Acis and Galatea* (1788), *Alexander's Feast* (1790) and the *Ode for Saint Cecilia's Day* (1790).

Publication of *A General History of Music from the Earliest Ages to the Present Period* by Charles Burney.

1791

Haydn attends the Commemoration concerts in Westminster Abbey and is deeply moved by the chorus 'The nations tremble' in *Joshua*, declaring that 'only one inspired Author ever did, or ever would, pen so sublime a composition'. He maintains that Handel was 'the master of us all'.

1796

Beethoven composes a set of variations for cello and piano on 'See the conqu'ring hero comes', from *Judas Maccabaeus*. In 1823 a friend reports him as saying: 'Handel is the greatest composer that ever lived . . . I would bare my head, and kneel at his grave.'

1799

Publication of *Anecdotes of George Frederick Handel and John Christopher Smith* by William Coxe.

1800

Publication of *An Introduction to Harmony* by the composer William Shield, who reinforces Handel's reputation as a religious composer with this anecdote:

> I have heard it related, that when Handel's servant used to bring him his chocolate in the morning, he often stood silent with astonishment (until it was cold) to see his master's tears mixing with the ink as he penned his divine compositions; which are surely as much the pictures of a sublime mind as Milton's words.

1818

25 December The Handel and Haydn Society of Boston, founded in 1815, gives the American premiere of the complete *Messiah*.

1843

The composer George Macfarren founds The English Handel Society. According to its prospectus, it aims to produce 'a superior and standard edition of the works of Handel'. The Society is disbanded in 1848, but publication continues for another decade and a total of twelve works are issued by Cramer, Beale and Company.

1846

The music publisher, Vincent Novello, issues an inexpensive vocal score of *Messiah*, followed by various other oratorios, and these are taken up enthusiastically by amateur choral societies whose performances of Handel have something of the aura of religious ritual. Wagner, who attended a performance of *Messiah* in London in 1855, noted 'the feeling among the audience that an evening spent in listening to an oratorio may be regarded as a sort of service, and is almost as good as going to church'.

1856

The German musicologist, Friedrich Chrysander, and historian, Gottfried Gervinus, found the Händel-Gesellschaft in Leipzig to prepare and publish a critical and uniform edition of Handel's complete works. Chrysander later takes over the edition himself and almost a hundred volumes are published between 1858 and his death in 1901.

1857

June A Handel Festival is held at Crystal Palace, London, organised by the Sacred Harmonic Society and attended by Queen Victoria and the Prince Consort. A choir of two thousand and an orchestra of five hundred, conducted by Michael Costa, perform *Messiah*, *Judas Maccabaeus*, and *Israel in Egypt*. Publication of *The Life of Handel* by Victor Schoelcher, translated from the French by James Lowe. This scholarly biography is based on years of research and also draws on Schoelcher's extensive collection of material by and about Handel, which he later donates to the Paris Conservatoire (it is now housed in the Bibliothèque Nationale).

1858

Publication of the first volume of *G. F. Händel* by Friedrich Chrysander. Two more volumes follow up to 1867, but this classic critical biography remained incomplete, covering Handel's life only up to 1740.

1859

14 April Centenary of Handel's death.
June A second Grand Handel Festival is held at Crystal Palace. A choir of 2,765 and an orchestra of 460 instrumentalists, conducted by Michael Costa, perform *Messiah*, *Israel in Egypt*, and selections from other Handel works. Handel festivals on this scale, and in the spirit of great national events, are subsequently held triennially, with the festival brought forward one year in 1885 for the bicentenary of Handel's birth. The last festival takes place in 1926, the year of the General Strike.

1861

Publication of *Autobiography and Correspondence of Mary Granville, Mrs Delany*, with reminiscences of Handel. Six volumes appear between 1861 and 1862.

1883

Publication of *The Life of George Frederick Handel* by W. S. Rockstro.

1885

23 February Bicentenary of Handel's birth.
A Handel Bicentenary Festival is held at Crystal Palace (see 1859) with performances of *Messiah*, *Israel in Egypt*, and selections from other Handel works.
Publication of *Handel* by Eliza Clarke in the series called 'The World's Workers'. It places Handel within the Protestant work ethic of the time and concludes:

Most emphatically may Handel be styled a 'World's Worker'. His quickness in production was from force of genius, perfect knowledge, and constant industry, and his masterpieces will endure and delight the world to the end of time.

1888

The first Handel recording – of a chorus from *Israel in Egypt* – is made on an Edison phonograph at the Crystal Palace, London, on 30 June during the Handel Festival. This is claimed to be the first ever recording of classical music.

1891

George Bernard Shaw, a Handel admirer, writes:

Why, instead of wasting huge sums on the multitudinous dullness of a Handel Festival does not somebody set up a thoroughly rehearsed and exhaustively studied performance of the *Messiah* in St James's Hall with a chorus of twenty capable artists? Most of us would be glad to hear the work seriously performed once before we die.

1906

Publication of *The Indebtedness of Handel to Works by other Composers* by Sedley Taylor – the first book to demonstrate the extent of Handel's borrowings and conclude that they were morally wrong. It stirs up much controversy.

1908

Publication of *Handel and His Orbit* by Percy Robinson – a response to Sedley Taylor's book, justifying Handel's borrowings.

1909

Publication of *Handel* by Richard A. Streatfield.

1910

Publication in France of *Haendel* by Romain Rolland. An English translation is published in 1916. This is a landmark biography as French musicians and audiences have previously been largely indifferent to Handel – Berlioz called him 'a great barrel of pork and beer'! Rolland's approach is impressive, and often modern in outlook: he has a clear and all-embracing concept of Handel as a composer of 'visual' music which can only come alive in performance:

> It is a music which paints emotions, souls, and situations, to see the epochs and the places, which are the framework of the emotions, and which tint them with their own peculiar moral tone. In a word, his is an art essentially picturesque and dramatic.

1920

26 June Oskar Hagan, an art-history teacher at the University of Göttingen, puts on a production of *Rodelinda* at the Stadttheater – the first staging of a Handel opera since 1754. This leads to the founding of the annual Göttingen Händel Festival. Successive artistic directors are Fritz Lehmann, Günther Weissenborn, John Eliot Gardiner (1980), and Nicholas McGegan (1990). Other German cities, including Handel's home town of Halle, begin to revive Handel's operas throughout the 1920s. Generally they are given in heavily cut and edited versions.

1923

Publication of *George Frideric Handel: his Personality and his Times* by Walter Newman Flower. A second edition follows in 1947.

1934

William Charles Smith, an English music librarian, begins his personal collection of Handel manuscripts and early printed editions.

1944

The conductor, Sir Thomas Beecham, an enthusiastic Handelian, writes in his autobiography:

> If Handel . . . were confronted with the gigantic crowds of singers that now strive to interpret his music, he would at once cut them down to a quarter of their bloated dimensions, or rewrite the orchestral portions of his scores for the largest combination of instruments he could lay his hands upon.

1948

Publication of *Concerning Handel, his life and works* by William C. Smith.
The Handel-Haus Museum is opened at his birthplace at Halle. The building was acquired by the city of Halle in 1937 (previously it was a furniture shop) and needed extensive restoration. It was further expanded and developed in 1984 and 1992.

1952

The Händelfestspiele Halle (Halle Handel Festival) is founded and continues annually.

1954

Publication of *Handel: A Symposium* edited by Gerald Abraham. It includes ten essays on major areas of Handel's music by leading scholars.

1955

The Georg-Friedrich-Händel-Gesellschaft (GFHG) is founded in Halle to publish an edition of Handel's music, the *Hallische Händel-Ausgabe* (*HHA*). The original intention is to supplement Chrysander's incomplete edition, but in 1958 it is decided that a new, complete critical edition will be produced. An annual scholarly journal, the *Händel-Jahrbuch*, is also published.

The Handel Opera Society is founded in London, conducted by Charles Farncombe, who remains the musical director until 1985. A total of twenty-eight works are staged.

Publication of *Handel: a Documentary Biography* by Otto Deutsch. A revised and expanded German translation, *Dukemente zu Leben und Schaffen*, is published as Volume IV of the *Händel-Handbuch* by the *Hallische Händel-Ausgabe* in 1985.

1959

14 April Bicentenary of Handel's death.

The Royal Opera House, Covent Garden, stages a production of *Samson*.

Publication of *Handel's Dramatic Oratorios and Masques* by Winton Dean.

Frances and Allen Kitching begin to mount productions of Handel's operas at the Unicorn Theatre, Abingdon. Fifteen works are performed up to 1975.

Anthony Lewis and Ivor Keys begin to mount productions of Handel's operas at the Barber Institute, University of Birmingham.

First recording of the *Music for the Royal Fireworks* with the original line-up of massed wind instruments, conducted by Charles Mackerras.

1962

Gerald Coke, a merchant banker and patron of the arts, buys William C. Smith's Handel collection and adds it to his own extensive Handel collection.

1965

Publication of *A Handelian's Notebook* by William C. Smith.

The Henry Watson Library, Manchester, acquires Newman Flower's extensive Handel collection, which includes most of the Aylesford Manuscripts originally owned by Charles Jennens.

1966

Publication of *George Frideric Handel* by Paul Henry Lang – the first significant Handel biography by an American scholar.
First recording of *Messiah*, conducted by Charles Mackerras, with reduced choral and orchestral forces and in a style informed by a re-examination of performance practice in Handel's time.
Glyndebourne Festival Opera stages *Jephtha*, in a revival of a production originally created in Germany in 1965. It has little success.

1972

Trevor Pinnock founds and directs the English Concert, a peri-od-instrument ensemble which soon expands into an orchestra. In the early 1980s Pinnock is one of the first to record most of Handel's orchestral works on period instruments. Since 2007 the director of the English Concert has been Harry Bicket.

1973

Christopher Hogwood founds and directs the Academy of Ancient Music, a period-instrument orchestra. Hogwood makes many Handel recordings, including a groundbreaking *Messiah* in 1980, in the version performed by Handel at the Foundling Hospital in 1754. Since 2006 the director of the Academy of Ancient Music is Richard Egarr.

1978

The London Handel Festival is founded by the organist and conductor, Denys Darlow, to specialise in reviving lesser-known works. The Festival expands in 1981 with the creation of the London Handel Orchestra and London Handel Singers. Laurence Cummings takes over as Musical Director in 2002.

Publication of the first volume of the *Händel Handbuch* by the *Hallische Händel-Ausgabe*. Volumes 1–3 (1978–86) contain the *Thematisch-systematisches Verzeichnis*, prepared by Bernd Baselt, and establish the catalogue of Handel's works identified by HWV numbers.

1979

English National Opera stages John Copley's production of *Julius Caesar* at the London Coliseum. Its success leads to many revivals.

William Christie founds and directs Les Arts Florissants, a period-instrument orchestra based in Paris, initially to revive neglected French music of the seventeenth and eighteenth centuries, but Christie also mounts successful stage productions of Handel's works, including *Orlando* (1993), *Acis and Galatea* and *Semele* (1996), *Alcina* (1999), and *Hercules* (2004). Christie's lead is followed in France by Marc Minkowski, who founds Les Musiciens du Louvre, Grenoble in 1982; by Hervé Niquet, who founds Le Concert Spirituel in 1987; and by Christophe Rousset who founds Les Talens Lyriques in 1991. All four orchestras make significant contributions to the expanding catalogue of Handel recordings on original instruments.

1980

Robert King founds and directs The King's Consort, a period-instrument orchestra, and The Choir of the King's Consort. King performs and records a wide range of early music, and specialises in reviving neglected Handel oratorios. He also researches and records the music performed at the coronation of King George II.

John Eliot Gardiner becomes the artistic director of the Göttingen Handel Festival.

1984

The Göttinger Händel-Gesellschaft begins to publish an annual journal, the *Göttinger Händel-Beiträge*.

Publication of *Handel* by Christopher Hogwood, with a chronological table by Anthony Hicks. A revised edition appears in 2007.

1985

23 February Tercentenary of Handel's birth. The Royal Musical Association holds a Handel Conference, organised by Stanley Sadie and Nigel Fortune. The subject of 'Handel's Borrowings' provokes renewed debate.

The National Portrait Gallery, London, holds an exhibition, *Handel: A Celebration of his Life and Times*, and publishes a lavishly illustrated catalogue book, edited by Jacob Simon.

English National Opera, at the London Coliseum, stages Nicholas Hytner's witty new production of *Xerxes* (*Serse*). Like John Copley's *Julius Caesar*, its success leads to many revivals and to further ENO Handel opera productions, notably *Ariodante* (1993, directed by David Alden), *Alcina* (1999, directed by David McVicar), *Agrippina* (2007, directed by David McVicar), and *Partenope* (2008, directed by Christopher Alden).

Premiere on Channel 4 television of *God Rot Tunbridge Wells!*, an ambitious and controversial drama-documentary about Handel's final days, directed by Tony Palmer, with a screenplay by John Osborne and music conducted by Charles Mackerras.

The Handel Opera Society in London mounts its final production: *Rodrigo*.

Publication of *Handel: the Man and his Music* by Jonathan Keates. A revised edition appears in 2008.

1986

The American Handel Society is founded by Howard Serwer, Paul Traver, and J. Merrill Knapp. Its aims are 'to foster study of the life, works, and times of George Frideric Handel, and to encourage and support the performance of his music'.

The Orchestra of the Age of Enlightenment is founded by a group of players as a self-governing period-instrument orchestra, working with a variety of conductors. It makes many Handel recordings and eventually becomes the resident orchestra at Glyndebourne Festival Opera for Handel and other early opera productions.

1987

Publication of *Handel's Operas 1704–1726* by Winton Dean and J. Merrill Knapp. A revised edition appears in 1995.
Publication of the *Handel Tercentenary Collection*, edited by Stanley Sadie and Anthony Hicks, including essays about 'Handel's Borrowings', originally given as papers at the 1985 RMA Conference.
The Handel Institute (Great Britain) is founded. Its aims are 'to advance education by promoting the study and appreciation of, and supporting and publishing research on, the music and life of George Frideric Handel and his contemporaries'. It organises study days and conferences, publishes a *Newsletter* twice a year, and liaises with other national and international organisations and societies dedicated to Handel.

1990

Nicholas McGegan becomes the artistic director of Göttingen Handel Festival.

1994

Publication of *Handel* by Donald Burrows – the definitive modern scholarly biography.

1996

Glyndebourne Festival Opera stages *Theodora* in a radical modern-dress production directed by Peter Sellars. This launches a successful trilogy of Handel productions, with *Rodelinda* (1998), directed by Jean-Marie Villégier in art-deco Hollywood style, and *Giulio Cesare* (2005) in British colonial style, directed by David McVicar. William Christie conducts all three productions with the Orchestra of the Age of Enlightenment.

1997

Publication of *The Cambridge Companion to Handel*, edited by Donald Burrows, with a series of essays reflecting the current state of Handel research.

2001

After years of planning and fundraising, the Handel House in London is finally restored and opens as a museum. It also offers regular concerts and special exhibitions.

2003

The Royal Opera House, Covent Garden, stages Francesco Negrin's production of *Orlando*.

2004

The Foundling Museum in London opens and the Gerald Coke Collection (donated to the Thomas Coram Foundation) is moved there, with study facilities for scholars. There is also a permanent exhibition gallery and occasional special exhibitions.

2006

Publication of Handel's Operas, 1726-1741 by Winton Dean.

2008

Harry Christophers is appointed Artistic Director of the Handel and Haydn Society, Boston.

2009

14 April 250th anniversary of Handel's death.

Handel online

Try putting the names of a few great composers into www.google.co.uk and the results are revealing: about 11,000,000 for Haydn; 14,600,000 for Vivaldi; 20,600,000 for Schubert; 34,800,000 for Beethoven; 51,100,000 for Mozart; 65,500,000 for Bach; and on top of the pile – by a long way – sits Handel with 94,800,000!

Meanwhile, the Google search for Bononcini, Handel's great operatic rival in London in the 1720s, gets only 139,000 results. And if you want finally to resolve the War of the Divas that raged between two of Handel's leading ladies, there's no contest: in cyberspace Faustina Bordoni romps home with a clear 12,000 results, while Francesca Cuzzoni can only manage about 4,710. Both formidable ladies, however, would be furious to discover that they are not remotely as popular as the castrato, Senesino, who polls 33,500!

It's an entertaining game and the numbers change every time you play it (the above results were recorded on 30 September 2008), but of course there is also a serious and useful side to the Internet. Searches for 'Handel Messiah' (820,000 sites) and 'Handel Water Music' (1,890,000 sites) will direct you to www.youtube.com where videos are available of extracts from these and many other of Handel's works. To complement this, retail sites like www.amazon.co.uk offer the chance to hear extracts from many recordings before deciding to buy them. So you could work your way through much of the music described in this book, listening to it online as well as reading about it.

Handel would surely have loved the Internet – just imagine the possibilities it would have given him for publicising and marketing his various artistic and business enterprises. And he would even have recognised some of the online jargon. On the Internet, everything musical is now divided up and categorised as *songs* – as it was in Handel's day. Read Charles Burney, and he constantly refers to the 'songs' in Handel's operas. He uses other words as well, like 'airs', but the underlying principle is the same: that a work is made up of a quantity of component parts, each of which can be enjoyed separately. Handel's publishers, with his blessing, certainly understood that fact when they issued selective extracts and anthologies of his music. Which is not to say that Handel did not consider and value the overall architecture of his greatest works, particularly his operas and oratorios, but he was pragmatic about what did and did not work in particular performance situations, and was forever changing around the component parts – the *songs*.

So let this book be a portal into a rich Handel cyberworld. Much that is available is ephemeral, eccentric, or misinformed, but there is also a great deal of serious and valuable information to be found online. Alongside the various Internet addresses already given in this book, the place to start onward surfing is www.gfhandel.org, a website devised and maintained by Brad Leissa and David Vickers. The site itself contains a vast amount of Handel-related information, including work-lists and bibiliographies, and it has a directory called 'Handel on the Web' which links to numerous other sites by category: e.g. 'Societies and Institutes', 'Handel Festivals and Conferences', 'Handel Museums', 'Collections', 'Musical Scores and Sheet Music', etc. Almost all of these sites link onwards to others – the possibilities seem endless and will no doubt increase through the anniversary year.

Further reading

Here is a selective list of books that I have found interesting and useful:

Handel by his contemporaries

Burney, Charles. *An Account of the Musical Performances in Westminster Abbey . . . in Commemoration of Handel*. Payne and Robinson, 1785.

Burney, Charles. *A General History of Music from the Earliest Ages to the Present Period* (1789). 2 volumes. G. T. Foulis, 1935, reprint of the 1789 first edition.

Coxe, Willam. *Anecdotes of George Frederick Handel and John Christopher Smith*. Da Capo, 1979, reprint of the 1799 first edition.

[Delany, Mary]. *Autobiography and Correspondence of Mary Granville, Mrs Delany*. London 1861–62. 6 volumes.

Deutsch, Otto Erich. *Handel – a Documentary Biography*. A. and C. Black, 1955.

Hawkins, Sir John. *A General History of the Science and Practice of Music*. London, 1776 (5 volumes). New edition, 1875 (2 volumes). Reprinted, Graz, Akademische Druck-u. Verlagsanstalt, 1969.

Mainwaring, John. *Memoirs of the Life of the Late George Frederic Handel*. Da Capo, 1980, reprint of the 1760 first edition.

Handel's world

[Handel House]. *Handel and the Castrati*. Handel House Museum, 2006. Text by Nicholas Clapton, Elisabetta Avanzati, and Patricia Howard.

[Handel House]. *Handel and the Divas*. Handel House

Museum, 2008. Text by Martin Wyatt, Suzana Ograjensek, Berta Joncus, and Nicholas Clapton.

Riding, Jacqueline. *The Purest Benevolence – Handel and the Foundling Hospital.* Handel House Museum, n.d.

Riding, Jacqueline, and Donald Burrows and Anthony Hicks. *Handel House Museum Companion.* Handel House Trust, 2001.

[Royal Society of Musicians]. *Handel in London.* Royal Society of Musicians, 1984. Text by Alec Forshaw, John Cruft, and Colin Master.

Simon, Jacob, ed. *Handel – a Celebration of his Life and Times.* National Portrait Gallery, 1985.

Early biographies of Handel

Abdy, Williams, C. F. *Handel* (The Master Musicians). Dent, 1901; revised 1935.

Clarke, Eliza. *Handel* (The World's Workers). Cassell, 1885.

Flower, Newman. *George Frideric Handel – His Personality and his Times.* Cassell, 1923.

Rockstro, W. S. *The Life of George Frederick Handel.* Macmillan, 1883.

Rolland, Romain. *Haendel.* Paris, 1910. Revised edition, Actes Sud, 2005. Trans. A. Eaglefield Hull, Kegan Paul, Trench and Trubner, 1916.

Schelcher, Victor, trans. James Lowe. *The Life of Handel.* Trübner, 1857.

Streatfield, R. A. *Handel.* Methuen, 1909; second edition, 1910.

Modern biographies of Handel

Burrows, Donald. *Handel* (The Master Musicians). Oxford University Press, 1994.

Hogwood, Christopher. *Handel.* Thames and Hudson, 1984; revised edition, 2007.

Keates, Jonathan. *Handel – The Man and his Music*. Gollancz, 1985; second edition, Bodley Head, 2008.

Lang, Paul Henry. *George Frideric Handel*. Norton, 1966.

Robbins Landon, H. C. *Handel and His World*. Weidenfeld and Nicholson, 1984; second edition, Flamingo, 1992.

Young, Percy M. *Handel* (The Master Musicians). Dent, 1975.

Handel's manuscripts

Best, Terence, ed. *Handel Collections and their History*. Oxford University Press, 1993.

Burrows, Donald, and Martha J Ronish. *A Catalogue of Handel's Musical Autographs*. Oxford University Press, 1994.

[Fitzwilliam Museum]. *Handel and the Fitzwilliam*. Fitzwilliam Museum, Cambridge, 1974.

Hyatt King, A. *Handel and His Autographs*. British Museum, 1967.

Tobin, John. *Handel at Work*. Cassell, 1964.

Handel's music

Abraham, Gerald, ed. *Handel: a Symposium*. Oxford University Press, 1954.

Burrows, Donald. *Handel – Messiah* (Cambridge Music Handbooks). Cambridge University Press, 1991.

Burrows, Donald, ed. *The Cambridge Companion to Handel*. Cambridge University Press, 1997.

Dean, Winton. *Handel's Dramatic Oratorios and Masques*. Oxford University Press, 1959.

Dean, Winton. *Handel's Operas, 1726–1741*. The Boydell Press, 2006.

Dean, Winton, and John Merrill Knapp. *Handel's Operas 1704–1726*. Oxford University Press, 1987; revised edition 1995.

Harris, Ellen T. *Handel as Orpheus: Voice and Desire in the Chamber Cantatas*. Harvard University Press, 2001.

Luckett, Richard. *Handel's 'Messiah' – a Celebration*. Gollancz, 1992.

Roberts, John, ed. *Handel Sources Series: Materials for the Study of Handel's Borrowing*. 9 volumes. Garland Publishing, 1986.

Robinson, Percy. *Handel in His Orbit*. London, 1908.

Sadie, Stanley. *Handel Concertos* (BBC Music Guides). BBC, 1972.

Sadie, Stanley and Anthony Hicks. *Handel Tercentenary Collection*. Macmillan Press, 1987.

Shaw, Watkins. The Story of *Handel's 'Messiah'* 1741–1784. Novello, 1963.

Smith, Ruth. *Handel's Oratorios and Eighteenth-Century Thought*. Cambridge University Press, 1995.

Taylor, Sedley. *The Indebtedness of Handel to Works by Other Composers*. Cambridge University Press, 1906; reprinted 1979.

General

Anderson, Nicholas. *Baroque Music*. Thames and Hudson, 1994.

Hayden, Ruth. *Mrs Delany and her Flower Collages*. British Museum Press, 1980; new edition, 1992.

Kitching, Alan. *Handel at the Unicorn*. Unicorn Opera Society, 1981.

Ledbetter, David, ed. *Continuo Playing According to Handel – His Figured Bass Exercises*. Oxford University Press, 1990.

Osborne, John: *A Better Class of Person (An Extract of Autobiography for Television); and God Rot Tunbridge Wells*. Faber and Faber, 1985.

Parker-Hale, Mary Ann. *G. F. Handel – a Guide to Research*. Garland, 1988.

Smith, William C. *Concerning Handel, his Life and Works.* Cassell, 1948.

Smith, William C. *A Handelian's Notebook.* Adam and Charles Black. 1965.

Finally, for more detailed information on literature about Handel, past and present, see the entry in *The New Grove Dictionary of Music and Musicians* (Macmillan, 1980; revised edition 2001), which includes a biographical article by Winton Dean, a complete worklist compiled by Anthony Hicks, and a bibliography of Handel's life and works. *The New Grove Dictionary* is updated and available online by subscription at www.grovemusic.com.

Acknowledgements

This book has been inspired chiefly by Handel's music – a never-ending source of delight. (As I write this I am listening for the umpteenth time to a wonderful aria from *Theodora*, 'As with rosy steps the morn', sung by the late Lorraine Hunt Lieberson.) I have been fortunate to have my listening enhanced by conversations about Handel with many of the singers, instrumentalists and conductors represented on the recordings recommended – creative artists who bring the music of Handel gloriously to life. My grateful thanks to them all, and in particular to Felicity Lott who also generously contributed the Foreword to this book.

My thanks also to my colleagues at BBC Radio 3, collaborators in the planning of celebration broadcasts for the 2009 Handel Anniversary Year, and to the ever-helpful staff of the Handel House Museum and the Foundling Museum.

I am especially grateful to Belinda Matthews at Faber who commissioned this book and followed its progress with enthusiasm and timely advice; to the dedicated editorial team of Elizabeth Tyerman and Michael Downes; and to Nicholas Kenyon who read the manuscript and offered characteristically helpful suggestions.

Finally, my thanks as ever to Helen and Laura: this book is for them.

EDWARD BLAKEMAN
DECEMBER 2008

Index

The main entry for each work is in **bold** type.

All works are listed under their first letter, even if they begin with the definite or indefinite article (e.g. under I for *Il pastor fido*)